A Safe Place
for Change

Skills and Capacities for Counselling and Therapy
revised 2nd Edition

Hugh Crago holds degrees in English language and literature, social sciences, and counselling psychology from universities in Australia, England and the USA. He is the author or co-author of eight books and some 120 articles, and retired as Senior Lecturer in Counselling, Western Sydney University in 2012. He has practised as a counsellor and therapist for nearly forty years, and with his wife Maureen was co-editor of the *Australian and New Zealand Journal of Family Therapy* from 1997 to 2009. Hugh continues to work as an individual and couple counsellor and group therapist in Blackheath, near Sydney.

Penny Gardner has lectured in Counselling and developed and taught in the Master of Psychotherapy and Counselling program at Western Sydney University since 2004. She has a wealth of clinical experience in a range of settings, using the model in this book with all age groups and client presentations.

A Safe Place
for Change

Skills and Capacities for Counselling and Therapy
revised 2nd Edition

Hugh Crago
Penny Gardner

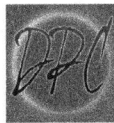

Digital Publishing Centre
an imprint of Interactive Publications
Brisbane

Digital Publishing Centre
an imprint of IP (Interactive Publications Pty Ltd)
Treetop Studio • 9 Kuhler Court
Carindale, Queensland, Australia 4152
sales@ipoz.biz
http://ipoz.biz
First published by IP in 2019
© IP, Hugh Crago and Penny Gardner, 2019

Printed in 14 pt Avenir Book on Adobe Garamond Pro 11 pt.

A safe place for change: skills and capacities for counselling and therapy, revised 2nd edition
ISBN: 9781925231885 (PB) 9781925231892 (eBook)

Contents

Preface for Trainers and Educators

This book was originally written for students of counselling and therapy in their first year of training. Subsequently we found that some trainers had set it as a text for second year students on placement. Since then we have realised that it is not simply a textbook, but offers much to practising counsellors. Many counsellors never experienced a sequenced training in basic skills, geared to the stages of the evolving therapeutic process, such as we have provided here. The teaching of skills seems often to be regarded by lecturers and trainers as less important, or less exciting, than the presentation of theories and models of counselling. To us, this seems to put the cart before the horse. Many practising psychologists and social workers may be surprised to discover here key understandings and skills that were lacking in their own professional education.

Theories and models are referred to all the way through this book, but its subject is the practice of counselling and therapy. When we look closely at practice, and understand fully what it is that counsellors are doing, some of the apparent differences between models and theories fall away. Our aim in this book is to emphasise the common ground that lies beneath most recognised approaches—the things that every counsellor or therapist needs to know (and know experientially, not just cognitively).

In some ways 'skills' is not the best word for what this book is about, though it is widely used and we have followed suit here. 'Skills' suggests something like driving, or being able to add up a column of figures, or throw a ball powerfully and accurately. Counselling skills are a little bit like these skills, but a whole lot different too. Counselling skills are really relational capacities, broken down into specific ways of talking (or sometimes, not talking) that will foster a strong therapeutic relationship. They cannot be fully expressed in 'rules' for how to talk or exactly what to say. Words may be important but words will never be enough without the therapist's presence, and 'presence' is not a skill but a quality possessed by a person, a way of being with someone else.

A Safe Place for Change is firmly based in the understanding that the relationship between clinician and client is the bedrock on which all effective counselling and psychotherapy rests. Without a solid, durable relationship (one that can withstand temporary challenge and rupture), no client, except for the most mature, self-aware and motivated, is likely to achieve more than temporary change—no matter what the theoretical model is employed by the professional.

Our approach in this book is 'relational' in the broadest sense. It was Freud and his colleague Breuer who established that clients would 'open up' and reveal long-buried traumas if only the therapist let them talk freely, without judging them or being too inquisitive. This clinical discovery has still to be re-learned by many professionals today, because their training emphasises knowledge about theories, models and 'techniques' rather than continuous practice in the subtle art of crafting a relationship that clients will perceive as trustworthy—a safe place for change. Many professionals fail to listen to their clients properly, and hasten too rapidly into offering information and strategies for behaviour change—which often address only the surface of the client's presenting problem. Beginning counsellors are (understandably) attracted to such approaches, because they seem to promise quick changes and offer a gratifyingly prominent role to the counsellor.

But to train students in this way is to mislead them. Patience and empathy are more important attributes for a counsellor or therapist to possess than an array of techniques for 'managing' anger, grief, compulsions, or whatever. Clients are more than simply bundles of diagnosable symptoms that can be addressed by one-size-fits-all 'treatments', as in the medical model. Clients must be 'held' by a person who adjusts sensitively to the clients' needs, instead of imposing their own needs on the client.

The idea that clients are entitled to be seen as wholes rather than as bundles of pathological behaviours and dysfunctional beliefs was the insight of Carl Rogers, who began publishing his ideas in the 1940s and 1950s. We follow Rogers in our belief that clients are people, unique individuals. They respond best to a professional who is sensitive and insightful enough to grasp the essence of who they are. When our clients are assured that we 'get them', there may well be room for techniques and strategies—if that is what our clients are actually looking for (see Chapters 5 and 7). Rogers developed Freud's ideas about the therapeutic relationship into an assumption (which he and his associates repeatedly tested in their research) that clients would change when they experienced empathy (the therapist's ability to 'feel with' them—neglected by Freud and many of his followers); unconditional positive regard (the therapist's capacity to suspend judgement and criticism); and congruence (the 'realness' of the therapist—the client's sense that 'she means what she says', that her words 'come from the heart'). In other words, what matters most is how the therapist is able to 'be with' a client, not what the therapist is able to 'do to' or 'do with' the client.

Irvin Yalom took Freud's ideas about 'transference' (that people will behave towards their therapist in ways they learned to behave with significant others), Rogers' ideas about 'congruence', and Franz Alexander's notion of 'corrective emotional experience' and developed them into his precept that the key moments in therapy are those when client and counsellor must face each other without masks, and speak honestly and openly from their in-the-room feelings (see Chapter 4). In these moments, said Yalom, clients experience something profoundly different from what typically happens in social conversation, something that catalyses change within them, not only at the level of realisations (cognitive learning) but at the level of felt experience (embodied learning). Such encounters (see Chapters 4, 6 and 9) are the 'breakthrough moments' that can occur once a sufficiently safe trusting and respectful relationship has been created between counsellor and client. If therapists attempt to 'bring on' these encounters too early, before the therapeutic relationship is resilient enough to withstand the stress of straight talk, their clients will typically flee from a challenge that they perceive as too great.

The landmark meta-study known as the Common Factors research (Wampold, 2015) offers substantial research confirmation of the whole relational tradition as we have sketched it here. The researchers found that of all the factors affecting the outcome of therapy, the most crucial was the strength of the counsellor-client relationship. The therapeutic bond (as perceived by the client) was more important than the theoretical model that guided the therapist, more important even than the approach and personality of the therapist ('therapist factors'). Recent neurological research into the structure and functioning of the brain has further supported the importance of the therapeutic relationship, and in this second edition we have greatly extended our references to this research, which confirms much that psychotherapists and counsellors have long known, but been unable to substantiate. Thus *A Safe Place for Change* rests within a well-recognised tradition of ongoing theory and practice. It is evidence-based, not simply a collection of appealing but untestable precepts.

Though we refer briefly to many models and ideas about counselling and psychotherapy, it is the humanistic, person-centred, relational approach that we hope students will learn from *A Safe Place for Change*.

They are more likely to do so if they are prepared to read the book cover-to-cover over the course of a semester, and then to re-read sections of it over the next year. It is written to make sense cumulatively, not to offer little 'nuggets of knowledge' that students can glean from skimming a few pages and then reproduce in their essays. Many students will expect to do the latter, and they will need their lecturers to deter them, by setting up exercises and discussions so that reading of the full text, as it unfolds in successive chapters, is required. While this may seem onerous to some students, the reception given to the first edition of *A Safe Place for Change* confirms that our writing strikes most students as accessible, interesting and, above all, practical. Our experience of teaching counselling (over 35 years between the two of us, in several different training programs, spanning both private institutes and universities) has convinced us that students overwhelmingly prefer textbooks that are clear and direct in their language, and acknowledge the kinds of difficulties that beginners face. Provided throughout are realistic examples that draw on typical clients and typical situations from our own experience. All identifying details have, of course, been removed.

We haven't attempted to cover everything the beginning counsellor needs to know. There are many aspects that are best left for trainers to tackle in their own way, with their own students. A text can only be an aid to learning. It is not an entire program in itself, and what happens in class is always going to take precedence, because it is person-to-person experience that fosters the most profound learning, and makes sense of words on the page—in education as well as in psychotherapy!

For readability, we have kept in-text references to a minimum. Deliberately, we have supplied references to classic works, not just recent summaries. Sound, clinically based analysis does not go out of date, as much scientific research does. Reading the actual writings of therapy pioneers offers a good corrective to still-prevalent stereotypes and misunderstandings ('Freud was sex-mad'; 'Rogers just said "Uh-huh" after everything the client said'; 'Family therapy is like spaghetti: everyone stuck together in a sticky mess').

Our clients have been wonderful teachers, and our experiences with them inform everything we have written here. We also want to thank the publisher who took on the first edition of *A Safe Place for Change*, Alan Fettling, and his colleague, Jill Henry. Alan and Jill were enthusiastic, courteous and helpful at every stage, including assistance with finding an alternative publisher when Alan found himself unable to continue with IP Communications. Similarly, we want to thank Dr David Reiter of Interactive Publications for taking on the second edition. We'd especially like to acknowledge the contribution made to this book by our students (past and present) at the University of Western Sydney. We thank our own therapists, who over many years created for us a 'safe place for change'. Finally, we want to express our appreciation to Meeray Ghaly, a former student in our program, who supplied the warm, witty and thought-provoking drawings, and who created 'the elephant' as a potent and ever-changing symbol—sometimes a big and unknown figure, sometimes a comforting presence, sometimes the problem itself.

– *Hugh Crago*, Adjunct Fellow, School of Social Sciences and Psychology, Western Sydney University; private practice, Blackheath, NSW
– *Penny Gardner*, Lecturer in Counselling, and Academic Advisor, Counselling, School of Social Sciences and Psychology, Western Sydney University, NSW

Chapter 1

So You Want To Help People?

Motives and hidden agendas

When you apply to a counselling training program—as run by a university, a private training college, or a large welfare organisation which conducts its own training—you will probably be asked, 'Why do you want to be a counsellor?' There are a variety of answers that applicants give to this question. The most common responses are:

- I just want to help people. I really enjoy solving problems and people appreciate the advice I give them.

- I'm really intrigued by people and their problems. I like to analyse what's really going on. Get to the *key issues.*

- People have always come to me with their problems. They say I'm a good listener. I feel so comfortable doing that for people.

- My parents brought us up to serve the community. Helping with problems is just something you do in our family. It comes naturally to me.

- A few years back, I was in a bit of a difficult spot, and I saw a counsellor. She was amazing! I'd love to touch people's lives like that.

All of these statements tell us something about the speaker's motivation for training as a counsellor. But there are areas that these speakers are unaware of, or unwilling to reveal. Rarely, for example, will would-be counsellors say,

- I like feeling that people depend on me. If someone doesn't need me, I feel empty.

- I feel kind of awkward around other people a lot of the time. But I enjoy observing people, and working out what makes them tick. I like the idea of explaining people to themselves. I feel in control.

- When I'm listening to someone else, I get really involved. I don't really know what I feel, their feelings are what I'm focussed on.

- It isn't so much the buzz I get out of helping people—it's more the fact that I can do this thing well. I'd really like to master all the skills, all the techniques, so I can be even better at it!

- I felt desperate, and this counsellor that I saw was able to help me. It seemed like magic. Everything started going better for me. I want to be like her, in fact, I want to *be* her!

Deliberately, each of the listed statements matches an equivalent statement in the first list. Each is the product of a different personality type, and a different orientation to helping. At a later point, you may wish to identify the personality types involved.

- The first applicant feels at her best when actively helping someone else. There's nothing wrong with enjoying being helpful—but she also admits to feeling 'empty' if she's not in this role. How will this applicant cope with the fact that as a professional helper, she will sometimes not be able to help? Sometimes she will have no option but to simply 'watch the train crash'. She will find that people aren't necessarily ready to change just because they seek her help. Will it feel like 'helping' if all she does is wait for her clients to be ready to do something for themselves? How is she going to feel when some clients act like they don't want her help? What will it be like for her when clients fail to return, with no explanation offered?

- The second applicant doesn't easily relate to people in social situations—in fact it makes him anxious—but the role of counsellor or therapist gives him a way of interacting with others while keeping at a safe distance. How easy is it going to be for him to express warmth and empathy for another person's distress? And what about when his clients reject his penetrating analysis of their situation because they need him to acknowledge how they feel? He likes being 'in control', but often, as a professional helper, you don't actually feel in control at all. What is that going to be like for him?

- By contrast, the third applicant will find no difficulty in entering into her client's feelings. But she admits that her own feelings get completely 'bracketed' in the process. As a counsellor or therapist, she will need access to her own feelings, because they will provide an invaluable source of information as to what is happening between herself and her clients. Focussing on what other people need may make her an excellent mediator, but what happens if her own needs are neglected? Will she 'burn out' by failing to notice the warning signs of her own anger, frustration or depletion? And if she enters too far into her clients' needs and feelings, how easy will it be for her to maintain a more objective position?

- For the fourth applicant, counselling or therapy is a performance—a set of skills and techniques which need to be mastered, and at which the applicant aims to excel, like a champion athlete or sportsperson. There certainly are skills involved in our craft (and this book is largely concerned with them), but they are not 'skills' in the same sense as the skills of swimming, golf or pole vaulting. We can certainly feel some satisfaction when we 'know what to say' and find that our clients respond positively to it, but often, the 'skill' involved is to say very little or even keep silent (see Chapter 2). Nor is counselling a performance in the same sense as ballet, singing, acting, or playing an instrument. The client isn't our audience, and the counsellor can't expect applause. This applicant may struggle to empathise with his client's distress, because he will be too busy thinking, '*What do I do next? What is the key that will unlock this problem?*'

- The fifth applicant wants to be a therapist because she wants to *be* her therapist. This is quite common in people who have had a highly positive experience of being helped. It isn't 'wrong', but it isn't enough. The applicant will enjoy the advantage of 'knowing what to say' or 'knowing what to do' with her clients, at least some of the time, because she herself has been a client, and has internalised a set of useful therapeutic responses. But when her clients' issues and needs are very different from her own, she may struggle. Moreover, she cannot be a clone of her therapist—any more than she can make herself into a carbon copy of a trainer, or a 'master therapist'. She needs to find her own way of being a professional helper, drawing on her own personality and her own resources. Finally, making yourself into a therapist may seem to some people to be a perfect way to avoid growing and facing new challenges!

- *Rarely do would-be counsellors present a wish to solve their own problems as a reason for becoming a counsellor. Yet at a deeper level, a wish to understand ourselves more fully—and maybe to heal something we dimly perceive to be damaged or impaired within ourselves— is probably what motivates most of us.* This is the 'wounded healer' model, proposed by Jung and supported by the fact that healers and shamans in many cultures (e.g. Native American, Mongolian, Balinese) ended up in this role because they were believed to be 'in contact with the spirit world'. Secular Western societies do not think of emotional healing as a 'spiritual' matter, so our type of wounded healer is somewhat different—hardly any schizophrenics in our society end up as counsellors, despite their intense experiences—but 'wounding' is still present in most of our healers. Like it or not, many of us have been drawn to this profession because of unresolved emotional pain or a sense of something missing in our lives. Just as with traditional shamans, these 'wounds' sensitise us to the vulnerabilities of others, and hence fuel what we call 'empathy' for those we work with.

Read more

Thomas Maeder's 'Wounded Healers' (*Atlantic Monthly*, January, 1989: 37-47) is an introduction to this topic for the general reader. Michael J. Mahoney's *Human Change Processes* (Basic Books, 1991: 348-353) gives an excellent summary of the evidence supporting the 'wounded healer' hypothesis. See also Ione Lewis' qualitative study, reported in 'Personal History in the Choice of a Career in Counselling', *Psychotherapy in Australia*, 10, 2 (2004): 2231, and Joseph Poznanski and Jim McLennan's study of the personal backgrounds of psychologists with different therapeutic orientations *Australian Psychologist 38*, 3 (Nov. 2003: 223–226).

Sometimes people do partly know about these 'hidden' sides of themselves. They just don't want to reveal all of that stuff when they're trying to impress an interviewer with what a good counsellor they'll make! Sometimes they genuinely aren't aware of it. One of the functions of a good training program is to help you discover hidden things about yourself, so that your own blind spots will not get in the way of your entering deeply into a client's experience, won't prevent you from being there for him or her in the most useful way. It isn't shameful to realise that your motives for doing counselling might be less than glorious—although many of you will have an 'internal critic' that may invite you to think it is! Having such motives just puts you in the same position as nurses who enjoy feeling competent when they 'manage' sick, helpless people, sales people who enjoy being able to talk customers into buying something, or teachers who enjoy their feeling of expertise—and even their feeling of frustration—as they patiently explain the same things year after year to successive groups of school students who 'just don't get it'.

Interestingly, when your clients come to you and start describing their problems, you will find that they do pretty much what most of you did in responding to our question, 'Why do you want to help people?' Your clients will start by giving you the surface of the problem, and the surface of themselves (more on this in Chapter 4). Often, that will be all that they are really aware of. If you listen well, many of them will reveal a lot more in later sessions. But in long term psychotherapy, over a period of years, clients may begin to discover things even further 'below the surface', including things that they may initially find it difficult to believe, or accept. For example, a person who has always seen herself as confident and robust may find that, deep down, she feels incredibly scared and vulnerable—but has 'cut off' her awareness of that vulnerability in order to survive and get ahead in the world. Or another person might realise that an episode of sexual abuse that took place many years before has in fact affected him profoundly, although he has always told himself that it 'didn't affect him much' and that it 'never worried him anyway'. It is important for you to know that these 'below the surface' parts of them are there, and can be explored, if clients so desire (many, of course, do not). If you have done a fair bit of exploration yourself, you will be far better placed to know how your clients may feel. *You can't take a client where you haven't been yourself* (see Chapter 8).

The problems clients present often seem insoluble precisely because they are presented at the surface level, at the 'safe' level, and because some important awareness is lacking or withheld (see Chapter 4). It is at the next level, where more of the reality of the person is revealed, that possible solutions may open up. Your job as a counsellor is to create the right conditions under which your clients can reveal more of themselves, both to you and to themselves.

Of course, this is only one way of seeing counselling. Some well-regarded current models of counselling do not see it as about 'revealing' or 'exploring' clients' inner worlds. Rather, they would talk about 'finding out about the problem', 'discovering exceptions to the problem' or 'entering into dialogue with the problem'. This sounds very different from the kind of counselling we have been talking about. But is it really as different as it seems? For more on this, see Chapters 5, 6 and 7.

Now back to you. Many applicants become interested in a possible career as a counsellor without any experience of what the role actually entails. In this they are no different from the average school leaver or university graduate, who may know little about the career she or he is embarking upon. Universities are full of people studying criminology because they 'love watching CSI' on television, and full of people who opt for nursing because they 'quite liked taking care of Mum when she got sick'. They have had a small-scale or vicarious experience of their chosen career, and on that slender basis have opted to pursue it as a vocation.

Typically (at least in our society) you don't know what a job feels like until you're actually doing it. Before that, you have to go on bits and pieces of experience, often indirect, and fantasies—ideas about what the job might be like—and these fantasies are probably shaped by some of your own private wishes and fears. If you secretly desire to be a powerful, expert person who can 'see into' others and solve their problems for them, then your conception of psychology might be informed by that fantasy. If you thrill at the thought of 'saving' your fellow humans from despair, drug addiction or suicide, then your fantasies about counselling might be shaped by that imagined gratification. And so on.

It is in the nature of most career fantasies that they rarely include the 'down side'. However, many applicants for counselling training do have some concept of what the drawbacks of the role might be. Frequently mentioned are, 'You might feel really drained by listening to people's problems all day', or 'You might feel bad because you can't always help people solve their problems'. Some will go straight to the bogeyman of all trainee counsellors: 'What if you have a client and they go and commit suicide? How are you going to feel?' In a broader sense, many of us share the fear that counselling may do damage—which also indicates that trainees (and most practising counsellors as well) feel partly or wholly responsible for their clients even though rationally, we can tell ourselves that our feeling of responsibility may be an illusion, and may not be helpful. *Learning to be responsible without feeling over-responsible is a vital part of learning to be a counsellor or therapist.*

OFFICIAL AND UNOFFICIAL THEORIES OF HELPING

How do human beings develop problems—the sort of problems that drive them to seek counselling? What are your beliefs about change, and how human beings can change? Before you read further, think about your personal answers to these questions, and jot them down. Your answers might be described as your 'implicit theory of counselling'—the set of assumptions you have accumulated over the years prior to your formal training. Here are some common answers that trainees tend to give at the very start of their course, and you may notice that one of these corresponds particularly closely with the answers you yourself came up with:

- *'People develop problems because they have bad childhoods*—like, they're abused, or their parents hate them—whatever. And then they don't really have a chance of being happy, because they're carrying all that baggage from the past. Counsellors can help them to look at what happened when they were growing up, come to terms with it, maybe let go of it, so they can be happier.'

- '*Some people just have bad habits*. They always look at the glass and see it's half-empty, whereas in fact it's half-full, only they never see that! Counsellors can help them to think more positively, and stop being so negative—they're really holding themselves back, only they don't realise it!'

- '*A lot of people are miserable because they're in bad relationships*. Often there's nothing wrong with them—it's the other person that has the problem! People need to start standing up to toxic parents and abusive partners. When they stop taking garbage from other people, they'll start to feel a whole lot different!'

- '*People could change quite easily if only someone listened to them properly*. The trouble is that we're surrounded by people who don't listen, they just preach at us, or tell us to 'quit complaining!' Counsellors can really listen, and just by being listened to, the person can start to feel different. Maybe this is the first time in their whole life that anyone has actually wanted to listen to them!'

- '*People have problems because they don't understand what's going on inside of them*. Maybe they're having a midlife crisis or something, or they've got some complex or phobia. When a counsellor can come into the picture and show them what's really going on, then they can start to change'.

Read more

As you'll see later in your training, these typical statements reveal underlying assumptions that correspond with particular major 'models' of counselling and therapy. Typical of the first 'theory of change' is Oliver James' popular book, *They F*** You Up: How to Survive Family Life* (2002; Rev. Edn Bloomsbury, 2007; first published 2002), a powerful if somewhat overstated argument that early interactions with parents and siblings have much more influence on the problems we later develop than genes do.

The 'bad habits' theory is well represented in the behaviourist and cognitive behavioural model, and has heavily influenced 'Positive Psychology', as exemplified by Martin Seligman's *Learned Optimism* (Knopf, 1991), and the much-publicised research on intimate relationships conducted by John Gottman (John Gottman and Nan Silver, *The Seven Principles for Making Marriages Work*, Weidenfeld & Nicholson, 1999).

Like the third statement, systems theory does, very broadly, claim that our problems are maintained by others with whom we interact, and that if we act differently towards them, our problems are likely to diminish. Family systems theory lies behind popular books like Harriet Goldhor Lerner's *The Dance of Connection* (Harper & Row, 2001).

The fourth statement, which sees good listening as the key to change, probably corresponds well with a central tenet of Carl Rogers, as described in *On Becoming a Person* (frst published 1961; Constable, 1967).

Finally, the fifth 'theory of change', while stated here in a very simplistic way, is essentially similar to any view that emphasises the importance of having insight (self understanding)—Freud's psychoanalytic approach is ultimately dependent on such a theory. Freud presented his ideas (as they were at the time) very readably in *Introductory Lectures on Psychoanalysis*, first delivered in person in 1915-16 (English translation, Pelican Freud Library, 1973).

Each theoretical model is, after all, the creation of a human being, and those who are attracted to a particular model are likely to share at least some of the assumptions of the founder. In fact, they may even share aspects of his or her personality! If you are interested in this idea, try reading a biography of the individual who formulated the ideas behind your favourite approach to counselling or therapy—people such as Sigmund Freud, Melanie Klein, Carl Rogers, Fritz Perls, B. F. Skinner or Gregory Bateson (neither Skinner nor Bateson were therapists, but they evolved the theories that led to revolutionary new approaches to helping).

As you progress through your training, you will see how what you currently believe about people and their problems is both true and not true, both useful and not useful. You will also start to realise that it isn't just your theory of change that matters, it's what your client believes that can make the difference. Some clients are determined to 'learn new attitudes', while others begin, 'I have to tell you about my past—I know my problems are all tied up with what happened to me when I was growing up in my family'. What happens when your theory of change doesn't fit the client's is something we will need to return to later in this book. For more on the client's theory of change, read Barry Duncan, Scott Miller, Bruce Wampold & Mark Hubble's *The Heart and Soul of Change: Delivering What Works in Therapy* (2nd Edn, American Psychological Association, 2009; originally published 1999 as *The Heart and Soul of Change: What Works in Therapy*).

COUNSELLING: THE INSTRUMENTAL VIEW

Now look back through the typical answers given above. How does each of them view the counsellor's part in the client's change? Do all of them, or most of them, have any common assumptions about the way that counsellors and therapists can help change to come about?

We're guessing that relatively few of you will spot the shared assumption, so we'll simply tell you what it is. *Four of the five statements give the counsellor an active role in the process of change.* Either the counsellor gives information, or the counsellor 'helps the client to understand' something, or the counsellor provides action strategies, or the counsellor 'really listens' (thus providing something nobody else has provided), and so on. The most basic fantasy that shapes trainees' assumptions about what a counsellor is, and about what she or he will do when she/he becomes a counsellor, is that a counsellor *does something to* a client, or *acts in a certain way with* a client, and that is what catalyses the change. It is true that good counsellors act in a certain way—but the 'way' that will reliably catalyse change within clients is not what most people imagine it to be. It does not reside in clever words, expert advice, or interventions that 'cut to the heart of the problem'.

Unfortunately, this concept of counselling is very prevalent, not just among lay people, but also among employed professionals who actually practise counselling—psychologists, doctors, social workers, welfare workers, nurses, and so on. Our society is convinced that counselling (or that even vaguer and more mysterious thing, 'psychotherapy') is a process in which *somebody does something to somebody*. Have a look at the following statements, all of which you will recognise from TV or press reporting:

- The survivors of the tragedy are receiving counselling

- The employees who were made redundant last week are being counselled

- Perpetrators of abuse need to be counselled, so that they learn that their actions are criminal and unacceptable

- There's something wrong with you—you need counselling!

- I don't think much of the idea of going for counselling. They try to psych you out, and write a book about what's inside your head. But seeing a Life Coach is OK, 'cos they just help you to sort out your goals and organise your life so you can be who you want to be.

In all of these examples, the way that the sentences are constructed shows that the speaker regards counselling as an instrumental process—it is something that is 'done' to the client, in order to achieve a desired effect (and the effect is one desired by the counsellor or by his employer, or by society generally, not necessarily one desired by the client).

Here are some examples of things you will often hear said by professionals in our field. The words we've italicised are the ones that indicate the professional's 'instrumental' thinking:

- We run a residential program for substance abusers. Of course most of them are pretty reluctant to commit to the program, but *we use Motivational Interviewing to get them in*. It makes a big difference.

- Statistics show that couples stay in treatment for an average of six sessions. So *we do family of origin work in session three, and by session four, the counsellor should be moving on to giving the clients homework based on Gottman's research.*

- My clients respond really well to a Narrative approach. *I generally start by externalising the problem*, because that stops clients feeling like they are the problem, and they start to realise that the *problem* is the problem.

- Well, I suppose *I work with the transference*. That's really where the work gets done.

All of the above represent variants of the instrumental view of counselling and therapy. As we shall see, this view is one dominated by the left hemisphere of the human cerebral cortex—the priorities of the left hemisphere include usefulness and pragmatism, a respect for 'rules' and a distrust of 'instinct' and emotion. If this is how many counsellors and therapists themselves talk, what wonder is it if trainees frequently believe that counselling is an active process in which they must do something to their clients, and that training programs are there to equip them with things to do—techniques, strategies, time-frames, models, and so on?

We are not saying that all of these assumptions are completely wrong. We are saying that paying too much attention to them now is not the best way to learn to be a counsellor. If there is a place for them, it will be much later in your professional development. When we say these things, some of you will already be feeling disappointed and a bit irritated, we suspect. 'Why are they rubbishing these ideas about counselling, if so many people have them? Is it just an ego-trip for them?' Secretly, some of you will already be saying, 'Yeah, but what would they know? I'm going to master those techniques, and then it'll be a cinch'. We can't stop you thinking any of those things, but we can present an alternative view of counselling which we have come to believe is much closer to the subtle reality.

In this book, we shall attempt to show you that counselling is an interpersonal process in which clients can change not as a result of the counsellor's direct interventions ('doing') but as a result of the way the counsellor is with them ('being'). If that sounds a bit Eastern, a bit Buddhist, a bit 'mystical', then maybe this is because counselling (at least in the form we shall teach in this book) shares some common ground with those non-Western traditions. And of course, today's counselling, which most people think of as a purely secular thing, fulfils some of the same roles as spiritual guidance might once have filled, in a time when people worked on the health of their souls, rather than going to the gym, and sought Heaven rather than 'happiness'.

COUNSELLING: 'BEING WITH', NOT 'DOING TO'

The principles underlying our 'interpersonal process' model of counselling were developed by American psychologist Carl R Rogers in his *Counseling and Psychotherapy* (Houghton Mifflin, 1942) building on a foundation laid originally by Sigmund Freud in Vienna half a century earlier. Rogers used as a point of departure Freud's idea of 'free association', in which a troubled person was invited to talk freely about whatever was on his/her mind, moving from one subject to another at will. Clearly, in order to encourage patients to talk freely, it was important to receive whatever they said calmly and matter-of-factly. Judgements and personal reactions from the therapist might get in the way of the patient's openness. In place of Freud's emphasis on understanding and *insight* (to be worked for by the joint efforts of patient and analyst) Rogers foregrounded *the experience of the counselling relationship itself*—the client would develop, grow, and change, because of the way the counsellor was with her, not because of anything decisive or authoritative that the counsellor did. All that the counsellor 'does' is to create the conditions under which this process of self-discovery, self-confrontation, and self-acceptance can occur. (For a more detailed account of Rogers' and Freud's contributions to our modern notions of 'counselling' and 'therapy', see Chapter 5).

Of course, not all clients want this from counselling, and some will be alarmed by it, or put off. These clients may need to be worked with differently, something we'll say more about later in this book (see Chapter 7). However, this is the model we shall be introducing, and we believe that it is by far the best one for any trainee counsellor or therapist. It teaches respect for clients, it teaches humility for counsellors. It puts you (and all of us) in touch with your own anxiety and with your own needs (to control, to compete, to 'rescue'). It is less likely to do harm to clients than any other model. It directs your attention, not to what you can *do to* clients, but to how you need to *be with* them. It is forms the bedrock of our approach in this book.

> 'Most of us have been dragged kicking and screaming to the realization that what really works in psychotherapy is the relationship between the therapist and the client. That's what does the work. We are all devastated by this reality because we spent years and a lot of money learning a particular technique or theory, and it is very disheartening to realize that what we learned is only the vehicle or springboard to create a relationship—which is where the real work happens.'
> – Daniel Stern (*Infant Mental Health Journal*, 2008): quoted in Allan Schore, Presentation at Australian Childhood Foundation Conference, Melbourne, August 2014.

Now, let's return to the point we reached some pages back, where we were dealing with your choice of counselling or therapy as a potential career.

TRAINING: A CHANCE TO FIND OUT WHAT COUNSELLING IS ACTUALLY LIKE

Nearly all of us have been 'on the receiving end' of teaching, and some of us have been on the 'receiving end' of nursing. By contrast, few people outside of the counselling world have much idea of what counselling actually is. Those who have sought counselling have had particular experiences of counselling, from the position of client, which may or may not give them much idea of what counselling actually is. In other words, they will have seen *a* counsellor who works in *one* way. For them, that experience will 'stand for' counselling as a whole. A much smaller number will have seen more than one counsellor or therapist, and hence have some basis for comparison. Counselling is something that is not easy to describe in words, and most clients either do not want to talk about such 'private' conversations, or, even if they do, fail to convey what they have experienced to their families or friends. Hence, fantasies have plenty of space in which to flourish—not to mention the stereotyped portrayals of counselling and therapy in movies and television sitcoms.

You may believe that the main function of a counselling training program would be to train you to be a counsellor—it sounds self-evident, doesn't it! And many trainers would agree with you. However, we think that what training programs really do—and all they *can* really do—*is give trainees a realistic experience of what it is like to be a counsellor, which is subtly different*. A training program should put your fantasies in perspective. It should require you to do what you will actually be doing as an employed professional—or as close as possible to it. Hence, most programs will ask you to try yourself out as a 'helper' to your fellow trainees. Hopefully, many will also offer opportunities for you to practise counselling with real clients, under close supervision, in a clinic or agency (sometimes called a 'placement', or 'internship'). After you have completed this experience, some of you may already be operating with the sensitivity and skill of a competent counsellor—which will of course grow with every new client that you see thereafter. Or you may have discovered that parts of yourself can block you from being with your clients in a helpful way. If this is you, there will need to be more self-exploration.

Importantly, another thing that a training program can do is to *give those trainees who've never seen a counsellor or therapist some sense of what it might be like to be a client*. The program cannot force its students to enter therapy; it can only recommend it. Fortunately, many students do take up the suggestion—often because something within the training program has 'stirred up' feelings within them that they realise they need to explore before setting themselves up to work as professional helpers of others. Aside from that, most training programs offer students some in-class experiences of being a client—if only for short periods of time, while acting as 'client' to a fellow student. This may sound very inadequate by comparison with a full experience of being a client for a year or more, but it is surprising how well these brief experiences can assist trainees to acknowledge more consciously what it is they might need to 'work on'. Finally, participating in a small experiential group with fellow students can put all of them in touch with feelings of vulnerability, fear of judgement, and emotional overwhelm—all things that a client often feels in counselling. We revisit this type of group experience in Chapter 4.

Training programs vary in how they prepare you to be a counsellor or therapist. We believe the best preparation includes experiential learning that pays attention to the development of the therapist's own self and the nature of the therapeutic relationship. Contrary to what many psychology programs teach, we do not believe that this relationship is one between a detached 'expert professional' and a helpless 'patient'. Rather it is a relationship between two human beings. It is at the level of your common humanity that you will best connect with your clients. Our approach provides you with the best preparation for this because you will have learned what it means to discover yourself. If you have received this kind of training, you will develop a confidence in your ability to sit with a range of people in distress and to know that your attentive presence is often all that is needed. Of course your abilities will grow with experience as this profession is one in which you will never stop learning.

Once embarked on your training program, you will start to encounter the reality of what this work entails. It will be (or at least, should be) confronting. Most of you will find that your existing ideas of what is involved in counselling will need considerable modification. If you have just read the preceding paragraph, then you will know what we mean! A few of you will immediately start to question your choice when you discover what you are actually going to have to do. Some of you will find it uncomfortable, but this will not deter you. A few of you will get a long way into the training program before finally realising that counselling is not for you.

It is important for you all to know that there is no shame in such realisations. In fact, it is much better for you to withdraw from a program than to continue purely because you feel you 'must' or in the flickering hope that maybe some day the role will feel less alien to you. By making a mature decision before you actually seek employment as a counsellor, you will be playing behaving responsibly towards your future clients—as well as honouring your own sense of what feels right for you.

YOUTH AND MATURITY: ADVANTAGES AND DISADVANTAGES

Two categories of individual typically self-select for counselling training programs. One consists of young adults who may elect to complete counselling subjects (units, modules) as part of their undergraduate degree, or who graduate as psychologists, social workers or welfare workers, and move straight on to a specialist counselling training as a further development of their professional skills. The other category consists mostly of older adults—from their early thirties right through to their fifties, sixties or even (occasionally) older. These are usually not 'helping professionals' by original training, but rather, are individuals who have decided to go back into formal education specifically in order to become counsellors or therapists. Both categories of applicant have some things in their favour, and face some challenges.

Older applicants have typically had a chance to experience many of the predictable stages of life, and the predictable 'landmark events': leaving home, living in a committed relationship with a partner of choice, perhaps the break-up of such a relationship (or several break-ups); the birth of children (or the failure to have children, or the decision not to have them); perhaps the loss of a close family member; living in new places, or new countries; learning new work responsibilities; having to take leadership roles (or failing to be offered them), and so on. None of these experiences, by itself, or even cumulatively, makes you a competent counsellor, nor does having gone through them necessarily mean that you are a 'better person' or have achieved any higher level of understanding of self or others. But frankly, they often help!

Most people with a reasonable level of openness to experience, and a willingness to be honest with themselves, learn the lessons of life bit by bit, and this confers on them a certain credibility when they come to interact with clients—not, we hasten to say, because they will be giving their clients little homilies based on their own experience, but because of the quality of empathy that will be available to them as they listen to their clients talk. A compassion that is rooted in a feeling for the 'human condition' is very different from a breathless, '*Oh, gosh, how terrible for you! I can't imagine what you must've felt!*' Not too many clients are going to feel supported or understood when they hear their counsellor make that kind of response!

On the other hand, older applicants can sometimes be anxious and driven, worried (at least initially) about whether they will be able to complete assignments or skills activities well enough to graduate. They have to juggle the demands of family and work, as well as their training program. They may be prepared to find out previously hidden things about themselves, but the cost of such self-confrontation may be very high—it may cost them their marriage, for example, a not uncommon outcome for mature-age trainees.

Some older applicants may have become prisoners of their particular life experiences—as when ex-alcoholics assume that they know every aspect of what another alcoholic is going through, and feel free to confront him with his 'stinking thinking'! Or when a parent who has raised children assumes that troubled clients will be able to solve their difficulties with their offspring in the same way the counsellor did (or will be unable to solve them, because they themselves failed to do so). These examples of what developmental psychologists call 'overgeneralisation' (assuming that your personal experience applies to everyone) are found just as readily in young applicants, but they can become more entrenched in older applicants. For some people, 'I went through it, and I know' becomes a rigid position, which they are unwilling to modify. Such applicants probably have no place in a counsellor-training program.

By contrast, most individuals in their early twenties have yet to sort out many of their life priorities, and may not yet have achieved functional autonomy as adults. Due in part to economic pressures or cultural expectations, they may still be living at home with their parents. Their experience of committed relationships may be limited. Most of them will not yet have experienced parenthood. In all of these ways, it is much harder to be a counsellor at the age of 23 than it as at the age of 33 or 43—even if you want to work only with children or adolescents. Of course, there are exceptions—young adults who, due to unusual personal qualities, or the early experience of suffering or loss, have achieved 'precocious adulthood', and whose resilience and self-awareness has enabled them not only to 'grow up faster' than their peers, but to achieve a higher level of empathy for others than would be normal for their age group. These are the type of readers that Alice Miller is addressing in her deservedly well-known *The Drama of Being a Child* (see Must-read books).

Young people, regardless of their prior life experience or level of emotional maturity, have abundant energy, and a willingness to believe in others that older people often lack. Altruism is not age-related, but it is probably easiest to sustain in young adulthood, before life's blows have fallen too heavily. This can be a great asset for a beginning counsellor. It can also be a liability—as when a young trainee is shattered when she finds herself with a client 'old enough to be her mother', and realises that she is totally out of her depth. *But what can I say to her? I haven't had kids—I don't even know that I want them—and she's having all these problems and I keep thinking, 'Why don't you just get over it?' and I know I can't say that!*

If you fall into this category, and are reading what we have just written, you may well be feeling upset, even angry. 'How dare these people tell me that I'm not 'mature enough' to be a counsellor! I *know* I'm going to be a great counsellor!' It's understandable that you would feel this. It's like your parents telling you that you're not old enough to know when you're really in love! And in fact, the two have a fair bit in common! Powerful convictions about what is 'right' for us are generally more based on the wishes and needs of infancy than on rational intellect. That does not mean such convictions are always wrong, but it does mean that they are potentially treacherous. Often, the only way we can learn which of these instincts to trust is to follow them—and then find that they have betrayed us. After we've done that a number of times, over a number of years, we can begin to say to ourselves, 'Yes, it feels right, but it's probably not going to work, and I'd better not do it'.

Think about it

Over a number of years teaching in several different training programs, one of us (Hugh) came to believe that the key 'age of maturity' for beginning counsellors is sometime in the early thirties. By then, he guessed, trainees would have lived long enough to be able to see some of the patterns of their lives repeating. They would thus be able to become 'curious observers' of their own lives—an ability which helps immeasurably with gaining realistic detachment when considering the lives of others. Recent research on brain development supports that guess. We now know that the full maturation of the brain is incomplete until the early to mid-thirties, and may continue even longer—into mid-life (see Kurt W. Fischer and Ellen Pruyne, 'Reflective Thinking in Adulthood' in Jack Demick and Carrie Andreotti, Eds. *Handbook of Adult Development*, NY, Springer 2003: 169ff). What this maturation makes possible is 'reflective thought'—the ability to stand back from ourselves to some degree, and to see ourselves simultaneously both 'from the inside' and 'from the outside'. Obviously, this level of brain development is not going to occur at exactly the same age for everyone. But it will probably occur at some point between the late twenties and the mid thirties, and when it occurs, it is likely to prompt a shift from 'just living' to asking 'Why am I living?' 'What do I really want?' 'Is the way I'm living working for me?' These are the questions that psychodynamically-informed developmentalists like Daniel Levenson saw as typical of the 'Age Thirty Transition', and the ages he assigned to this period (he saw it as occurring somewhere between 27 and 33) correspond quite well with what neurologists are now saying about brain maturation. See Daniel Levinson, Charlotte Darrow, Edward Klein, Maria Levinson & Braxton McKee: *The Seasons of a Man's Life*, Ballantine Books, 1978); Eric Kandel, *In Search of Memory:*

The Emergence of a New Science of Mind, Norton, 2007).

So, it makes sense that the late twenties-to mid-thirties is not only the stage at which *clients* start to seek change in their lives, but also the age at which *you* may start to think, 'Maybe I could be a counsellor'. The two go together. Reflective thought is necessary for a full competence as a counsellor—and for a satisfying experience of self exploration as a client. Anyone who has worked in a campus counselling service will recognise what I mean. The majority of clients in their late teens or early twenties come for only one or two sessions. Once they gain a 'handle on the problem' or feel that their difficulties are diminishing, they will want to believe that counselling is over. There is a deep wish not to be dependent, and to take back control over their own lives as quickly as possible. Of course there are exceptions, but we are talking about a statistical generalisation. Young adults in their early twenties are not often ready for in-depth counselling or therapy; by their early thirties, there is typically a willingness to engage in greater depth, and with less fear of dependency or stigma. Similarly, some very young counselling trainees like to feel that they 'haven't got any real problems' and can leap straight to learning 'techniques' to help others. They don't like the idea of going into anything too personally painful, or anything that might make them feel dependent on a parent-like therapist.

In a way, trainees in their early thirties combine the best of both worlds—they should have sufficient experience and maturation to have begun to reflect on the events and patterns of their own lives, but they still possess some of the energy and faith of the younger adult, that faith which can be so important in nurturing change in others.

WHAT LIES AHEAD FOR YOU?

We have tried to be honest with you about some of the challenges that learning to be a counsellor will bring, whether you are an older or a younger applicant. The real proof of your suitability for counselling will not be found in any set of principles that we can set out, but in what happens within you as you engage with the training program. Depending on how thorough the process of selection has been, up to one third of a class will not complete the course, and many of these will drop out during, or at the end of, their first year. Counselling is definitely not for everyone. Some of those who drop out will have been drawn to the training—often unconsciously—because it promised them personal development: greater self-knowledge, and new skills for living: a kind of personal 'therapy' in fact, if not in name. In a year or even a semester of training, these students will have realised some important things about themselves: their time will not have been wasted. They have clarified that they need to heal themselves, rather than assume the uncertain and sometimes burdensome role of being a healer of others. What they have studied should assist them with their own relationships at home and at work, and enhance their people skills generally—perhaps more than they realise at the time.

Those who remain at the end of the first year should have a much more realistic sense of what being a counsellor means. They will be aware of the ways that the role will challenge and unsettle them, and be prepared to undertake further personal work to tackle these challenges. But they will also have begun to develop a sense of joy and excitement about their participation in helping another person—feelings that will sustain them through the difficult process of learning professional competence.

What lies ahead of you in your first year? First, you can expect a lot of emphasis on self-examination—facing yourself honestly, discovering things about yourself you didn't know, comparing yourself with models of how human beings ideally should be (but rarely are). For most students, this is an exciting journey of discovery, but it can also be somewhat alarming. You may notice that your own experiences resemble those of people with 'serious problems', and wonder if you are therefore 'crazy'. You may wonder whether perhaps you are 'not normal' because your experiences don't fit what is described in textbooks of human development.

All of this will happen *even if you are doing a program of study that is primarily cognitive in focus*—a program where you are asked to read, think, discuss, and write assignments, as you would be in most university subjects. Just reading and thinking about the subject matter of human behaviour and human distress—which you will inevitably relate to yourself—will challenge you, and may even stir up long-buried pain. In programs that include more intense interaction with other students, where you are required to *talk about* your discoveries, and challenged by the way others react to *you*, rather than just to your *ideas*, this challenge will be much greater still.

What are called 'skills' in counselling and therapy are not things that can be learned by rote. Trainees may acquire phrases like, 'What I hear you saying is …' or learn to ask, 'How does that make you feel?' But such responses are pretty useless without the empathy, curiosity and honesty that good counsellors possess. Empathy, curiosity and honesty are *capacities* rather than skills—they can be 'developed', but they cannot be 'learned' in a mechanical way and trotted out on demand. Most trainees already possess these capacities, at least in some degree, and they can be expanded (those who do not possess them at all will probably not belong in a training course of this nature). So, as you start working through this book, and begin to practise the 'skills of holding' (Chapter 2) or 'exploring' (Chapter 3), you will rapidly find that things which appear very straightforward when you read about them are, in fact, not straightforward at all.

Some of you will be immediately challenged by the very idea that you will often need to sit back and listen to your client, without saying anything much at all, even if your client is in distress. It will feel 'wrong', it will feel restrictive, you will 'stiffen up' and for a time, struggle with the whole idea. Here again you will be developing not just a skill, but a *capacity*—the capacity to 'hold' another person without having to be active or vocal, to remain calm in the face of their pain or confusion. Similarly, the 'skills of encountering' (see Chapters 4 and 6) will demand a capacity to say openly what is not normally voiced in social situations, and a capacity to risk a higher level of interpersonal honesty than most of us normally trust ourselves to display. So, even in learning 'how to do counselling', you will be, constantly, learning about your own limitations and potentials, discovering your assumptions (the things you take for granted), and questioning habits of behaviour that previously felt like 'part of you'.

Counselling is a practical art. It cannot be learned solely by reading, watching demonstrations, discussing, listening to lectures, researching, and writing assignments. These cognitive activities are only adjuncts to your most important avenues of learning, which will be largely experiential. *Experiential learning* (learning from direct experience) is of central importance in any 'applied' subject—like teaching, nursing, and medicine. You can't learn to teach without standing in front of a class, you can't nurse without spending time on a hospital ward. And although you can sit and practise in a simulator, you won't get your license without actually driving a car in traffic, and doing a reverse park under stress! And you can't learn to be a counsellor without counselling—and (we strongly believe) knowing what it is like to be counselled.

In learning counselling, however, you will be asked not just to engage in relevant experiences, but also to reflect upon them, to analyse them, and (probably) to write about them. All of these latter activities will assist you to get more understanding of yourself and others out of the experience. So, unlike in most subjects, you will find that your written work—the more academic side of your studies—will often be focussed on your experiential learning, rather than on what you have read or heard in lectures. In marking our students' assignments, we're less impressed by the student who has read and cited twenty books and articles than by the student whose bibliography contains only five, but who shows that she is able to apply what she has read in a thoughtful and appropriate way to experiences she has gained through skills practice, personal therapy, or experiential group work.

Self-awareness, experiential learning, and regular simulated counselling sessions are core to most reputable counsellor training programs. Your course will not be boring! But if you have been trained to write university essays in psychology, other social sciences, or even humanities, you may initially find it difficult to adjust to assignments that ask you to write personally, yet at the same time require you to develop a different kind of 'objectivity' from the kind that most academic programs insist upon. Objectivity is not achieved simply by avoiding the pronoun 'I', and substituting 'the present author'! Nor does drawing upon experiences of your own necessarily make your assignment 'purely anecdotal' and therefore worthless. The kind of objectivity we seek in counselling programs is the ability to stand back from yourself and your experiences and to reflect upon those experiences, not just as *you* see them, but as others might see them. You cannot expect that everything about you is going to be fine, normal and not open to question. This doesn't mean that your lecturers will ask you to produce harshly critical self-judgements. But it does mean that they will ask you to pay attention to what you do, and to the effects that your behaviour has on others, and then to write about this in an honest, 'transparent' way.

Spending time each week or fortnight in a small group with other students, where your main task is to share your honest reactions to each other, is a vital part of many training programs, and it is designed deliberately to develop these capacities. Small, interpersonally-focussed groups can be very effective learning tools (see Chapters 4 and 6). Yet even when groups are run to high standards of respect, support and confidentiality, a minority of students always find them difficult. It can be very challenging to be in a small group for 90 minutes where nobody sets a nice safe topic of discussion and where you must evolve rules and standards for yourselves! But in fact, almost any aspect of a personally-focussed counsellor training program can be confronting. Even writing an assignment that requires recounting painful personal experiences, or reflecting on one's personality or parenting, can have a similar effect—and sometimes does. If you enter a counselling training program expecting to 'sail through' with no distress, no embarrassment, and no painful self-realisations, then you are under an illusion. These things will almost certainly happen. You can choose to see them as opportunities for learning, or you can choose to reject the program because your feelings have been hurt. It's up to you.

Counselling is not always easy or pleasant. Occasionally, you are going to be confronted—even spoken to aggressively—by a client, and many times you are going to feel helpless, confused or vulnerable. Unless you have had such experiences in a safe environment, where others can assist you to examine your own reactions, and to understand what is going on (both for you, and for the person who confronts you), you will be ill-prepared for the work. While it is good that counsellors are sensitive, it is also important that they be able to tolerate situations of vulnerability or confrontation without undue anxiety, defensiveness, or panic. Hopefully, by the end of your first year of training, you will feel an enhanced ability to do just that, and you will embark on seeing clients under supervision with more confidence.

We have come to the end of our first chapter. We hope that we've made you think harder about some of your beliefs and assumptions about counselling. We also hope that we've helped you to realise that the time you spend learning to be a counsellor is going to be eye-opening and perhaps disquieting. If you can live with that, then you stand a good chance of eventually becoming a counsellor. If you can't—if you need to go on believing that you can be a great counsellor without ever having to look at yourself, or go through any uncomfortable realisations—then you are probably not ready to be a counsellor at this point in your life. And hopefully, sooner or later, someone will be honest enough to tell you that.

Chapter Summary

- Different personalities see the world differently
- People present themselves to the world at a superficial level that also protects them against uncomfortable self-knowledge
- Your wish to be a counsellor will reflect both reality and fantasy, both conscious and unconscious elements.
- One job of a competently-led training program is to assist you to understand yourself and your motives for doing this work more fully; in doing that, you will simultaneously be enhancing your understanding of others.
- The model of counselling employed in this book is one which emphasises being with clients rather than doing to. It is a process-oriented, relationally-driven view of counselling that emphasises the person of the therapist, rather than a content-driven, technique-oriented view.

Chapter 2

Being There: Developing The Capacity For Holding

Holding: the 'default setting'

Client: She didn't really say much at the end of the session. I'd cried a lot, I was pretty wrung out—but I somehow didn't need her to say anything. I just needed to know she was there, and she cared. She didn't need to say it in words. Actually, that probably would've got in the way.

Counsellor: He's very upset, very distressed, and I suppose I'm just trying to stay with him, so he knows he's not alone. I suppose I'm just being there.

Both these statements refer to what we call the capacities involved in 'holding'. The counsellor uses the phrase 'staying with' and 'being there', the client just experiences the effects of the non-anxious, empathic way the counsellor is relating to him. 'Empathy' is a term most often associated with psychologist Carl Rogers; it was psychiatrist and pioneer family therapist Murray Bowen who talked of the therapist's 'non-anxious presence' (although he probably drew the idea directly from psychoanalysis). Both capacities—empathy, and non-anxious 'being with'—are what make a good counsellor or therapist effective from the very first session. Other qualities may be required later, but these two are crucial. While we will speak in this chapter of skills involved in holding, the ability to sit with clients calmly and tune in to their feelings without losing our own objectivity is not a skill that can be mastered in a mechanical way. It does not reside in a form of words that we can learn by rote. It generally develops as we become more experienced in being with a variety of clients, and realise that we do not necessarily need to 'do' or 'say' anything for the client to settle, and start to work. The paradox here is that 'holding skills' are often skills of *not* saying, or *not* doing, and thus they may not seem like 'skills' at all—yet they are incredibly effective because they create a space for clients to fill.

The skills of holding are basic to virtually all forms of counselling and psychotherapy. They lay the foundations for a helpful relationship with a client. Holding skills allow clients to talk freely, and encourage them to say more about what they have already said—thus they give the client a lot of control over the content of the session (of course there are times when that may be counter-productive, but we'll come to that later in the book). When we employ holding skills competently, clients trust that we want to understand them. At a deeper level, holding helps clients to feel safe and looked after. If those words ('safe' and 'looked after') sound a bit childish—then they should. The fact is that most clients do feel a bit like children when they enter a therapeutic relationship, and the relationship itself recreates some aspects of early childhood feelings. In fact, it is usually the 'child' part of a client who needs something to be different, and hence seeks counselling.

There are several key ways that we can behave so that clients feel safe and looked after:

- We can be respectfully silent. This means not offering a response until the client seems to need one (purposeful use of silence)

- We can accurately reflect back or paraphrase something clients have just said, and accurately summarise a series of things they have talked about

- We can offer empathy, in words and non-verbal responses (which often communicate to clients more fully and effectively than words)

We return to these shortly. But first, a brief mention of non-verbal 'attending' to our clients—the messages we send with our faces and bodies—which of course form an important part of all three forms of holding—and perhaps the most important part, since most of us respond powerfully to non-verbal messages even though we may not be consciously aware of what it is we are 'receiving'.

Some counselling texts offer elaborate rules for non-verbal attending, and the more elaborate they are, the more they confuse trainees. For example, you may get instructions like: 'Maintain eye contact, but not too much'; 'Maintain eye contact but woops, people from some non-Western cultures find it invasive and disrespectful!'; 'Sit facing the client; woops, no, don't sit facing the client, sit three quarters turned towards the client!'; 'Sit close but not too close'; 'Sit distant, but not too distant', and so on. How on earth do you find your way through this apparent minefield?

We think it's better if you simply pay attention to how your client responds to you. If what you are doing is 'wrong' or uncomfortable for your client, you will pick up little cues that indicate their discomfort. And in a classroom practice session, you can ask straight out: 'How did I go?' 'Was I sitting too close/distant?' 'Did I look at you enough?' The answers that you get should tell you something about how your personal style affects another person—but it will also tell you something about *what they need from you*. Both are valuable. A few of you may not possess this level of sensitivity to others, and may benefit from individual coaching. However, individuals with inadequately developed social skills should probably not have gained admission to a training course in the first place.

A key exception to this would be if your difficulties stem from cultural differences. In other words, within your own culture of origin, your behaviour would come across as sensitive and appropriate, but within a Western cultural framework, it may seem awkward, intrusive (over-close) or even uninvolved (too distant). If this is the case, just experiment, and discover how easy or hard it is going to be for you to adopt a different set of 'automatic' behaviours when working with clients who do not belong to your own culture. By the same token, if you were born into the Western cultural framework, you will need to discover which of your taken-for-granted behaviours may not fit for clients from non-Western backgrounds, and when necessary, modify them accordingly. This is no different to adapting sensitively to clients with, for example, a trauma history or any other set of formative experiences that have led them to see the world differently from the way you do.

Most texts include a section on 'minimal encouragers'—sounds or words such as 'Mmm', 'uh-huh', 'yes' or 'right', which encourage clients to continue with what they are saying. We see these, not as 'skills' but as responses that nearly all of us possess as part of the normal social repertoire. In this sense, they are not things that students have to 'learn to do' because most people do them appropriately anyway. Minimal encouragers only become a problem when counsellors do them too often, or in a way that strikes clients as intrusive. It can, however, be a problem when a counsellor uses none at all for long periods, causing some clients to feel uncomfortable at what appears to be a complete lack of response. Again, the best way for trainee counsellors to guard against these (relatively rare) problems is simply to *check* with their 'client' after the end of a class practice session: *Did you notice me doing too much? Or too little? Did it get in the way when I said 'Wow!' that time?* Most students will never have a problem with minimal encouragers.

WHY HOLDING MATTERS

In *holding*, we do not go much beyond what clients themselves have said. We do not ask questions, direct clients' attention to new areas, or tell them what we think is the problem. We try to hold up a mirror to their view of the world, to 'echo back' to them their own reality.

Here is another client, speaking directly after a first counselling session:

Client: I can't remember much of what we talked about, to be honest. I suppose I just told her what I've been going through—the time went really quickly, and I don't think we actually got very far, you know, but it's funny—I felt like she understood me somehow, even though I don't think she actually told me what she thought, or suggested anything.

Again, this is how 'holding' tends to be experienced—it does not translate into words particularly well, and so client reports of good 'holding' tend to be vague and unspecific—another indication that they are responding from the 'child' part of them. If you employ holding skills well, clients will feel comfortable, and will probably want to come back for another session, but they won't necessarily know why. Nor will they relate what they've felt to anything you have done. And yet you have done a lot. This level of attention from another person—attention without crowding or pressuring—usually feels extremely pleasant, but most people rarely experience it except within a counselling relationship—one of the ways in which what counsellors and therapists offer differs markedly from the norm of social intercourse (see Chapter 5).

This client's counsellor may well have 'reflected' what he said, or made one or two empathic responses (see below). The client can't recall these responses explicitly, but instead, talks about the overall effect of being responded to in this way. *He was being affected at the level of relationship—the level of the 'right brain'.* Had the counsellor said something apparently authoritative—like offering a diagnosis or supplying some advice on how to tackle his problem—the client might well have remembered it, which might seem a better outcome. Yet it would not necessarily be better at all. If the counsellor had diagnosed or advised, it might well have taken the client off in directions quite different from those he would otherwise have been taken. And an early intervention might also have stopped the client from 'listening to himself' and instead encouraged him to look to the counsellor for leadership, structure and direction.

Think about it

In striking contrast to what clients feel, trainee counsellors mostly get anxious that they have not done enough, claiming that 'all I did was listen'. For them, 'being helpful' translates into 'doing something', which in turn usually means 'Saying more'. It is very hard, at first, to accept that your clients may need you to be quiet more than they need you to question, advise or inform them! These anxieties of new counsellors are partly due to the same 'instrumental' understanding of what counselling is which we noted in Chapter 1. They may also stem from hours of watching television counsellors—real ones like Dr. Phil and fictional ones like Paul in *In Treatment*—see further below.

Being on the receiving end of holding is very different from watching it when someone else does it, and it is something you can only experience when you take the role of client yourself in a classroom practice session, or in ongoing therapy with your own therapist. If your counsellor reflects well, using natural language that connects, *you will feel it in your body as you settle into the sense of being understood.*

If clients don't feel held initially, they are unlikely to go on to do real work with you—they will not go near the bits of themselves that really hurt. They may go through the motions, and try a few new behaviours in their lives, but they will not feel safe, they will not fully trust, and so they will not 'drop down' into deeper feelings and less comfortable thoughts. So holding skills are fundamental, not only to the first few sessions, but to the entire process of counselling and psychotherapy. They are the 'default setting' to which all competent counsellors and therapists easily and naturally revert whenever necessary. Even after a good relationship has been established, you will still need to return to holding skills frequently, and especially when there has been a temporary 'failure of empathy'—which is when a gap has opened between you and your client, when your client feels taken aback by something you've just said. In the language of 'holding', you may have 'let the baby slip'. Which brings us to a discussion of where the 'holding' metaphor actually comes from.

THE METAPHOR OF HOLDING

'Holding' is a metaphor derived from the way that caregivers (which mostly, but not necessarily, means 'mothers') physically relate to their babies. British paediatrician and psychoanalyst Donald Winnicott noticed that mothers (or most mothers, anyway) learn to hold their baby firmly enough for it to feel secure (it can't slip or fall), but not so tightly that the baby feels uncomfortable, or unduly restricted. The mother adjusts the way she holds the baby, so that her baby can feel comfortable. She is sensitive to its movements, and accommodates to what it seems to need—more support, or less, gentle patting or rocking, or just being still.

Psychoanalytic developmentalists guess that, for a baby, to be held in this way provides a *bodily experience of safety*, the feeling of being looked after, cared about. Of course the baby can't use words like 'safety' or 'being cared about'. It doesn't yet have any words. And the baby is probably only aware of those feelings when, momentarily, the 'holding' slips, and it no longer feels what it has, until then, taken for granted.

Read more

Apart from technical writings for his fellow analysts, Winnicott produced some books that were written for a non-specialist audience, in fact, for ordinary parents—for example, *The Child, the Family and the Outside World* (Penguin, 1964), in which he tries to convey to mothers that their babies have 'thoughts', and answers the question, 'Why do babies cry?' Some of you may be dubious about reading something written so long ago. If you have recently studied psychology, sociology, social work or nursing, you may well have been told that unless a reference is less than five years old, it is out of date, and not worth bothering with. This rule is derived from the physical sciences, where it makes some sense because research findings are constantly being published and new research generally supplants (or calls into question) earlier work. In our field, however, outstanding work based on clinical observation and analysis can remain relevant for a very long time. The human brain hasn't altered in any fundamental way since our ancestors were living in trees or caves! And far too many counsellors and therapists pick up words like 'holding' without any first-hand acquaintance with the writing of those who first used them. This contributes to loose use of such words, and to the employment of metaphors without any thinking-through of what they mean. In this book, we have tried to explain the metaphors we use, so you can see where they come from, and what they are intended to convey.

The counselling equivalent of 'holding' happens partly at a verbal level, and partly non-verbally. We may not physically hug or hold our clients—over the years counsellors and therapists have learned that such actions, at least in our culture, can have unintended, unfortunate consequences. And our 'babies' are not infants who cannot communicate with words, but adults, or children old enough to speak fluently.[1] Although there may be occasions when even an adult may enter a space that does not permit any words (for example, silent weeping, or frozen fear), adults and older children will normally communicate in language. So, the counselling equivalent of 'holding' happens at both a verbal and a non-verbal level. At a non-verbal level, it can happen through the counsellor not speaking at all, but being comfortable to leave a silence. A comfortable silence is very different from an uncomfortable silence (where perhaps the counsellor is feeling anxious and 'stuck' because she doesn't know what to say or do).

Ideally, you as counsellors will be sensitive to the needs of your clients, giving them the sense that they are heard and understood ('holding them securely') but not intruding into their space with unnecessary comments and questions (which is the verbal equivalent of 'squeezing a baby too hard' or prodding it sharply). Conversely, if you respond carelessly and imprecisely, clients may feel that they are 'on their own'—judged, or misunderstood. Then you would be, as it were, 'letting the baby slip'. Being silent when the client really needs you to say something would be a non-verbal example of 'letting the baby slip'. Again, the client might feel alone, wondering what you think of what she/he has just said, longing for some acknowledgement from you—but getting only a blank look and no words at all. That is not a comfortable silence!

Because it is so hard for most trainees to remain silent in response to a client, particularly to one in distress, your trainers may commence the teaching of 'holding skills' with reflection of content and feeling (which we'll come to later in this chapter) rather than with purposeful use of silence. The mental discipline involved in formulating a good reflective response will actually assist you with learning how to remain silent. As you start to feel more comfortable with reflecting, and realise that a good reflection will often prompt the client to go further, you will relax, and become less anxious about having to say something and more sensitive to when your client needs to speak without interruption. However, we will start here by discussing the skill of purposeful silence because you should at least understand what is involved, even though you may not yet be ready to practise it.

'STAYING OUT OF THE WAY'—PURPOSEFUL USE OF SILENCE

Remaining silent sounds very easy, but in practice it is probably one of the hardest skills for a beginning counsellor to master. Partly, this is because the normal expectation in social conversation is that you should 'keep your end up', and say something as soon as your conversational partner pauses. A girl, in particular, grows up learning that being a good conversationalist means she must step in quickly, as soon as it is 'her turn'. If there is a pause, she learns to say, 'Wow! That's amazing!', ask a question, change the subject, or recount an experience of her own that seems relevant to what is being discussed. Silences often leave people (not just women) feeling uncomfortable.

In many social conversations, whether people know each other well or are hardly acquainted, participants seem to compete for talking space. They are in such a hurry to say their bit that they crowd each other, talking over each other in their anxious haste. When most people (including new counselling trainees) watch a film or video recording of a whole counselling session, it will likely seem very slow and even boring. Partly, this will be because there are some pauses, and because, when the counsellor does respond to the client, it will be after a few seconds, not hot on the client's heels. The 'anxious haste' of social conversation will not be present. As we anticipated earlier, a real counselling session may seem disappointingly slow compared to an heavily edited, or semi-scripted session on TV, where things seem to happen quickly, the counsellor always seems to know what to say, and the clients always respond spectacularly with tears, anger, or profound realisations.

Even a show as powerful and realistic as *In Treatment* (the US version of an Israeli series about a therapist and his patients) is not, in fact, as 'realistic' as it seems, because its twenty minute 'sessions' would in fact occupy forty-five or fifty minutes in real life, and because it is scripted and acted for maximum dramatic impact. In other words, the awkward pauses are kept to a minimum, and the hesitations, repetitions and false starts that typify almost any conversation (therapeutic as well as social) are not present. If you watch this kind of show, you will feel, 'Oh, I could never do this'. In some ways, Jennifer Melfi (the therapist who attempts to work with Mafia Boss Tony in *The Sopranos*) is a better example of a counsellor fumbling around for words, and trying out responses that often sound 'stiff' and forced, because the rapport between her and Tony wavers so much, depending on Tony's attitude that day! But even *The Sopranos* is far from adequate as a representation of 'real' counselling or therapy. We are shown only segments and have little sense of how things are unfolding overall, because the presentation skips over whole months of sessions. And of course, Tony is a far from typical client (though he is a typical *sociopathic* client, by turns charming, seductive, evasive and belligerent!)

WHY IS IT IMPORTANT TO 'WAIT BEFORE RESPONDING'?

- First, because if you do, you will often find that your client has something more to say. If you rush in with an immediate response, you will cut across this.

- Second, because leaving a pause gives the client some space to think about what he/ she has just said, or to 'collect his/her thoughts'. (This is one important aspect of how the experience of counselling and therapy actually encourages the development of the capacity for 'reflective thought', mentioned towards the end of Chapter 1. Some therapies refer to 'slowing down the process' so that clients become more self-aware. In long term therapy (see Chapter 9) clients often do learn to talk more slowly—in part because at the same time that they are speaking, they are internally checking whether what they are saying is fully true for them.

- Third, and most subtly, a pause communicates the message that your client, not you, is in charge of the session.

In counselling, clients need to be able to move freely around in the conversational field, at least at first. They need to sense your interest in whatever they want to say. But they should not feel that you are 'pushing' them or 'steering' them in a particular direction. They need to feel safe to talk about their problems in any order, at a pace that is right for them. They cannot do that if you are continually interrupting, asking questions, or offering your own opinions and experiences, as you might in normal conversation.

Of course we do not mean that you should leave long pauses (e.g. several minutes) before saying something in response to your client. The key principle is to leave *some* space before you rush in. You will soon get a sense of how long to leave, because if you stay quiet for a few seconds, you will find that some clients begin to speak again almost immediately, while others may take a bit longer. Still others will 'freeze', and it is clear that you do need to make some response (a reflection is the safest kind of response at this early stage in the counselling relationship). Such clients become *more* anxious if they are simply listened to than if they were being asked a series of questions, or given a lecture on their problem. These are the clients who look to a counsellor as an authority figure who will, like a doctor, rapidly tell them what is wrong, and offer a 'prescription'. And the practice of many helping professionals (psychologists as well as medicos) actively supports this perception. However, the majority of clients (at least in our experience) will not react in this way. They may initially feel a bit 'thrown' because the counsellor doesn't behave like a busy GP. But with good quality listening, and no unnecessary interruptions, they will relax and tell their story (see Chapter 4), beginning to feel understood in the process.

What we are saying, then, is that your job in the initial stages of the counselling relationship is to be sensitive to your client's need to talk, and to allow this to happen with as little interruption as possible. Wait until your client has clearly reached a temporary 'resting point' before you come in with your contribution. If you find that as soon as you start to speak, your client starts up again and talks over you, then let her finish, and try again later. There is no cast-iron 'rule' that you 'must' follow (e.g. 'Always leave five seconds before responding to anything your client has said'). Each client is different, and each counsellor is different, so you will need to be sensitive to what *this* client seems to need from you. You will find that we repeat this message throughout the rest of this book, because it is a principle that holds for almost every aspect of the counselling process.

Practice task

As a part of your training, you will probably be asked to engage in some version of the following. It will seem absurdly simple and perhaps rather boring, but wait and see what it reveals about you!

Pair with another trainee. One of you talks for, say, two minutes about a problem or issue she/he is currently facing. The other must simply listen for the whole time, without saying anything at all. Then reverse roles. Your tutor, or another student in the 'observer' role, will keep time for you. If you are the client, the time will go very fast, and you may well feel that you are only just getting started. If you are the counsellor, you will more likely feel overwhelmed by the amount that the client has said! At the end of the second two minutes, tell your partner honestly what it was like to have to listen without saying anything. Some of you will find it hard; others will find it much easier.

It's worth repeating this exercise on a later occasion, with a different partner, but this time with a longer (say, five minute) time allocation. Again, each of you should check out your own thoughts and feelings while in the role of silent listener. The observer could ask you:
• If you wanted to say something, what was it?
• What might you have been *feeling* that led you to want to speak?
• What might you have been *thinking*, that indicated to you that you needed to speak?
• How fast, or slowly, did the time pass for you? What do you think this might indicate about you?

These questions can fruitfully be discussed when the larger group reconvenes, and you can share your experiences with other trainees.

PERSONALITIES MAKE A DIFFERENCE

Personality differences will emerge sharply as you develop the capacity to 'stay out of the way'. If you are naturally introverted, and especially if your stance towards strangers is relatively withdrawn and guarded, you will have little difficulty in staying silent and waiting for your client to continue. But you may fail to recognise when your client is struggling, and really needs you to 'come in' with a contribution –such as a reflection, or an expression of empathy. If you don't, your client may be left feeling alone, judged or even foolish.

However, most of you will experience the opposite difficulty—you will find it very difficult to shut up! Individuals who take an active, problem solving stance in their everyday life—compulsive rescuers (Point Twos on the Enneagram, Pia Mellody's 'Co-Dependents')[2]—will want to rush in very quickly, almost as soon as the client has made the briefest, most superficial presentation of his/her difficulty. They will often interrupt or talk over the client in order to do so. They will feel anxious to show *that they can help*, even though, at this early stage, that is probably not what the client needs. If this is you, then you may be thinking, *'But I'm not anxious at all! I just want to be helpful! It's a good feeling!'* It's natural that you would think this, at this early stage of your training. Many of us are completely unaware of the level of anxiety we carry, and display, in ordinary conversation. And people don't usually identify 'wanting to be helpful' as a manifestation of anxiety. But it often is. Part of your development as a counsellor will be to realise when you actually are feeling anxious—which in turn will assist you to know more accurately when your *client* is feeling anxious.

Because 'helping' is so often interpreted as an active process—*doing* something or *saying* something (usually giving advice or information)—it is hard for many trainees to grasp that the majority of clients do not actually take in much of what is said to them in a first session (sometimes the first several sessions). So whatever advice, information or analysis the counsellor offers will often fall on deaf ears anyway. You can actually research this for yourselves once you begin to conduct a series of whole sessions with clients. You can ask your clients at the second session what they can remember from the first. Most clients will reply at an extremely general level—like the client whose words we quoted at the beginning of this chapter. They will retain little of what you actually said, though they will often remember aspects of your *presence*—how you were with them. Advice or information often gets 'bracketed' (although some clients can recall it when prompted to do so). There could be no clearer evidence that premature intervention is simply a waste of time!

At this point, some of you will still be worried. But how do I know when a client needs me to say something, or needs me to stay quiet? What we have said so far has not helped to reassure you, probably because your anxiety is focussing you on the details of what the client is saying, and you are trying hard to remember the specifics. In order to know when your client needs you to intervene, you need to be taking in information about *process*—how the client is behaving, rather than what she is talking about (the *content*). As you sit with a variety of different student clients in practice sessions, you will gradually become less worried about retaining all the details of what they are saying, and begin to relax. This, in turn, will assist you to pay attention to the subtle cues that will let you know whether the client is happy for you to remain silent, or needs you to participate more. Most of you will be able to recognise these cues easily, once you realise that it doesn't matter if you miss some details—the client will always repeat them later. You will have shifted your attention from yourselves (what *you* need in order to feel comfortable) to your client—what *he or she needs* in order to feel comfortable. And that is where your attention should be.

Be guided by how your client behaves. If she seems happy to continue talking without interruption from you, then let her do so. Sit back, and let the patterns gradually emerge from the details. If she seems to need more from you, then try some simple reflections (see below) and notice whether this helps. If you start to say something in response to a client, and the client interrupts you to explain something more, it is likely that he *needs* to say more, or that he wants to pick up on something you have said and wants to run with it. Of course, if your client never stops talking, or refuses to talk at all, that is a different situation and we'll consider those situations in Chapter 4.

THE METAPHOR OF 'REFLECTION'

Reflecting means saying back to the client in your own words a close approximation of what you have heard the client say. It is also called paraphrasing and sometimes *active listening*. Some textbooks divide reflecting into reflecting *content* and reflecting *feelings*, although a lot of the time, both will be involved. The term 'reflecting' suggests a mirror; and as with 'holding', it is useful to tease out the implications of this metaphor. Our reflection (in words) 'holds up a mirror' to what our client has just said by 'showing himself to himself'. However, a real-life mirror shows us two things simultaneously: first, it shows what we already know about how we look; second, it shows us what others see, but we do not—for instance, that we are unusually pale, or that our hair has become messed up without our realising. Think of reflecting as a verbal equivalent of a mirror, showing our clients what they are already aware of—but more than that. The 'more than' might take many forms. It might include the intensity with which a client feels something (an intensity he is unaware of), or the contradictory nature of what he has just said (he might not realise just how confused he is), or the relative importance of one element over the others. Here is a brief example:

Client: I'm really worried. She goes up and down like a yo-yo, and I never know what to expect. One day she's really sweet and it's like 'This is the person I was so attracted to'. But then the very next day, she'll be dark and bitter, and she's telling me things like, 'I know this isn't going to last'. And then of course I start thinking, 'Maybe she's going to give me the flick'. I just don't know where I stand with her.

Counsellor: You're really put in a difficult spot because she seems to change so rapidly from the person you know into a scary stranger. It leaves you questioning whether or not she really wants to be with you.

Notice that the counsellor's reflection doesn't include everything the client has said, and it may not prove completely accurate, but it does capture the main things. The counsellor uses her own words, but she doesn't go beyond what the client himself has talked about—she doesn't interpret or hint at a meaning that the client is unaware of. We call this 'staying close to the client'. Now, here is an example of reflecting which goes a little further—but still stays with what is actually present in the client's words and manner:

Client: Yeah, I try to talk to him all right, but he just doesn't listen. I might as well save my breath. I've told him hundreds of times how selfish he is, wanting to go out with his mates when I'm stuck at home with this little one [indicating her baby] and he says all the right things, yes, he understands, blah, blah, blah, but he just never gets it. He just goes on doing exactly what he wants, and I'm left here by myself.

Counsellor: So you're feeling like you've tried as hard as you possibly can to get through to him, but he just doesn't seem to get the message. It's frustrating, and it feels so unfair that he can go out, but you get left home with your baby.

[Here the counsellor has emphasised the client's frustration—present in her voice, although she has not actually used the word—and her sense of unfairness, again not mentioned explicitly. Can you see how the counsellor doesn't just echo back the client's content, but also picks up on key feelings that accompany what she is saying?]

Unlike a mirror or a still photograph, however, a verbal reflection within a therapeutic conversation is both temporary and insufficient. Anything we 'play back' to a client will necessarily be brief and inadequate. It is really just a 'snapshot' of how the client was, a minute or two ago, when they made their last statement. By the time we utter our reflection, the client may already have 'moved' a bit, be in a slightly different place. So we need to keep pace with him, 'updating' our reflections so that they capture at least some of what is new or different in what he has just said. Although we talk of *a* reflection, the real skill involved is the skill of offering *ongoing reflections*, a whole series of them. This is where another metaphor is useful—the metaphor of 'walking with the client'. Trainers and textbooks often use this metaphor to convey the activity of 'keeping pace with' the client, while not getting 'ahead' of her, or 'lagging behind' her. Here is an example of ongoing reflections, not always entirely accurate, but getting progressively closer to the client's central concerns. The client is talking about his work, where he is in charge of a dynamic business:

Client: So what I find is that the people I've put in charge of the various sections—there's six of them altogether—just don't take the sort of initiatives that I need them to take. They kind of sit there and they do their job, fair enough, but they don't look beyond it, they don't look around them and see what's there!

Counsellor: You don't find that your subordinates are doing their job properly, and that frustrates you.

Client: Well, it's not that they aren't doing their jobs properly. They're all very competent, I mean, I picked them because they were so good at their jobs! It's what they fail to see that makes me so irritated. They seem to expect me to do all of that, and I resent it.

[Client 'corrects' the emphasis of the counsellor's first reflection, which was a bit too general, and failed to recognise what is most important to him.]

Counsellor: OK, so you know they're really competent, yet somehow, they don't seem to look beyond what you ask them to do.

[Counsellor repeats the client's original words, 'look beyond it'. This doesn't seem a big advance, yet the client seems happier with it.]

Client: That's right. I thought when I appointed them that they'd see what needed to be done, and get on and do it. But instead, they sit around almost like they're waiting for me to approve before they're prepared to do anything over and above their job descriptions!

[When your reflection is accurate, your client will often let you know ('That's right') and then expand on what he or she has said before.]

Counsellor: You don't like it that they want you to approve of what they do.

Client: No, what I mean is, they don't get in there and think for themselves! I've given them all this trust and responsibility, and they just sort of refuse to take it—like they're scared or something! I can't imagine what they're scared of.

[The counsellor is too confrontational, too blunt, so the client again 'corrects' him, taking the focus away from his own feelings, and back to the behaviour of his subordinates. He also displays high expectations and a lack of understanding of his subordinates, providing the counsellor with insight into the way that the client's own attitude might be part of the problem.]

Counsellor: OK, so what you're saying is that they act like they're scared, but there's nothing for them to be scared of. Is that right?

[Sensibly, the counsellor again sticks close to the statement the client has just made. The counsellor 'puts on hold' his impression that perhaps the client's own attitude may be part of the problem. One of the hardest things about reflecting is learning to sit on your own hunches about what the 'real' problem is, and staying with the client's reality. It can be very tempting to show our clients that we are clever and can 'figure them out' quickly. The time for offering your feedback to clients will come much later, when your relationship is more firmly established, and you are more attuned to each other but often, with good reflections, your client comes closer to what is really going on and your hunches get confirmed without needing to voice them.]

Client: Yeah, that's part of it. Look, I built up this company, I made it what it is, and I did that by taking initiatives—taking calculated risks. And they paid off. That's what I want them to do, but they've let me down. I picked them, but they've disappointed me. They don't seem to be able to match up to what I hoped for.

Counsellor: In a way, you really hoped you'd chosen well—they'd be able to do what you did, and take the same risks you did. But they seem to hang back from that, and you're pretty disappointed in them. It's like they can't live up to your example—is that right?

Client: That's exactly right. I do feel disappointed.

[The client picks up on the word 'disappointed' when the counsellor uses it back to him. He is now somewhat more aware of his feelings, because the counsellor has found the 'right word' for them—even though it is actually the client's own word!]

Client: And I hand picked men who I thought had the same way of working that I did. I'm starting to wonder whether my judgement was poor!

[The counsellor has now pin-pointed the emotional 'core' of the client's message, and the client responds with emphatic agreement—and then moves into a new dimension of the problem, which he feels safe enough to mention now that the counsellor has demonstrated his full understanding].

Read more

As you start to grasp the basics of reflecting through practising the skill with each other in class, it makes good sense to read the work of Carl R. Rogers. Rogers' best explanations of reflection ('paraphrasing')—and indeed, of his whole approach—can be found in his earlier works, such as *Counseling and Psychotherapy* (1942) and *Client-centered Therapy* (1951) where he wrote in scholarly depth about his practice, and explained the reasons for his innovations. In his later books, enthusiasm and evangelical zeal began to dominate evidence and careful reasoning. It is also worthwhile to have some understanding of the philosophical basis of Rogers' 'client centred' approach—now called 'person-centred'—since this bears very directly on his notions that the client, not the therapist, should be in charge of the process, and that the therapist's job was to 'stay with the client's present awareness' so that it could deepen and develop over time (described in vivid detail in his essay, 'A Process Conception of Psychotherapy' in *On Becoming a Person* (1961), first published in *American Psychologist*, 13 (1958): 142149.

The most direct way in to understanding Rogers' approach, however, is to read transcripts and view films of his actual work with clients. Trained as a psychologist, Rogers wanted to document therapeutic techniques and evaluate their effectiveness—in today's terms, he advocated 'evidence based practice', and rigorously applied evaluation tools to his own work with clients. Long before video and audiotape recording, he produced many sound recordings on 78rpm disks, and, later, visual records on film. A number of these are commercially available on videotape or DVD.

Our own students sometimes comment unfavourably on the transcripts they read (many of them are reprinted in Barry Farber, Debora Brink and Patricia Raskin, Eds, *The Psychotherapy of Carl Rogers*, Guilford Press, 1996). Some students describe these transcripts as 'boring', 'repetitive' or even 'intrusive'. Yet when we look at the actual films from which some transcripts were made, a very different impression emerges. We become aware of Rogers' *timing*—his reflections do not crowd the client in any way. Because the printed transcript of the recording doesn't indicate short pauses, only longer ones, the therapeutic interchanges can seem to occur more rapidly than they actually do. Seeing Rogers' face, and hearing the tone of his voice, supplies the missing dimension—empathy—without which the words on the page can seem cold, uninspired, or repetitive. Most important of all, the films enable us to see how Rogers' clients respond to his ongoing series of reflections. Nearly always, they seem to feel understood, supported by his understanding, safe to go further—although sometimes frustrated with him for not offering them advice or taking away their anxiety and self-doubt!

When you read the counsellor's part of the dialogues we have provided in this chapter, and the rest of the book, we hope you will be able to imagine the counsellor speaking quietly, with empathy, and with respect. Just reading the words 'cold' may give you the same misleading impression as our students gained of Rogers' practice—you will need to 'feel into' the counsellor's words, re-creating the tone of voice and the emphasis as you might need to hear them if you were the client.

What we are attempting to do, in offering reflections, is to temporarily see the world as the client sees it, *experience the world as the client experiences it*. It is this effort to put yourself in the client's position that convinces clients they are safe with you. It can be quite magical to feel understood—that the counsellor 'gets you'—and most especially for clients whose past experience has been marked by lack of understanding, and responses from other people (usually parents) that have invalidated their experiences. Reflecting is a way of validating a client's experience without necessarily agreeing with him or her. It's as if you are saying to your client, 'Yes, this is how it feels to you' not 'Yes, this is how it feels to you, *and you are right*'.

Think about it

When baby birds are very young, they are unable to digest the food that their parents bring them, so the parent bird first swallows the food, and then brings up the partly digested food and offers it to the baby bird from its beak. This process may seem messy, even disgusting, to us humans, but it serves a very important function for birds, and I believe that humans have our own (verbal) equivalents—and the activity of reflecting is one of them. It can be quite useful to think of counsellors taking the client's 'raw food' and partly digesting it, then offering it back to the client. Like any analogy, this one can only be pushed so far. But the idea of 'operating on' the raw 'food' in order to make it more 'digestible' by another person helps us to gain a different perspective on what we do in counselling when we paraphrase or reflect. In birds, pre-digesting does not totally change the food, it remains recognisably the same, but it is 'softened' and hence made easier to swallow and then digest. As so often in nature, what animals do with physical actions, we humans do with words, and converting a client's thoughts and feelings into words that are our own, yet which retain key elements of the client's original experience, does very often make them more acceptable to the client—and oddly, more interesting, more worthy of the client's curiosity. Clients will sometimes say 'like you just said' when you have reflected what *they* just told *you*!

Reflecting is well explained in most textbooks of counselling skills, but it is much easier to explain than it is to put into practice. Many of you will struggle with the skill of reflecting for weeks or even months. You will complain that reflecting is 'So frustrating—there's all these things I want to ask!', that 'The client's not getting anywhere—I just keep saying the same thing!' Your frustration probably comes because you have been very invested in the questions you wish you could ask, instead of this 'tedious' reflecting, which does not allow you to demonstrate your insight and cleverness! If you stick with trying to reflect, however, most of you will eventually reach a point where you offer a really accurate reflection, and your client responds emphatically and positively to it—an 'Ah hah!' moment. Then you will begin to realise how much impact your 'babyish', 'boring' reflection can actually have on another person. Conversely, when (as a client) you experience the dynamic effect of a good reflection from your counsellor, it may well assist you to gain more confidence in the skill. Ideally, you should have both experiences—as both counsellor and client.

KEY POINTS ABOUT THE SKILL OF REFLECTING

- *Reflecting means using your words, but sticking as closely as possible to what you think the client means.* Beginners sometimes confuse reflecting with a kind of mechanical repetition of what the client has said, which they refer to as 'parroting back' or 'sounding like a tape recorder'. The difference between this and genuine reflecting is vast, and your clients will be aware of it (see below).

- *Oddly enough, putting a reflection in your words rather than theirs seems to assist clients to feel understood better than if you mechanically repeat what they have said.* At first, even hearing a fairly mechanical reflection may feel good to clients. But if you persist in simply echoing back their exact words, they will notice this, and become irritated or restless.

- *Of course, you will often end up using one or two of the client's own words in constructing your reflection*—like 'disappointed' in the example we quoted most recently. What happened in that example is typical. If you use a client's own word as part of your reflection, the client may spark up: 'That's exactly right! That's just the word for it!'—as if *you* had come up with the word, and the client were hearing it for the first time! There could be no more convincing proof that *many people do not 'hear' themselves as they speak*. They may even be quite unconscious that they have used a particular word. When you reflect well, you make them more aware of what they themselves are saying. 'Hearing themselves' in this way is, for many clients, the first step in an ongoing process of becoming more self-aware, and a vital part of what makes counselling effective.

- *Reflective responses should normally be kept fairly short.* Don't try to say back everything you've heard. Focus on what seems to be the most important point to the client (even if it doesn't seem the most important bit to you!)

- *If feelings are to the fore in what your client is saying, then your reflection should pick up, and acknowledge, the feelings involved.* 'You're saying that when she talks to you like that, you feel really confused and irritated'. *If factual details are to the fore, then your reflection may not need to incorporate feelings*: 'So what you're telling me is that this man is your boss, and you have to do what he says, but actually he's asking you to do stuff that's not part of your job description at all'.

- *In reflecting, you are showing clients your intention to understand them.* At first, many of your reflections will only be partly accurate. You may miss the mark completely. If so, your clients will implicitly 'correct' you—rephrasing their own statement to draw your attention to the bits that you have 'got wrong' or left out. Or they may explicitly correct you, by saying 'No, not really, it's more like …' These corrections are a necessary part of the process. You do not need to take them as criticisms or as evidence that you have 'failed', though it can feel a bit this way for you. Instead, each correction will assist you to approximate the client's meaning more closely. What clients will usually value is your attempt to understand them, even though that attempt is not yet completely successful.

- *Think of reflecting as an evolving series of responses from you, which gradually enable you to come closer and closer to what your client is actually 'on about'.* When you do 'hit the mark', your client will often respond dramatically. 'Yeah. That's exactly what I mean'. Or, 'That's it! That's just what's been going on, only I couldn't really put it into words before'. This is the process of *attunement*—and when you 'attune' to your client, you are essentially doing what a caregiver does with an infant: showing your client that you care enough to 'stay with her' and keep trying until you correctly understand what she needs from you.

- *Over this series of interchanges between you and the client, her central concerns should gradually become clearer.* For example, she may use a number of different feeling words at different times, and at first, you may be confused as to what feeling is most central. However, as you continue to 'try out' your developing understanding on her, listen carefully to her 'corrections' and incorporate them into the reflections you then develop, you will find that one or two 'intensity marker' words keep coming back again and again in what she says.

- These intensity markers may be adjectives ('silly', 'irritating') or they may be acknowledgments of her own feelings ('I just feel worthless') or judgements of her situation ('It's so unfair'), or repeated figures of speech ('I'm like a fish out of water'; 'I'm just left out of the picture'). *Intensity markers will guide you to the emotional core of what the client is saying.* These are the words or phrases which, when you use them yourself in reflecting, will often prompt the kinds of strong positive response mentioned above: 'That's exactly right!', 'Got it in one!'

- Typically, when you reflect well enough, clients will do one of several things:
  - *Offer more detail on the subjects they've already raised.*
  - *Bring up a new subject* (i.e. expand the picture that they are offering you) or decide it is now safe to share with you something that earlier seemed too risky to expose.
  - *Reveal a greater depth of feeling* in speaking of the subject they have been discussing

(we call this 'dropping down' to a more authentic level of emotion).

- [Rarely, but significantly] *Pause and think before continuing*, as if your response has stimulated some mental activity.

- *By contrast, if you reflect poorly (or not at all), you can expect your clients to*:
  - 'Spin their wheels', *simply repeat what they've already said*, in only slightly different words
  - *Come to a halt, in apparent confusion*, as if not sure what to say next
  - *Ask self-doubting questions* like, 'Am I making sense?' or 'Do I sound crazy?' (Of course, clients may sometimes ask, 'Do I sound crazy?' for reasons other than simply because you have reflected poorly.)
  - *Question*, or *challenge us*: 'Aren't you going to tell me what you think?'; 'I don't know if you can help me with some strategies, I really feel that I need something'.

Beginning counsellors tend to take requests for information or 'strategies' at face value—perhaps because they fit with their own expectations of what they 'should' be providing for clients. But in fact clients are not really wanting advice or strategies when they make such comments. What they want is to know that you understand them. Requests for advice or opinions are often clients' oblique ways of signalling to us that our reflections have been inadequate, that we need to try harder. We say more about this in Chapter 4. Of course, there will be occasional exceptions, where a client may provide feedback that is not an accurate guide to how well you have reflected, or where you may need to override the client's response. But these are rare, and require individual guidance from your tutor or supervisor, when you start working with non-student clients.

The great thing about reflecting is that by focussing all your attention on listening to the client, and then framing an appropriate response, you soon lose your own anxiety about 'what to say'. And you actually free up your own thinking about the client's situation. *If you are really 'in synch' with your clients, this may result in the client's thinking also being freed up.* You may not need to say anything to achieve this result! (We often find that during a session we come up with a new insight into the client's situation, and if we just hold onto it quietly for a few minutes, the client will then come up with the same insight, as if by magic, even though we haven't said a word.)

By contrast, what usually happens to beginners is that they are so anxious to come up with 'something to say' or 'something helpful' that they listen only half-heartedly. In other words, the client's anxiety and 'stuckness' transfers itself to the counsellor, and in skills practice sessions these trainees turn to their observer and say, 'Help! I don't know what to say!'

Read more

We have just provided a long list of specific instructions to help you reflect better. At the end of the day, though, this is 'left hemisphere learning'—it works 'from the outside in'. As we emphasised throughout this book, following rules faithfully and trying to 'get them right' will not necessarily give you the capacity to reflect accurately, though it may help you to 'step towards' it. Good reflecting comes from feeling deeply connected with your client, deeply present to them. What is happening there is what neurologists like Allan Schore are calling 'right brain to right brain communication'.

More exactly, older parts of your brain are resonating with the older parts of your client's brain. These older parts are the structures we call the 'limbic system' or the 'limbic lobe'—brain structures that we share with all mammals. They are primitive (in the sense that they evolved long before the 'thinking brain', the cerebral cortex that makes us human). They represent instinctive responses to situations, telling us (for example) if we are in danger, or whether we are safe. When we as counsellors can 'tune in' to what our clients are experiencing (not just through words, but through picking up their body language as well) and mirror it back to them accurately, then we are connecting with their limbic systems. The result will be that they will feel deeply understood, they will feel safer, and they will start to 'settle' (come into their bodies and connect with themselves—a good therapist will notice this when it happens). Less of their energy will go into protecting themselves from fear and pain, more will be available for self-awareness.

Connecting with our clients in this way is not something that we can 'will' into existence. We can't 'make it happen'. We can't 'do anything' to make it happen except drop our own agenda of questions, speculations (about what may be happening for the client) and judgements. When we allow these concerns to drop away, we will start to open our hearts to our clients. That may sound corny or 'unscientific' but in fact it is precisely what brain science suggests we need to do. When our hearts are open, we will automatically know what to do, what to say (we may not need to say anything at all). The right words will come. They will well up out of our interconnectedness with our client. And those words will seem right to our clients because they will sense that interconnectedness too. One limbic system will 'speak to' another with or without words. It is that state of being which enables change to occur. (Alan Schore, *The Science of the Art of Psychotherapy*, Norton, 2012: 152–208).

The reflecting exercise

At some point early in most counselling training programs, your trainer will introduce you to a standard way of practising reflecting. The exercise is generally done in triads (groups of three). Once you are familiar with the roles and responsibilities involved in this exercise, you can practise it outside of class, too, with two others who want to gain more experience and master the skills of reflecting. Ideally, you should practise every week.

Practice task

The first person will be the client, and will speak for a short time, perhaps only five minutes initially (gradually increased over a number of weeks to ten, fifteen and twenty minutes).

We believe in asking trainees in the role of client to talk about a real issue that is current in their own lives, rather than talking about simulated problem (which is what 'role playing' really means). Of course, talking about something immediate and personal is much more threatening—but it is also a lot more like real counselling. Student clients do not have to put energy into 'being someone else' or attempting to portray a problem they may not personally have ever experienced. Your student clients can be asked to take responsibility for the issue they select to talk about, so that they avoid choosing something that is huge and overwhelming (on the one hand) or something so trivial that it permits no in-depth exploration (on the other). Most trainees are perfectly capable of making this responsible choice. How deep they choose to go, as the session unfolds, will then have a lot to do with how competently you, their student counsellor, are able to reflect back their meaning and the level of intensity with which they express themselves.

Penny has experimented with providing non-threatening yet personal topics for student 'clients' to talk about for the first few practice sessions in the course. Such topics might include: something you love about your life; a favourite hobby and why you enjoy it; a wonderful experience you have had; etc. This enables students in the client role to get used to talking freely with a fellow student, but without needing to 'find a problem' to talk about. In fact, as people talk about almost any topic, they will probably begin to touch on problematic aspects of their lives—but then it will happen naturally.

The second person will be the counsellor, and her instructions are simply *to reflect for the entire time*. Most trainees initially find this extremely difficult.

The third person occupies the role of timekeeper and observer. At the end of the designated time, the timekeeper will 'call time', and then ask the client to talk for a minute or so about how she experienced being the client. 'What was it like for you talking with Sue?' 'Did you notice that your feelings changed at any point?' 'Was there anything Sue said that was particularly helpful for you?' 'Did anything Sue said get in the way a bit, or feel 'not quite right'?

Then the observer feeds back her own observations of the counsellor's behaviour (*but not her thoughts about the client or his problem*). For example, she may notice that a couple of times, the counsellor slipped into offering a response that was not a reflective one (perhaps asking a question); or the observer may have noticed that the counsellor's response on one occasion prompted the client to 'withdraw' or pull away, verbally or non-verbally—perhaps because the client felt judged or somehow intruded upon. The observer may also notice examples of good reflecting, which prompted the client to say more, go deeper, or whatever. *It is important that the observer direct her comments to the counsellor, and not try to analyse the client, or tell the counsellor how she (the observer) would have done it better!* In other words, the observer's feedback is at the level of factual observations, not value judgements. It will take some of you a while to master this difference, and your tutor will assist you. By practising the making of dispassionate observations of behaviour, observations that don't contain a critical or judgemental aspect, you will in fact be training yourself for the important skill of confrontation, which we discuss in Chapter 6.

Once you have completed the first round, the roles then shift, and the observer takes the role of counsellor, while the counsellor goes into the role of client, and the client becomes the observer. This is partly to give the client a rest from being exposed and vulnerable, and to offer the counsellor the experience of being 'on the other side of the table', so to speak.

Some common challenges you will encounter as you participate in this exercise:

- In the 'client' role, you may find it hard to launch into talking about something quite important and personal, only to have the 'session' stopped after what may feel like hardly any time at all! This takes quite a bit of getting used to, and initially you will feel 'rudely interrupted' or even that you, as the baby, have been 'dropped'! Part of the reason for the debriefing component of the exercise is to give you a chance to acknowledge whatever feelings you are left with when the 'mini-session' ends. However, even if you and your student counsellor were given a whole therapeutic hour, without interruption, you might still find that your session ends before you are 'ready' and you might still feel 'dumped' or 'thrown out in the cold'. This happens in real counselling sessions all the time, and it is useful to be aware of how clients may feel when told that their time is 'over for this week', or 'We have to finish now'. As the client, you may also find yourself feeling quite critical of your student counsellor, or alternatively, you may find yourself admiring her skill, and wishing you could do as well. Your feelings towards the person who is trying to help you may tell you something objective about him/her, but they will definitely tell you something about *you*—whether you tend to idealise a helpful person, or find fault with her, whether you tend to put energy into 'looking after' your helper, instead of into being honest with him, and so on.

- In the 'observer' role, you may find it difficult to keep your triad partners to time. You may be hesitant to interrupt the client if she/he is in the middle of something. You may not want to be 'bossy' in indicating too obviously that it is time to stop. (If this is you, ask yourself what your anxiety might be telling you about yourself. You may be an Enneagram Nine, the type who privileges others' feelings and agendas over his/ her own, excels at empathy, but finds it difficult to interrupt or take control.) Again, observing time limits in class exercises is excellent practice for the real-life necessity of ending appointments on time! Learning to interrupt people, politely but firmly, is one of the skills you will need as a counsellor, and if you do not possess it now, regard these training exercises as a chance to develop it!

- Trainees in the 'observer' role may neglect to 'debrief' the client first. This usually occurs because they are insufficiently aware of how vulnerable the client may feel, and think that 'She only talked for a few minutes, she didn't seem upset, so we'll skip that bit'. If the client's first response is a face-saving 'It was great, she really did a great job, I thought she was excellent', observers may hesitate to prompt the client with further questions: 'When did you feel most at ease? Was there a point where you felt at all uncomfortable?' As we mentioned earlier, observers are actually being trained in (gentle) confrontation through their role, although they may not realise this. They are also being trained in persistence! These are capacities they will need as counsellors!

- Trainees in the 'observer' role may be too 'nice' in their feedback to the counsellor, out of a wish to save face for him/her. Alternatively, they may be too judgemental and prescriptive in their feedback to the counsellor (perhaps because of a wish to show how much they know!). Personality differences among trainees emerge strongly at such times. Again, here is a chance for you to learn some things about yourself that you may not have been aware of before. Can you see the value in learning these sorts of things before you start seeing clients 'for real'? Do you want to be like the young professional whose ex-client reported, 'Well, I went to see him a couple of times, but every time I started to get upset, his eyes would wander around the room, and he seemed sort of bored and uncomfortable'?

- Your tutor may need to coach 'observers' intensively on how to offer feedback in the form of observations of behaviour, rather than in terms of judgement.

- Trainees in the 'counsellor' role will find it very difficult, at first, to simply reflect. They may need your help, as observer, to concentrate on doing so. They will typically be wanting to ask questions, or make comments.

- Trainees in the 'counsellor' role may also need respectful coaching in how to make better reflective responses. Observers (or tutors) can ask questions like, 'What's the thing the client keeps coming back to again and again?' or, 'What feeling has the client mentioned several times already?' Having established what the client's main concern is, you can then concentrate on how to reflect it back, in a way that the client can accept and connect with.

In our experience as trainers, most students take at least six months to start to master the skill of reflecting adequately. Some 'get it' earlier than this, and others may take up to a year. This may sound a very long time to grasp such a 'simple' skill—but of course, it is not a 'simple skill' at all. The skill of reflecting requires the capacity to focus intently on what is important to the client, not on one's own anxieties about 'what to say next', and it is hardly surprising that this cannot be acquired rapidly and easily by the majority of students!

SIMPLE EMPATHIC RESPONSES

'Just empathising' involves picking up a client's unstated, but obvious, feelings, and voicing, simply and genuinely, your appreciation of what she/he is feeling, at a point where you sense that the client may need you to do so. Examples:

- *That must feel very disappointing*
- *That sounds just awful!*
- *You sound like you're really mad about that!*
- *Seems like you just keep getting rejected again and again, and it really hurts!*
- *Talking about this must cost you a lot*

Our experience is that students overuse this skill or come up with 'formulas' (*'That must be hard'* is at the top of the list!) which allow them to avoid connecting with the world of the client fully (because they leave out what 'that' actually is!). We ask them to try to supply the 'that' as well: e.g. *Listening to her go on talking about such painful stuff must be hard.*

How does this differ from an *empathic reflection*, of the kind we have just been discussing? When you reflect, you are saying back to clients in your own words what they have said to you. If they have stated feelings, then you 'mirror back' the feelings they have already expressed. But quite often, clients do not express feelings in words. Rather, they tell their stories in such a way as to give us a fair indication of what they must be feeling, but without saying it. The feeling may be contained in their tone of voice, their facial expression, or the way that they sit in their chair. When you pick this feeling up, and offer them an unforced, natural response of your own—not a paraphrase of what they have said—then you are 'empathising'.

Empathic responses hover somewhere between the instinctive behaviour most of us display in social settings, like minimal encouragers, and the purposeful, consciously learned skills (like reflection) that distinguish counselling as a special type of conversation—'therapeutic conversation'.

We see empathic responding as a 'skill' because as a counsellor, you would normally think before empathising, whereas in a social setting (e.g. with a friend), the empathic statement would just 'come out', without any conscious decision on your part. Thinking first doesn't necessary make an empathic statement less genuine: you have to feel it first, or you would sound artificial and 'wrong' saying it. But it's a good idea to think first, in order to check whether you are saying it *for the client or for yourself*. Is it really necessary to say it at all? Will it perhaps get in the way if you indicate your own response in this manner? Or will the client feel supported—held—if he hears you saying what he has been feeling, but not expressing?

After all, you may have all kinds of personal reactions to what your clients tell you (shock, dismay, worry, pity, irritation) but you would not put most of those reactions into words— at least, not without careful consideration first. Counsellors put empathic responses into words when they judge that clients need that extra holding, that explicit indication that the counsellor knows where they're coming from. Thus, counsellors often respond with simple empathy when they see that clients are very distressed, or very agitated, and need something more than just the kinds of reflections they've been offering them—a more immediate, human reaction from us. In exactly the same way, a parent might murmur softly to a small child, 'It's really bad, isn't it. It really hurts.'

Practice task

What if you can't empathise, or actually find it very difficult to sit with a client who is feeling something very strongly? Some of you may feel uncomfortable when your client cries. Others may feel the same discomfort at the thought of a client becoming angry—even though the client's anger is not directed at them. And so on. A useful class exercise is for everyone to identify the emotion that they feel most uncomfortable sitting with, and then to have someone else in the class take, for a few minutes, the role of an angry client, a weeping client, an anxious client, or whatever. Student are then asked to sit with the 'client' while he or she expresses that feeling, and to notice what they themselves think and feel in response. This can sometimes lead the student to identify where she or he has previously experienced discomfort in a similar situation (*It was a huge shock when I saw Dad cry for the first time—I remember thinking that this shouldn't be happening, something was badly wrong with the world, and I must have caused it somehow*) or to think about the 'programming' around emotions that she or he may have received in childhood (*It's not nice to be angry. We don't raise our voices in this family*). In turn, these perceptions may need to be further explored in your personal therapy. While there are certainly approaches to counselling and therapy that do not require the counsellor to engage deeply with clients' feelings, being able to identify (and appropriately express) the full range of your own emotions is an important prerequisite for helping clients to feel held and understood. If you are obviously uncomfortable in the presence of their feelings, they will almost certainly notice it (*I started to tell my counsellor about how my partner came home two whole hours later than he said he would. I told her how I just wanted to smash something! She said, 'Sometimes things happen for us to be late'! She sounded just like my mother! Mum always told me that 'No one likes an angry person.*

EMPATHIC SENTENCE COMPLETION

Sometimes counsellors and therapists convey empathy by completing their client's sentence for him/her. Some trainers refer to this scornfully as 'second guessing the client', and consider it very poor practice. But when well done, by a counsellor who is thoroughly familiar with how her client thinks and feels, it can produce the same effect as a good reflection, or a statement of empathy. 'She really understands—she knows exactly what I'm going to say'. Obviously, you are more likely to find yourselves sensitively completing clients' sentences in later sessions. Unless you are extremely well-attuned at a very early stage of the process, it is presumptuous and arrogant to try such a way of showing empathy with a new client. It can also feel 'crowding' to clients (you are holding the 'baby' too tightly!)

SUMMARISING

We haven't said much about summarising (or 'summarisation', as some textbooks call it) because there is no need. In some ways, summarising is simply an extension of reflection—a somewhat longer reflection, but one which 'condenses' the essence of the client's presentation so far, a spoken 'précis' of the main things the client has talked about. A summary does not need to include every detail, and indeed, it should not. If a summary goes on for too long, the client will not benefit very much, and may even end up being confused.

The real aims of a summary are:

- *to show the client that you have been listening attentively* (particularly when they have talked for a long time)

- *to offer the client a coherent statement* of what you have heard (which may assist the client to see the pattern or organising ideas in what she has said)

- *to help to organise the client's account a bit*, so that he can stand back from it, and consider what parts are most important;

- (sometimes) *to provide a platform for you to make an intervention that goes beyond holding*—perhaps, to state a pattern you can see in the client's account, or to challenge something that does not quite add up in what they have been saying. To make that kind of intervention 'cold' is to risk taking clients by surprise, or weakening their sense of being understood. The summary underpins the intervention, reminding clients that yes, you do know what is most important to them, that you have not forgotten anything important. In a way, a summary of this kind gives you the right to offer a new perspective, or to challenge. A good summary can shade into the statement of a theme in what the client has presented. Most of this is discussed in depth in Chapter 6.

For beginners (for more experienced counsellors too, when a session has temporarily lost direction) summarising can assist clients to re-focus on what is most important to them, assisting them to grasp onto their central concerns again. Often, in first sessions (and sometimes for several sessions), clients pour out a lot, and in the process end up feeling confused and lost.

They may even say, 'I'm confused now', or 'Am I making sense at all?' A good summary from the counsellor can reassure them that they are not 'crazy'. And then they can pick up their account and go somewhere with it, somewhere that *does* make sense to them.

Many students pick up the idea that it is necessary to end every session with a summary ('So today we've talked about ... and explored ... and you realised that ...'). Whether an end-of-session summary is a good idea or not will depend on the nature of the session itself and how the client is feeling as the end nears. Again, anxious beginners look for rules to follow, rules that will make them feel (temporarily) as if they are 'in charge' or are 'doing something'. What counsellors should be paying attention to is: *what does this client need now?* (As opposed to what do *I* need now?)

THE PLACE OF HOLDING SKILLS IN ONGOING COUNSELLING

Holding skills are employed all the way through the counselling process, from beginning to end. Earlier, we described holding as the 'default setting' of all counselling and therapy. Whenever the counsellor's response hits a jarring note, or when a confrontation produces resistance and defensiveness, the best thing to do, nearly always, is to fall back on reflecting and empathy. However, holding skills have a particularly vital function in the first few sessions. They are the skills that contribute most to the creation of a reliable counsellor-client relationship. Indeed, in a first (or even second) session, holding skills may be all that you will use. This will typically happen when clients talk readily, and so 'staying out of the way' is really all you need to do for a while. Although holding skills can be difficult to take on board for many trainees (because they run counter to normal expectations of one's role in a conversation), they are the key skills to possess if you want to be a really good counsellor. They are also 'low risk' skills—they are unlikely to do harm because they do not go beyond what the client is offering. For these reasons, it is worth spending a lot of time practising until these skills come naturally. You will really be training yourself in a completely different way of being with people. It's not surprising if that takes some time. If, after months of practice, you are still finding holding skills tedious and irritating, then perhaps you are not training for the right profession.

Holding skills can achieve far more than just establishing a trusting relationship in the opening sessions, or helping to restore that relationship if, later, it is temporarily ruptured. In fact, when holding skills are employed with a high level of sensitivity and sophistication, they can take the place of skills of exploring (like questioning) and even skills of encounter (like confrontation). Just by itself, good holding can take clients all sorts of places. So please don't tell yourself that these are 'just beginner skills' that you can forget about once your work with a client really gets going! A sexual assault survivor recently addressed a workshop for professionals, reporting her experiences of seeing a succession of helpers. The first three that interviewed her left her feeling completely unsafe, she said, because they seemed intent on sounding like experts. The fourth was different. This woman simply said, 'You must have had just a horrific time'. Simply hearing those words (which, clearly, were uttered from the heart) enabled the client to open up and describe what had happened to her, in a way that she had found herself unable to do with any of the others. Never underestimate the power of reflection and empathy! By contrast, if you use language that 'sounds professional' when responding to clients—*Have you experienced any suicidal ideation?*—then they may well feel alienated. *Have you had any thoughts about maybe wanting to end it all?* is much more likely to preserve the connection between you.

Think about it

Staying silent and empathic reflecting are positions that you will learn with some difficulty, 'against the grain', and often feeling deskilled. Inevitably, once you progress to later stages of training, and begin seeing clients with no tutors peering over your shoulders, most of you will tend to revert to more 'natural' styles—which for many of you will involve 'doing to' rather than 'being with', and (probably) asking more questions and doing less holding. And of course, several of the types of counselling and therapy that are particularly in vogue at present depend on such active, question-asking styles (more on this in Chapters 5 and 8).

However, even when you have been trained to use such models, it is still important to be able to 'stay out of the way' at times, to listen attentively and to reflect back what you have heard. We tell our students, 'Yes, the model we're teaching you is quite different from the structured models some of you have learned. Those models can be very useful. But what we are teaching you here is a set of skills (and a framework for understanding them) which is essential for any model. Some models will call on holding skills more, and others less, but you will always need them. And once you have mastered these fundamental skills, you will find that you actually operate other models better, and use their specialised skills more sensitively and intuitively'.

CHAPTER SUMMARY

In this chapter we have mainly focussed on three central holding skills:

- *appropriate use of silence*: the capacity to remain silent tells clients that you are not anxiously rushing to 'take your turn in the conversation', or feeling the need to get your word in. Your silence allows space for them to think about what they have just said, and maybe develop it further in a direction of their own choice.

- *Empathic responding and summarising*: these skills show clients in a more active, verbal way that you are listening and trying to understand what is important to them. Like the appropriate use of silence, these skills encourage clients to go further, to open up new subjects, or to reveal more of the depth of their feelings.

- *The conscious choice to express empathy*: this assures clients that you sense their feelings, even though they may not have expressed them explicitly. In turn, showing clients your empathy can encourage them to voice their own emotions more openly.

- *Holding skills are vital in the first few sessions*—where they can sometimes be the only skills you will use. They may also be vital in much later sessions, when your client may have felt misunderstood or judged by you.

- *Holding skills alone*—and especially reflecting—*can, when done really well, take your clients a long way towards their goals*, without your needing to venture into most of the more 'advanced' skills.

- As with learning a foreign language, *it is not that difficult to acquire rudimentary holding skills. But to employ them with sensitivity, tact and appropriateness is like learning to speak a language fluently and idiomatically*—the way a native speaker would speak it. In fact, learning how to hold your client is rather like learning your client's language—even if that language is English!

Chapter 3

The Story Unfolds: The Skills Of Exploring

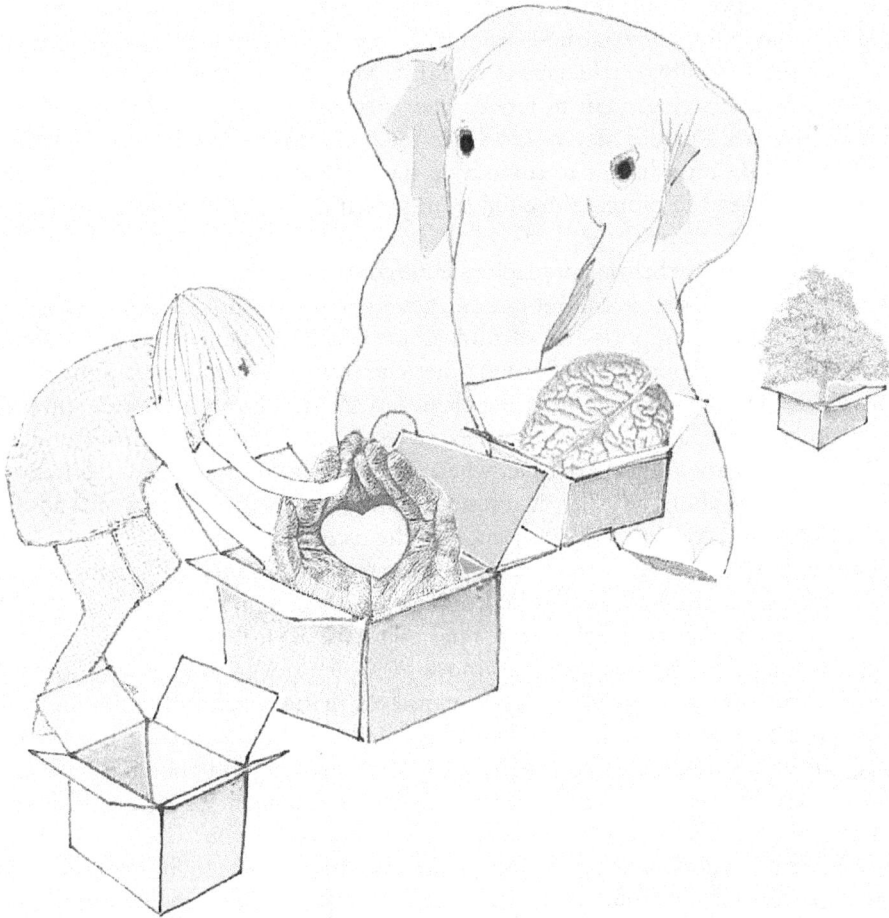

THE METAPHOR OF EXPLORATION

At around nine months, infants become mobile. They begin to crawl or pull themselves along, and soon, to walk upright. They can now explore their environment. Of course, they have been exploring since birth, but they have been restricted to the area within reach of their almost-stationary bodies—their exploration has consisted of gazing, grasping objects, and tasting or chewing those things they can convey to their mouths. Infants learn a great deal about the world in these limited ways, but when the infant turns into a toddler, its horizons broaden enormously. Now it can venture forth and choose its surroundings. It can actively search out people it wants to engage with, or things it is curious about. It can learn much more about its environment, and simultaneously, learn more about itself.

A toddler is capable of exploring on its own, but there are times when its caregivers need to assist that exploration. Sometimes, the child will become frightened by something new and alarming, or simply by how far he is from Mummy. His exploration ends in temporary disaster, and he may initially be reluctant to repeat it. Most toddlers will quickly try again; a few will need active encouragement to retrace their steps if that means risking another bad experience. Sometimes a parent may need to take the child's hand, steady it as it reaches for something, or actively introduce it to something new that it may otherwise have avoided. Sometimes we may need to protect the child from potential danger by warning it not to do something, or not to go somewhere.

In counselling, when we help clients explore some concern that they have brought to us, we may act in all of these ways at times. But just as a good parent does not force new experiences on her child, but instead, supports and encourages his natural tendency to explore things of importance to him, so a good counsellor takes her cue from the client's own priorities, and encourages the exploration of things that the client has already shown interest in, or anxiety about. Sometimes clients, like toddlers, may need to be actively protected from what might be risky or dangerous for them—for example, when they have been severely traumatised—but deciding what to leave alone, or what to restrain clients from exploring, demands advanced levels of sensitivity, and considerable experience on the counsellor's part.

In Chapter 2, we saw how Donald Winnicott's metaphor of 'holding' a baby stood for the complex-yet-simple business of *creating a safe space* for a patient or client. Good holding enables a client to hear her own voice, to see her own face, to feel her own feelings. As we said last chapter, some clients will 'shift' or 'move forward' as soon as they have listened to themselves in this way, or (as it were) seen themselves in the mirror. 'Finding out about myself through talking to you' is the way one of our clients put it (and no, she hadn't studied counselling; the words were quite unprompted. All the counsellor had done was reflect).

The next stage after holding is exploring, and, in this chapter, we have employed the metaphor of exploration because it conveys, better than any other word, the idea of an active process of investigation and discovery. In this process, we assist clients to find out more about the things they have talked about. Reflecting is one way of assisting exploration, because a good reflection can help clients to step beyond their current awareness. Exploring can also be done by asking questions. Not just any questions, though. The questions that best assist the process of exploring are those which open up possibilities, rather than closing them off. That is why your trainers will speak of 'open questions' and 'closed questions'. Closed questions limit the client's options (typically to 'A' or 'B', 'Yes' or 'No'); open questions, by contrast, leave the field wide open. It is the client who will decide what the options are.

THERAPEUTIC QUESTIONING AND DIAGNOSTIC QUESTIONING

Let's begin with an example of open and closed questions.

Open: What was it like to talk to your Mum again, after all that had happened?

Closed: Was it really hard to talk to your Mum again, after all that had happened?

In practice, the difference between closed and open questioning is not as absolute as it appears in textbooks. While a closed question may indeed point clients' answers in a certain direction, clients who actually want to explore their experience will sometimes answer as if an open question had been asked, not a closed one. In other words, they will say what they need to say, regardless of what you have asked. This is just one of several ways in which clients may get us back on course, and remind us of what is central to them:

Counsellor: Was it really hard to talk to your Mum again, after all that had happened?

[Closed, because it could be answered with a simple 'Yes', or 'No', and implies that the counsellor *expects* that the client might have found the experience 'hard']

Client: What it felt like was really weird—as if we didn't really know each other, as if we weren't in the same family, only at the same time, we knew we were—does that make sense?

[The client has ignored the counsellor's invitation to say, 'Yes, it was really hard' and leave it at that. Because she wants to talk about the experience, she answers in a much less 'closed' fashion, offering more information than the question strictly required.]

A counsellor's preference for open questions is one mark of how therapeutic exploring differs sharply from the diagnostic questioning associated with medicine, nursing, and legal and forensic investigation. Nurses, doctors, psychiatrists, detectives and lawyers typically ask questions in order to eliminate possibilities, to distinguish between fact and fiction, to establish the truth. You might imagine such questioning as like a 'grid' or a 'sieve'—it serves to separate one thing from another, and in this process, some data is discarded, and other data is retained for further processing. Diagnostic questioning is vital to the professional disciplines we've just mentioned. It serves an important function when the professional has already formed an idea of what may be going on, and wants to refine this through targeted inquiry. But in counselling and therapy, we do not normally 'have a suspect' (as a detective does) nor are we mainly concerned to find a 'diagnosis' (as a medical professional might be). So our emphasis in counselling is on *widening the range of possibilities*, enabling both the client and ourselves to 'see further' than we did when the client first told their story.

Professional psychology has adopted a medical model in advocating formal 'assessment' as the first step towards a 'treatment plan'. This makes sense in lots of ways, but it can equally be argued that the kinds of difficulties that bring clients to counselling do not really lend themselves to 'diagnosis' of the neat, behaviourally-oriented categories found in the *DSM* (*Diagnostic and Statistical Manual of Mental Disorders*). Such diagnosis may indeed be useful at first—providing a sort of 'road map' of a particular set of difficulties that a client may report—but it becomes increasingly less useful the further the therapeutic relationship progresses, and the better we come to know our clients. Thus, the emphasis of counselling—certainly since Carl Rogers—has been on the whole person of the client, not simply on his or her problematic behaviour. So to us, it makes sense that we can learn more about the client's presenting difficulties by finding out more about the 'whole' client—who he or she is, how she or he came to be that way, how he or she experiences the world, and what she or he is good at, as well as what she or he struggles with. 'Treatment' often simply means 'the alleviation of symptoms'. Working with the whole person, as we are teaching you to do here, can certainly lead to symptom relief, but for counsellors committed to the relational approach, the goal goes well beyond simply lessening symptoms. Rather, such counsellors conceive of their work as a healing process in which the relief of presenting symptoms is something that happens along the way, rather than the destination itself. See Chapter 9 for more on this.

Exploring and 'assessment' need not be mutually exclusive. In helping clients 'explore' their concerns we are likely to come across much of the same information that we would have discovered had we employed a series of targeted diagnostic questions. The difference is that we will have discovered this information as one aspect of a wider-ranging interest in the client's story, so clients are less likely to feel that we are disregarding what is of most importance to them. We are less likely to give the impression that we are trying to work out 'what is wrong' with them. And at the very beginning of the counselling relationship, it is crucial to show clients that we are interested in what matters to them, because that is the foundation of a therapeutic relationship—one in which clients will be prepared to trust us with what is really bothering them. They need to trust that we want to see the whole of them, instead of rushing to 'deal with' just one part of them and ignoring the rest.

Read more

Research into the different 'world views' of the brain's two hemispheres casts a lot of light on whole issue of asking clients lots of questions early on. We might say that the right hemisphere 'accepts things as they are', whereas the left hemisphere wants to isolate, question and arrange in order to understand. The right hemisphere (on its own) sees things 'whole', whereas the left hemisphere (on its own) breaks things up into parts—and does the same with people. Hence, questioning is the left hemisphere's 'default setting'. When the left hemisphere is dominant, we want to *find out*, ask why? and how? We want to know the details—who did what? We want to get the client's story in order, and we are concerned with which parts of it are more important, which bits should we pay most attention to? (The left hemisphere organises and evaluates.) This is exactly the sort of thing that happens in much psychological and forensic questioning. But as we'll see throughout this book, in counselling it is vital to start by getting a sense of the whole—the right hemisphere's priority. See Louis Cozolino, *The Neuroscience of Psychotherapy*, Chapter 6, 'One Brain or Two?' (NY, Norton, 2002: 105ff.

The whole issue of the different 'world views' of the two hemispheres is discussed in great detail, with a mass of research evidence, in Iain McGilchrist's long but wonderful book *The Master and his Emissary* (2009). Although McGilchrist's work is not aimed specifically at counsellors, influential therapists like Bonnie Badenoch are increasingly quoting him.

When we ask our clients why and how questions, we engage their left hemispheres. Questions of this type take clients into the 'world according to the left hemisphere' and unfortunately, the answers they give are not necessarily all that useful. Unless the right hemisphere is equally engaged, the client will offer answers that sound plausible, but which may actually be wide of the mark. Meantime, clients' left hemisphere dominated exploration may interrupt their connection with the counsellor—they need to 'conduct an internal search' in order to find the answer (which often means the answer they think we want them to offer). As we argue throughout this book, it is the right side of the brain which is crucial to the building and maintaining of the therapeutic relationship and the right hemisphere of the client must be engaged early on, or the relationship will become more like that of teacher and student than therapist and client. Eugene Gendlin's chapter 'Dead Ends' (in *Focussing-oriented Psychotherapy*, NY, Guilford, 1996: 7–15) explains this really well, and his technique of 'focussing' shows us how we (and our clients) can learn to use our right-hemisphere awareness in the service of gaining direct sensory information about the issues that are bothering us.

THOUGHTFUL QUESTIONING

Many trainee counsellors find it quite difficult to restrain their questions, because questions come naturally, while reflections don't. Yet questioning is widely believed to be one of the most important tools a counsellor has. So why do we ask you to wait before developing your questioning skills?

- *Because beginning counsellors often use questions for the wrong reasons*—to 'sound like an expert', to keep themselves 'safe' (offering a reflection exposes you to the possibility of being 'wrong'), to gratify their personal curiosity ('I wonder if she dumped him for the same reason I dumped my ex?') or to progress a (probably premature) 'diagnosis'.

- *Because asking questions is (potentially) more intrusive than reflecting*, and hence you need to have 'held' your clients adequately before you move into questioning them. You earn the right to ask questions, just as, much later, you earn the right to challenge your client, or give her feedback on how you experience her behaviour.

- *Because successful questioning depends on the counsellor's level of experience, and sense of timing.* A competent counsellor senses when her client is ready to be asked something, and the question then opens up important areas for exploration (the subject of this chapter). Yet the same question, asked too early, can cause the client to 'baulk' or to become defensive. As counselling progresses, other things being equal, a question that a client might have considered abrupt and threatening in the first few sessions may come to seem perfectly reasonable.

- *Because, in asking questions, you are beginning to participate in a more overt way in the counselling process.* Every question you ask tells the client what you consider potentially important—as opposed to what the client considers important. Your pattern of questioning, over a whole session, or over several sessions, implicitly reveals your choice of focus.

So, in learning to 'explore', you will need first to learn to *follow your client's lead*. In other words, to employ questions in a way which points the client in a certain direction—but only in directions that you anticipate will feel natural and appropriate to the client. You will still be exercising some control over the direction of the discussion—but only insofar as you are directing attention *to one aspect of what the client has already presented*, instead of another. But how do you know which aspects are important, and which are not? This is something we will return to as we offer examples of the exploring process in action.

QUESTIONS THAT FOLLOW THE CLIENT'S LEAD

Here is an example of a series of questions (or reflections that serve the same function as questions) that explore a topic the client has already signalled as important to her.

Client: I'd like to do it, but there's a fear there.

Counsellor: There's a wish to get in there and make it happen—but there's something scary that gets in the way.

[Notice that this is a reflection, not a question, but as good reflections so often do, it prompts the client to respond as if a question has been asked.]

Client: I don't know about 'gets in the way'. I'm not sure really. But maybe it's something to do with what might happen if I do go ahead and do this.

Counsellor: Something might happen … so, do you have any ideas about what might happen?

[The counsellor repeats the key words in the client's statement, which could act as a 'prompt' with or without the question that follows.]

Client: Not really. It's just a feeling of 'something terrible's going to happen' or 'someone's going to explode' or something like that.

[The client doesn't think she has 'any ideas' about 'what might happen', but in fact she does. Her response clarifies what sort of thing might happen, and how she feels about it.]

Counsellor: Who do you think might explode?

[The counsellor instinctively goes for clarification of 'someone's going to explode', rather than following up the vaguer, 'something terrrible's going to happen'.]

Client: I might. I might just lose it, and that'd be terrible.

[The client's response makes it clear that it is her own 'explosion' that she fears, not someone else's. So now different possibilities open up—is it that this client is afraid of letting her own emotions out, because that is not something she has ever really done? Or is the client aware that when she 'loses it', she has in the past caused destructive interactions with others? The counsellor doesn't know, and simply continues to explore.]

Counsellor: You might sort of explode, and that would mean you might 'lose it' … What would be bad about 'losing it'?

[The client has told the counsellor that she fears 'losing it', but the counsellor doesn't yet know why. The answer to 'what would be bad…' will help to clarify which of the two possibilities above is more likely.]

Client: I'd feel embarrassed and ashamed. I'd feel I'd lost control.

[The client's response shows us that shame is central to her fear of loss of control.]

and so on.

Here the counsellor follows the leads provided by her client, in a step by step process. Her questions are simple, common sense ones. The reason that they work so well is that the counsellor is not assuming she knows where the client is going, or where the client will end up. She is not 'knowing more than the client', and steering the client in the direction of her own assumption about 'what the real problem is'. She is paying attention to the way the client's answers change slightly, to reveal a different dimension each time. It is as if her message is, 'You've told me something new—so, tell me a bit more about that new bit!'

In the above dialogue, notice how the client first presents an emotion, but it is vague and global: 'a fear'. This may be something that the client does not fully understand, or has not ever really thought about (after all, who wants to think about something they're afraid of?). So the first step is to ask 'what's the fear about', that is, 'tell me more about the nature of this fear'. Instead of asking, the counsellor has offered a reflection—but it serves the same purpose. When the client then offers 'something might happen', the counsellor responds by asking *what* might happen. 'Something might happen' then turns into two alternatives, 'Something terrible's going to happen' (vague) and 'someone's going to explode' (more personal and specific), the counsellor now exercises a judgement that the more specific phrasing is the one to follow up. Each question offers the client the opportunity to define more fully the territory that is being explored.

As we said earlier, exploration isn't simply guided by the principle of 'following what is important to the client'. In the example, the counsellor's responses are also being influenced by an appreciation that the client is struggling with a child part of herself, a part that feels small and helpless in the face of an undefined and unknown fear. When the counsellor uses words like 'something scary', she is using language that is appropriate to the 'child within' the adult client who is speaking. In the course of the brief dialogue, the client actually moves from that infant space to a more adult one, able to identify that the 'explosion' she fears is a breaking out of her own emotions, rather than some 'storm' that comes from outside herself. Daniel Stern's *Diary of a Baby* (Basic Books, 1990) is an imaginative guide to how emotions like anger or fear might feel to an infant. Effective therapists need to have a 'felt sense' (Gendlin's term) of what sorts of fears a client may harbour when they say, 'Something terrible might happen'.

Don't worry too much if all of this sounds highly sophisticated and difficult. A good counsellor will instinctively use words appropriate to the client's ego state (the term used in Transactional Analysis to identify the inner 'parent', 'adult' and 'child'). 'Tune in' accurately and sensitively to your client's words and body language, and your reflections and questions should be appropriate. This paragraph is just to indicate to you that exploration is shaped by general understandings of what clients struggle with, and what gets in the way of their ability to resolve their problems unaided.

Read more

In 'A Process Conception of Psychotherapy', which we mentioned in Chapter 2, Carl Rogers documented the precise ways in which a client's verbal statements changed over the course of a therapeutic relationship. He noted that clients moved from the vague and 'experience-distant' to the specific and 'experience-near', from the impersonal to the personal, from thinking to feeling, and so on. Rogers' intention was to show that these shifts occurred naturally and inevitably through the provision of an empathic, non-judgemental, honest relationship with the counsellor. He would probably not have placed much emphasis on the counsellor as an active participant in this process, although careful study of Rogers' work shows that he did in fact 'model' the shifts in his trademark empathic reflections. In other words, when he 'paraphrased' (reflected) his clients, he tended to translate the client's impersonal language into more personal wording, the client's general phrasing into something more specific and concrete, and so on, thus encouraging his clients to pick up and use similar language. If your client say, 'There's a feeling of sadness', and you reply with 'Tell me more about this sadness that you feel', then that would be an example of what we are talking about.

At the other extreme, Bandler and Grinder, later known as the 'inventors' of Neuro-Linguistic Programming' (NLP) analysed videotapes of several celebrated therapists operating in the 1970s (including Virginia Satir, Milton Erikson and Fritz Perls). Bandler and Grinder concluded that although these professionals worked in quite different ways, informed by very different theoretical frameworks, all of them asked questions that pinned down the vague statements that clients made, and all of them progressively required their clients to shift from the cognitive to the emotional, from the impersonal to the personal, and from the general to the specific. Bandler and Grinder employed a framework taken from linguistics to analyse this type of questioning, but it is not necessary to understand that framework or to use that terminology to see that what is being described in their two early volumes, *The Structure of Magic I* and *II* (Science and Behavior Books, 1975, 1976) is very similar to what Rogers was talking about. The difference is that Bandler and Grinder place all the emphasis on the therapist's 'magic' interventions rather than on the client's unaided journey towards responsibility and self-knowledge (as Rogers saw it). In fact, most of the therapists Bandler and Grinder studied were simply noticing little 'missing bits' in clients' statements, and prompting the clients to fill them in—common sense, perhaps, rather than 'magic'. 'Someone might explode', says the client. 'Who (or what) might explode?' the counsellor asks.

SPEAKING FROM THE SELF

In English, we often say, 'You feel so bad' when in fact we mean '*I* feel so bad'. Because this way of speaking keeps disturbing feelings or perceptions at a safe distance from self, some counsellors insist that clients always substitute 'I'. Sometimes this makes a real difference straight away—clients sound more genuine, more authentic, and may even recognise that 'speaking for self' can render them more vulnerable, while also being more empowering. However, the impersonal 'you' is so ingrained in colloquial English that to insist clients replace it with 'I' early in the counselling process is to risk irritating and alienating them. Such coaching fits much better at a later stage, when rapport is well established, and client and counsellor know and trust one another. Some clients can then be safely challenged to speak in a way that allows them to connect more directly with their thoughts and feelings. With others, it will never be worth it. 'Rules' like 'always insist that your clients speak for self' are misleading until you have the experience to tell when you are better off ignoring them!

Moreover, when clients talk in a vague, general and impersonal way ('There's a fear there'), their chosen wording often points to the possibility that what they're dealing with may be based in some very old experience—possibly dating from their infancy. Experts guess that a very young child experiences feelings as somehow coming from 'outside' itself. So in a real sense, expecting an adult client to 'take ownership' of such a primitive fear, anger, or whatever, may be targeting a speech habit and failing to realise how deep the client's emotions go. As counsellors, we need to notice when our clients talk from this very young part of themselves. At times we can pick up this 'young part' when the client's voice suddenly gets higher in pitch, more breathless and uncertain, perhaps. Or we may notice it in their body language—as when a client may temporarily seem to 'shrink into herself', huddle down in her chair, and hunch over. But we can also notice it when clients' actual wording—as in 'There's a fear there'—temporarily ceases to reflect the perception of an adult whose feelings 'belong to her' and instead reflects the perception of a small child, whose feelings may not be experienced as having anything to do with her. (Again, Stern's *Diary of a Baby* is a vivid portrayal of how, to a toddler, her own feelings may seem completely external to herself.)

EXPLORING 'GAPS' AND 'MISSING BITS'

In the example of questioning that we gave earlier, the counsellor was inviting the client to be more specific about what she had just said. But it would be equally true to say that the counsellor was nudging the client towards supplying something that was missing in her statement. Such 'gaps' are often highly significant, but we cannot know exactly what that significance is unless we ask about them, and consider what the client says in return.

Counsellor: Last session you talked a lot about your Mum. And today you've said quite a lot more about her, and how you related to her. I suppose I'm wondering—where was your Dad in all this?

Client: [dismissively] Oh, yeah, well he wasn't around much. Mum was the one who counted when I was little.

We are asking you to be conscious counsellors—aware of what you are doing and why. You might want to pause and think at this point what it might mean that the client has not mentioned her father up to now. When you have come up with your own list, compare it with the possible meanings we have suggested below.

- She has few memories of him because he was away so much. So it simply doesn't occur to her to talk about him [*a straightforward, 'factual' explanation, which may not, however, be sufficient in itself.*]

- She resents him for not being a part of her life, and so claims he 'didn't count' [*Strong feelings can actually alter what we remember and what we forget. Maybe the client's father was 'around' more than she recalls? Or maybe he was physically around, but emotionally unavailable?*]

- Her parents separated when she was little and her mother did not encourage contact with her father. It has never occurred to her to ask whether there might be another side to the story. [*Children often accept unquestioningly the account that a parent gives them, or a parent's account conveys a strong 'don't ask me any more!' message, which they naturally do not challenge.*]

- Her father abused her, or treated her (or her Mum) badly, and she knows this, but doesn't want to talk about it because it is too painful, or because it might unleash a volcano of long-dormant rage. [*A trauma-based explanation, informed by the knowledge that children will protect themselves by repressing or 'cutting off' distressing memories.*]

One of these may be true, or none of them may be true. At this stage, you don't know, and although it is perfectly OK to guess, you should not assume anything. You have to be ready for your guesses to be wrong. It is not a quiz show, in which you're expected to push the buzzer before the client does. In fact, there is no point in getting there before the client, because if you do, the client will simply not engage with your clever answer to a question that he may not even be asking himself. Even if you are right in your guess, your hasty assumption may forfeit the chance that the client will embrace the same possibility. *Somehow 'being clever' disconnects us from our clients.* Penny vividly recalls two occasions where she figured out what was going on for her clients in the very first session and told them. Neither client came back!

Now the dialogue continues:

Counsellor: You said he wasn't around much ... could you tell me a bit more?

['Could you tell me some more?' and its variations ('I'd be interested to hear more about that', 'Could you say some more?') are extremely useful prompts, because they are nice and open, leaving clients lots of room to answer as fully, or as briefly, as they choose.]

Client: Um ... I think he worked as a truck-driver, I'm not sure, so he would have been away a lot.

Counsellor: You think he was a truck-driver, but it sounds a bit like you don't really have a clear sense of when he was there and when he wasn't?

Client: That's right. I don't have many memories of him, actually.

Counsellor: I guess I'm wondering—so even when he was around, he didn't make much impression on you? Was that because he was quiet, or was there some other reason, do you think?

[The counsellor offers one reason, while leaving open the possibility of others. This kind of question combines a 'closed' bit with an 'open' bit, and is particularly useful when clients are having difficulty coming up with ideas of their own.]

Client: [pause] No, actually, he wasn't quiet at all, he used to rant and rave and we were all glad when he left to go back to work.

Counsellor: He used to really, um, rant and rave—it was a relief when he left. So what was that like for you, when he used to carry on like that?

[The client has indicated that her father's behaviour was distressing, so the counsellor acknowledges this in a reflection before asking her a question that might open up more of that experience. Notice that the counsellor does not rush into pursuing the topic of possible domestic violence, even though she realises it may have been present. There will be plenty of time to do that later. Right now the key thing to do is to stay close to what the client experienced.]

Client: Oh, awful I suppose, although I don't really remember much about it until later, around the time he actually left Mum..... That was a bad time [picking up a cushion from the lounge and hugging it] ... I was about six I think.

In this process, a significant gap in the client's account has gradually been filled in. Now we have some ideas as to why she did not mention her father in her initial 'story'. A painful period of her early childhood was involved and, like many people, this client prefers to avoid thinking about it. That does not mean that as a counsellor, your job is to force her to talk about it! She may need to talk about it, or she may not, and at this early stage, it is not for you to 'know' what she needs. She has probably built a wall around these early experiences for very good reasons, and this must be respected. Take your cue from her. If, next session, the client starts off by telling you how significant it was when she talked about her father's 'ranting and raving', and how it brought back 'a flood of memories', then it probably makes sense to go further with the exploration of this area—after you've checked to find out how tolerable that 'flood of memories' actually was for her. But if the client does not make any mention of it, and redirects attention to a different area of her account, then the wise counsellor will leave well alone until (perhaps many sessions later) there will be an indication that the early memories of an angry, frightening father might be relevant to how the client is reacting in the present—to a partner, for example.

Read more

Why would a child build a wall around an experience, or bury it so deeply that later, they find it difficult even to remember that it occurred? We have come to realise that human beings instinctively protect themselves from painful, frightening or overwhelming experiences in this way. Freud called it 'repression', and theorised that it occurred automatically (unconsciously) in early childhood as a 'defence' against a feeling that was impossible for the child to tolerate. Since Freud's pioneering work, we have learned more about the ways that children (and indeed adults) can protect themselves against traumatic experiences—including 'dissociation', in which the person feels completely 'outside' what is happening, or may experience himself as 'floating above' it. The key thing about any form of dissociation is that it is often so effective that even many years later, the original painful experience may be difficult to access. It is not a deliberate obstruction. Clients are not 'holding out on you'. Often, as clients feel safer in the counselling relationship, they will automatically feel more able to talk about such things, and even explore them in more depth. Judith Hermann's *Trauma and Recovery* (Basic Books, 1992) is a sound guide to 'dissociation' and Babette Rothschild's *The Body Remembers* (Norton, 2000) presents a wealth of practical experience on how to work with clients who have suffered trauma. Bessel van der Kolk's *The Body Keeps the Score* (Alan Lane, 2014) readably describes the abundant research evidence that supports our current thinking about how childhood trauma affects the body and the mind, and how trauma is best addressed in therapeutic work.

What's Really Happening? What, When and How Questions

Von Ranke, a great nineteenth century German scholar, famously observed that the job of the historian was to establish *wie es wirklich war* ('what really happened') or *wie es eigentlich war* ('what actually happened'). He meant that there might well be a gap between the literal facts of an important event in the past, and what people believed had occurred. Every historian knows that even eye-witness accounts of a famous event may be distorted and misleading. It is in the nature of human memory that we are more likely to remember something that felt familiar or recognisable than something that was completely different from what we expected. Our brains make new experiences conform to the pattern of what we have experienced in the past. We recall things differently depending on how long it is since the event that we are remembering. Each individual will remember an event slightly differently according to his or her mental state at the time he or she is asked about it. Past experiences of sadness are more likely to be remembered in vivid detail when we are asked about them at a time when we feel sad—though our current sadness may be for a completely different reason. People will even recount a memory differently depending on who they are talking to—some details will 'come out' for one conversational partner, while for another person, different details might emerge.

Read more

Intending counsellors and therapists should know something about the tricks that memory can play on all of us. While undergraduate psychology texts will contain some of this material, we particularly recommend two very readable books by experts who can write for the lay reader, Daniel Schacter's *Searching for Memory* (Basic Books, 1996) and Douwe Draaisma's *Why Life Speeds Up As You Get Older* (Cambridge University Press, 2004; first published in Dutch, 2001). Both summarise a great deal of fascinating research in a readable way, and illustrate the principles of how memory works with vivid, evocative examples and photographs. Lenore Terr's *Unchained Memories: True Stories of Traumatic Memories, Lost and Found* (Basic Books, 1994) is a fascinating account by a forensic psychiatrist of the process of dissociation. If you doubt the whole concept that traumatic memories can be completely lost to consciousness, only to re-emerge many years later, then you should try this highly readable book. Please note that these are not 'false memories' created by the questions asked by a professional: they are real memories (later confirmed by other witnesses) triggered spontaneously by things like seeing the sunlight on a small child's golden hair, or standing next to a particular model car at a particular time of day.

At the time von Ranke wrote, intellectuals believed in a truth that transcended individual personalities and individual memories. These days, intellectuals often deny that any such 'truth' exists, and maintain that everything is relative. However, most therapists would agree that there are situations where careful questioning can often establish a fuller, more objective, and more specific account than the one that a client initially offers. The resulting account may not be 'the whole truth' of the situation, but it is a more useful basis for counselling intervention than the client's original presentation, which might be quite misleading. By saying this, we do not want to imply that clients lie or deliberately misrepresent a situation (although a small number may do so). But inevitably, because of the way our minds work, clients will present 'their own truth', and they will remember details selectively. They may be 'eye witnesses' to their own lives, but they are not necessarily unbiased or objective witnesses.

For example, it is extremely common for clients to talk about a particular behaviour that distresses, frustrates, or bothers them. The behaviour may be their own (for example, compulsive counting or hand-washing; sudden explosions of anger that alienate the people closest to them, or a pattern of 'bailing out' on relationships at the first sign of conflict). Or it may be that someone else's behaviour causes the problem for them (for example, clients may describe the 'lazy' or 'irresponsible' behaviour of their son or daughter, or the attitude of a work boss, who treats them with 'contempt' and 'constantly criticises' their performance). In instances like these, it is important for you to help the client explore the behaviour, and its context, more fully. Typically, clients will only talk about the part that most affects them, and (if the behaviour is someone else's) will leave out any consideration of how they themselves may be contributing to the continuation of that behaviour. If the behaviour is their own, they may leave out how it affects others in their world, and they may also omit key details, presenting their actions as a mystery, or as something over which they have little or no control. In most cases, the clients will be telling 'the truth'—as it appears to them. The behaviour will *feel like* something that they have no control over, or something unconnected with them. Here again we may be dealing with a 'child part' of the client, which has not yet learned to connect feelings with self, or actions with consequences.

'What?', 'When?' and 'How?' questions help us to get a fuller and more accurate picture of the behaviour in question, and help clients to see that the problem behaviour is not something that occurs in a vacuum, but in a particular interpersonal context ('context' means 'what lies around' something—its 'setting' if you like). Such questions also address the 'adult within' clients, assisting them to move beyond the perspective of their 'child within'. So answering these questions sometimes forms part of the 'taking back of responsibility' process. Broadly speaking, 'blamers' often need help to take more responsibility for what goes wrong, instead of assuming it's someone else's fault; self-blamers, on the other hand, often need help to do the opposite—to cease assuming that all the responsibility lies with them, when in fact it may be shared with others). The first step in achieving a fuller picture is exploration of the problem in its context.

Client: He's just impossible! He never does anything I say, he always has an excuse why he can't do it.

[She sounds like a 'blamer', but the counsellor doesn't rush to assume that this is the whole story.]

Counsellor: So you ask, and he always palms you off … So when does this mostly happen?

[The counsellor briefly reflects what the client has just said to maintain connection, before asking the 'when' question.]

Client: Oh, all the time. It's constant. It's the air I breathe, you know, it's how I live.

[The client's statements vividly express how 'big' the problem feels to her—huge and overwhelming. If the counsellor's aim is to focus on her experience of the situation, then it would be important to explore those feelings of being surrounded, impinged upon—deprived of control. However, in the following dialogue, the counsellor chooses first to gain a more detailed picture of the whole situation, including how both the client and her son behave.]

Counsellor: It feels like you can't get away from it—it's with you all the time. Is that right? [client nods emphatically] Can you give me an example of a time when you asked him to do something and he wouldn't do it?

[Asking for an example is a good way of pinning down clients who speak in dramatic but unspecific ways, as this one is doing.]

Client: Oh, God, I could tell you a million! Well, I suppose … like, last weekend, I asked him to please tidy his room before he went out. He just flatly refused, you know.

Counsellor: So you asked him to tidy his room—OK. What did you actually say? Can you remember roughly what you said?

[We already know that she will have difficulty answering this question. She is struggling with her own feelings of helplessness, rather than noticing and remembering what was actually happening between her and her son. In fact, this is how most of us are in similar situations! Our attention is wholly focussed on the thing that is most distressing to us, and details that seem unimportant pass unnoticed.]

Client: Um, ah…I probably said … well, to be truthful, I usually say something like, 'I don't suppose there's any hope of you tidying your room before you leave is there?'

Counsellor: How would you say those words? Could you say them the way you would say them to him?

[The client has answered in a general way, 'I usually say…' so asking how she would say the words encourages her to provide more information.]

Client: I don't suppose there's any hope of you doing something about your room before you walk out the door, is there?

[Slightly different wording, but uttered in a high-pitched, pleading voice.]

Counsellor: OK, sounds like you feel a bit tentative around making the request, is that right? You're kind of expecting that he's going to refuse?

['Tentative' comes from the client's tone of voice, as well as from her actual words.]

Client: Well, yeah, of course—I already know he's going to say no, and probably bite my head off, too.

[At this point the counsellor might well be guessing that part of the problem is that the client is fearful of having her 'head bitten off' so is reluctant to make her request firmly and assertively. However, the counsellor does not rush to tell the client this, or to start coaching the client in 'how to be more assertive' with her son. Instead, she persists in exploring the whole event. The truth is, we will all have ideas about how people *should* be behaving—how it is appropriate to behave—but we need to hold these ideas lightly and not invoke them prematurely. See Chapter 6 for more on the role of the therapist as 'expert on human relationships'—and the potential risks involved in this.]

Counsellor: All right. So, that's what you probably said, and what did he say when you said that?

Client: Oh, he always just says, 'Not now, Mum, I've got important stuff to do. I'll do it later'.

Counsellor: So you ask in a very polite, fairly tentative way, and he tells you that he isn't prepared to do what you're asking. Instead, he says he'll do it some other time.

Client: Yeah, absolutely typical of him.

Counsellor: So what did you say then?

Client: I think I said, 'OK, suit yourself!'

[The client may not, in fact, be accurately remembering what she said, or what her son said. However, what she believes she said is still a guide to how she experiences such confrontations, and what she experiences is that she is helpless, and the other person—her son in this case—is the one who controls the situation.]

Counsellor: So you didn't make any agreement about when he was going to do it? You didn't take him up on his offer to do it later?

Client: Nup. He never does it later anyway, so what's the point? [sighs.]

Counsellor: He makes a half-hearted offer, and you don't take him seriously. Is that typical of how you and Tim are with each other?

[Notice that the counsellor is now more forthright in how she speaks about the situation. She is able to do this because the client has gradually revealed more of the reality of her own behaviour, and has accepted the counsellor's rephrasings without demur.]

Client: Yep. Pretty much. I just feel so mad with him—he doesn't realise how mad I get, you know?

[The client may also be hinting that if she happened to be mad at the counsellor, she would not show it in any obvious way, and so the counsellor would not know about her anger. This is a possibility that the counsellor needs to 'hold lightly'. It is certainly not something to be 'interpreted' or focussed on right now, just something to be filed away, mentally, for future reference. Again, the counsellor persists in gathering more details of the situation, understanding what is going on.]

Counsellor: [gently] You feel mad, but it sounds like he doesn't know you're mad. What do you think's going on there?

Client: Because I don't tell him, well, I kind of tell him, I probably roll my eyes and sigh or something, and then just walk out of the room.

Counsellor: You give him sort of hints that you're mad, but you don't say anything.

Client: No, I guess not.

Counsellor: When this particular incident happened, what can you tell me about what led up to it? Had the two of you been getting on well, or not so well that day?

[Here the counsellor widens the context by asking about what preceded the 'incident'. The counsellor is wondering whether there has already been a difficult or conflicted interaction between them, which may have influenced what happened.]

Client: Just a normal day, I suppose. I don't really expect him to care about what I feel. He just does his own thing, you know. With his friends. They're his number one priority.

[The counsellor recognises the feeling of hurt and rejection implicit in this statement, but does not follow it up now. This is an example of the many choice points that counsellors are faced with in responding to clients.]

Counsellor: Did anything happen between you and him that day, that you think might have left you feeling that he didn't care about what you felt? I mean, earlier than you going into his room and asking him to tidy it before he left?

[This is a 'closed' question, where the counsellor is clearly 'fishing for something', but by now, the counsellor has sufficient ground to make a closed question permissible, because the client is likely to be willing to give a full answer, not a 'yes or no' response. Some textbooks call this kind of question a 'probe', an unfortunate choice of term, as it suggests a surgical operation!]

Client: Um … can't remember … um, I guess there was one thing, but I didn't give it any thought at the time … he came and asked me for the billionth time if he could leave school at the end of this year, and get a job. I said 'No'. I know he doesn't like school much, and he's not doing much work or anything. But he just can't drop out, you know, he's got to finish, so I didn't discuss it with him, I just said no. He knows I won't

52

agree.

Counsellor: So earlier that day he asked you something, and you refused, and then a bit later, you asked him to tidy his room, and he refused. Is that sort of a pattern between you—sort of, 'If you won't give to me, I won't give to you'?

In this dialogue, some of you may be struck by how long it takes the counsellor to explore the situation that the client presents as problematic. This is not how it would have unfolded in most normal conversations, is it! You'll also notice how the counsellor proceeds step by step, pausing to summarise her understanding of the situation at intervals, so that the client has a chance to accept or reject her summary. This counsellor could not have acted as she has in this dialogue if the client had not earlier indicated her acceptance of the counsellor's emphasis and direction. Imagine that the client had reacted, early in the dialogue, like this:

Client: You keep asking me about what I said. I know you're the expert, and I'm sure you know what you're doing but—I just keep thinking, isn't it him that's got the problem? I mean, if he doesn't change, then how is anything I do going to make any difference?

[Assertions that someone else is 'to blame' or 'has to change' often point, once again, to understandings that originate in early childhood, when—as an infant—you cannot really do much to make things better for yourself, unless your parents pick up on what is wrong, and step in to correct it. This view seems so 'natural' and 'right' that it is hard for many adult clients to relinquish it, nor can we expect them to do so quickly.]

Here the client has politely 'corrected' the counsellor's focus, insisting that the problem lies with her son, not with her. Most probably, the counsellor would either back away from that line of exploration, or else dealt with the impasse by some form of confrontation/immediacy (see Chapters 4 and 6). As it is, however, the counsellor has managed to gain the client's co-operation in filling in a great deal that was missing from her original presentation of the problem between her and her son. In the process, she has introduced the client to the possibility that she herself plays a role in maintaining her son's problematic behaviour. This is quite a sophisticated way of working, so don't be alarmed if you find yourself thinking, 'But I could never do that!' Experience helps us develop competencies that we cannot possess as a beginner: there is really no way this can be speeded up.

TIMING AND CHOICE POINTS

Explorations like the one demonstrated in the above dialogue lay the groundwork for behaviourally-oriented interventions (see Chapter 7) in which the professional helps the client to change aspects of their own behaviour towards a significant other person, thereby facilitating a change in the other's behaviour as well. Such interventions typically form part of 'active' approaches to change such as cognitive-behavioural therapy, and some forms of family therapy. Our point right now is simply that careful exploration must precede any such intervention. You cannot suggest behavioural changes until you are sure what is going on, and until your clients have actively co-operated in the exploration, enabling them to feel ownership of what you are discovering together.

In the long dialogue above, we drew your attention to 'choice points' where the counsellor could have gone further into the client's feelings, or stayed with trying to establish the facts—'what actually happened'. Such choice points are part of what makes counselling and therapy an art, not a science, and they are reasons why manualised treatments and formula approaches, which work well with some clients, do not fit for others. Manuals (including this book!) can tell you what to do and say in a general way. But they can't tell you which path to take when you come to a choice point in your exploration. That only comes with good listening, sensitivity, and experience. What you can do, even as a beginner, is to pay close attention to how your clients respond to an exploration that you invite them to undertake. Do they seem interested, curious, and emotionally involved? Or do they seem as if they're just going through the motions, for the sake of pleasing you? If the latter, then probably, the path you hoped to explore might not be the most relevant or useful one right now.

The choices you make around what aspects to explore are going to be influenced by how you think change occurs—your 'theory of change'—and by how your client thinks change occurs—your client's 'theory of change'. Your choices will also be shaped by what you know of this particular client. Does she feel things vividly, but fail to notice the details of her interactions with others—as in the long example given above? In that case, you might choose (as the counsellor in the example does) to focus on the specifics of what, how and when. In that case, your theory of change might say, 'Emotion-governed clients need to learn how to notice and think, instead of being driven by their feelings'. But alternatively, it might be useful to stay with the client's feelings of helplessness and powerlessness, and invite her to explore those feelings in more depth. What do they remind her of? When has she felt that way before? What was it like then? And so on. In this case, your theory of change might say, 'Clients change when they recognise, investigate and accept their feelings, instead of pushing them away, or denying them'. We'll have more to say about 'theory of change'—yours and your client's—in Chapter 5.

WHAT'S IT LIKE …? QUESTIONS THAT EXPLORE EXPERIENCE

A rounded picture of a client's situation involves not only establishing 'what typically happens', as we've just been discussing, but also exploring how the clients are affected by the situations they find themselves in. This involves asking questions that focus on the client's experience. At the two 'choice points' in our demonstration dialogue, the counsellor chose not to ask more about the client's feelings. Now, we need to say something about how you might go down the path of exploring feelings, and what sorts of things you might find.

Many lay people now believe that all counsellors do is ask, 'How did you feel?' or 'How did you feel about that?' at frequent intervals. There are lots of jokes about it. Counsellors on sitcoms do it, and distressingly, many professionals actually do it too! The question, and the jokes about it, both reflect the 'expressive-cathartic' theory of change, which roughly means that repressed or held-back feelings ('conceal don't feel') underlie most of our problems, and that resolving those problems is going to occur when we acknowledge and express those feelings openly. That theory began with Freud's early work and continued through others like Wilhelm Reich, Fritz Perls, Arthur Janov (who originated the term 'primal scream') and many body-based forms of therapy.

We discourage our students from asking 'How did you feel?', because that question assumes that 'feelings' are the most important thing involved for this client (which is not necessarily the case). The words 'how do you feel?' limit the client's field of potential response—making the question more 'closed' than 'open'. When we want to help clients explore their experience of something, we generally prefer to ask them, *'What's it like to…?'* or *'What's it like when …?'* This form of words allows them to respond in several different ways, not necessarily related to feelings. For example, some clients may respond by telling you what they *think* about the experience. Clients who typically respond cognitively (with thoughts rather than with feelings) may need to be helped to explore their feelings, which may be out of awareness, or seem 'unacceptable'. Clients who typically respond emotionally (by accessing feelings) may need to explore the beliefs or thoughts that accompany those feelings. Here is a brief example, taking up the same client and her son, but this time with the counsellor choosing to explore *her experience* of the situation:

Counsellor: What's it like, when your son fobs you off like that?

Client: I feel so rejected. It just feels awful.

Counsellor: So when you feel that rejection, that awful feeling, what are you thinking?

Client: I don't know, really. [pause] I suppose I think 'he doesn't care about me'. He prefers his friends to me—actually, he prefers his father to me. I've always been second best. In Tim's eyes, I'm the poor relation. An embarrassment.

Other clients again may take up the hint offered by 'What's it like?' and offer an analogy or a metaphor to convey their experience:

Counsellor: What's it like when your son fobs you off like that?

Client: It's awful. Like being told that you don't count, like having a door shut on you.

Counsellor: So it's like you're left out in the cold, and don't matter to your son? Like he doesn't care about you?

Client: Well I know he does care about me. But why the hell doesn't he show it?

By asking the question, 'What's it like for you?' or 'What's it like when …', we allow clients the choice of how to respond, and when we hear that response, we will learn something about the way that they typically process experience—cognitively, affectively (in terms of feelings) or perhaps through some impulsive action. That knowledge, in turn, will assist us to know how we can best communicate with them ('using their language') and also how they may need to change to gain new perspectives and access the possibility of new actions.

EXPLORING CONNECTIONS BETWEEN PAST AND PRESENT

Experience-related questions lead naturally into explorations of past experiences that strike the client as similar to the one they are talking about. Questions that connect past and present are typical of psychodynamic work, but in fact they have come to form a part of most counselling approaches. For example, a CBT practitioner might be concerned to establish a 'schema' (thought-pattern) that is governing his client's behaviour in a certain situation, and he will assume that this schema will probably have been formed a long time ago, often in childhood.

Client: It's awful. Like being told that you don't count. Like having a door closed on you.

Counsellor: Like having a door closed on you … does that remind you of anything? Have you had that feeling before, at some time in your life?

Client: I'm not sure [pause while client searches within]. It's sort of like when Mum left, and didn't say goodbye. She just took off, and she didn't tell us she was going. Dad was devastated. I thought it must be my fault, somehow. I don't know why I thought that—I just did.

Counsellor: It was the same sort of feeling. Can you say a bit more about what it was like when your Mum left, and didn't say goodbye?

Client: I didn't believe it at first. Dad said I kept asking when Mum was coming home. I think it was how he was that really got to me first [bringing her hand up to her throat]. He just kept crying. I'd never seen him cry, it was terrible.

Counsellor: And you said that at first you thought it must be your fault?

Client: Yep, I did think that. For years I think. I used to lay in bed at night and think, 'Why would Mum go like that, unless it was me? I used to be a bit naughty, and one day I'd wagged school with a girlfriend, and she was really mad about that. That wasn't long before she went. Now, I realise it probably wasn't anything to do with me. Dad and her'd had a lot of fights. But that's what I thought then. That she left 'cos she couldn't cope with me any more.

Counsellor: How would you connect up what you felt like back then, and how you feel now, when your son refuses to do the stuff you ask him to?

Client: Feels like someone's shut the door in my face [low, intense voice]. Because I've been bad. Like somehow I caused this. It's my fault I have a son who defies me. I must be a terrible person.

[Here is the 'schema' that governs this client's reaction to being rejected or abandoned. And we know that this is what children typically feel in such circumstances, so it is plausible that the schema did, indeed, originate in childhood although there is no way of proving that conclusively.]

When counsellors ask clients whether a recent experience reminds them of something from the past, it is often assumed (by the counsellors themselves, as well as by the clients) that the past experience has somehow 'caused' the more recent one. This is a misleading oversimplification (see the box that follows). Rather, it might make sense to say that our memories tend to link similar experiences, past and present, in ways that we are often not aware of. What we feel now may colour our memory of a somewhat similar event that occurred in the past, and what we felt then may lend a particular 'overtone' to what we are experiencing now. An earlier experience does not 'cause' another—but whenever our minds encounter something that our brain associates with an intense experience in the past (or series of experiences), feelings and thoughts from the earlier experience will flow into our current feelings and thoughts. The result is that we may feel 'taken over' by something we do not understand—feelings and meanings that do not necessarily 'belong' to our current experience at all—and we tend to act on the basis of that confusing mix, instead of pausing and thinking. (*What is going on here? Are my feelings of dismay and hurt an appropriate response to what my partner said a minute ago? Or are they somehow 'bigger' than her words warranted?*). Exploring the resemblances between past and present can assist clients to become more aware of which parts of what they feel and think 'fit' the experience that has triggered them, and which parts may in fact belong somewhere else in their history.

Read more

Research has shown that, contrary to what most of us believe, memories are not really stored in some sort of mental photo album or video library. Instead, what seems to happen is that an experience in the present will trigger an 'engram'—that is, a pattern of neurones firing in a particular sequence. It is this brain event that corresponds with what we call a 'memory'. When something happens to us, our brains automatically activate a pattern corresponding to similar experiences in the past. The present experience will be understood through the lens of similar past events, and hence, as mentioned earlier, we 'remember' what is familiar, in preference to what is new and unprecedented in our experience.

    The last decade or two of research into the brain's older and more primitive organs have helped us to understand why very early experiences might shape our adult perceptions. The amygdala, a small bulb of tissue that forms part of the limbic system—the part of the brain that we share with all mammals—appears to play an important part in processing memories in infancy, before a child acquires the ability to speak. As adults, none of us can retrieve such memories out of storage, because they were not encoded verbally (in words) in the first place. Instead, they were encoded in engram patterns that correspond to sensations—body feelings. But as adults, experiencing similar sensations can trigger a flood of meanings that our brains have in the distant past attached to those sensations: *I'm shaking and my heart's beating at a million times a minute—I've been left all alone and I'm terrified*. In reality, this person is not alone. Her boyfriend has just told her he can't come round that night because he's got work commitments. But body feelings that are familiar to her (and frightening) have already kicked in as she reads his text message, and her brain instantly tells her that she has been abandoned. For that moment, she returns to being a small child whose mother has walked out the door and (as far as the child knows) may never come back.

Neurological insights into memory may supply a scientific basis for aspects of Freud's theory that were long thought to be questionable or speculative—past experiences (including long past experiences of which we have no conscious recall) *do* influence our present reactions, and we *do* find ourselves in the 'grip' of particular feelings that remind us of similar feelings in the past. Hence, the meanings that we associate with those feelings may also be formed by past experiences that seem similar. And all of this happens automatically or, as Freud would have said, 'unconsciously'. These processes are involuntary and instantaneous. Too often, it is assumed by parents (and sometimes professionals) that they are deliberate. In addition to the references on memory provided earlier in this chapter, Joseph Le Doux: *The Emotional Brain* (Simon & Schuster, 1996) is very useful on this whole area, as is Daniel Siegel's *Mindsight: Change Your Brain and Your Life* (Scribe, 2009). You can read more about 'schemas' (where current developments in cognitive therapy converge with the psychodynamic approach) in Jeffrey Young, Janet Klosko and Marjorie Weishhaar's *Schema Therapy: A Practitioner's Guide* (Guilford, 2003).

It's our conviction that the common *metaphors* that clients use to convey their experience of emotional states may even correspond to *real experiences they have had in the distant past*, although it is not often that this can be established in any definite way. After all, doors really are shut when parents walk out, and babies really can feel suffocated when they're held too tightly, or the blanket gets too tight around them. We won't go further in this book, but just remember that when your client is talking, there is a lot to listen for, and both the words clients typically select, and the order in which they arrange them, are often significant. It doesn't matter if you are not aware of these nuances at this stage of your professional development. But as you gain more experience, and relax and listen more and more sensitively, you will begin to notice them.

'WHAT DOES THAT MEAN TO YOU?'

Sometimes clients will use words that are in common use, and it is easy for you to assume that you understand what they mean. They will tell you they are 'anxious', or 'upset' or 'tense' or 'confused'. But such a word may not necessarily mean the same thing to your client as it means to you. Asking clients directly may help to clarify a 'personal meaning' that such a word may have. For example,

Counsellor: So when you say you're 'tense', Kate, what does being 'tense' mean to you?

Client: Well, it means I'm on edge. Like I'm expecting bad things to happen at any moment. Don't understand why, but I just am.

Or, alternatively, it can be useful to ask clients about the 'body experience' associated with a particular word:

Counsellor: So Kate, when you feel that 'tense' feeling that you've talked about, what are you noticing in your body? What happens to you?

Client: Um, well, um, I know my throat gets tight. And I get this sort of 'rushy' feeling, as if my heart's going too fast or something. Kind of like a panic attack, only not as bad.

We've already looked at the way that people's past experience may shape their ideas about what a particular event means. In the extended example of the woman and her son, the client interprets her son's defiance as meaning that she 'doesn't matter to him'. She tells herself, 'I've been bad and therefore I deserve to be treated this way'. Her mind turns automatically to these possible 'life and death' meanings, rather than other, more rational ones. What we've thought before, in similar circumstances, we tend to find ourselves thinking again.

Sometimes clients will use a word in a way that suggests that it has a particular significance to them, yet doesn't say explicitly what that significance is. In those cases, we can ask meaning questions, to encourage an exploration of that dimension of their experience. Let's imagine a different client dialogue developing from the same starting point as our example above:

Counsellor: What's it like for you, when your son fobs you off like that?

Client: It's awful. It feels like I don't matter to him.

Counsellor: What does it mean to you … that you don't seem to matter to your son?

Client: It means I've failed as a mother. And if I've failed as a mother, then I've failed as a person. I know I don't need to feel that way, but I do. Being a success was always tied up with being a good Mum. That's what my Mum always said: 'If you can be a good mother, then you've done the most important thing in the world'. I didn't think much about it back then. Now I know she was right.

Here the client has identified a 'chain' of linked beliefs (in CBT this would lead to a 'core belief' or a 'schema'). She has also identified the person who, she believes, was the actual source of her beliefs about what makes a 'good mother'—her own mother.

Explorations of meaning are only as useful as clients' readiness to entertain them. For some clients, exploring what a particular behaviour means to them may lead to a mini-revelation. Perhaps it is something they have been dimly aware of, but not thought about or examined previously. Articulating the meaning helps them to understand why they react so strongly in a particular situation. In a few cases, it may even help them to act differently when faced with the same situation in the future. This is what Freud meant by 'insight'. More often, clients are not profoundly changed by their realisations unless the meaning that has emerged is one of which they have been completely unconscious. Such meanings are unlikely to come to the surface in the early stages of a therapeutic relationship. They emerge only gradually, in the course of a long, co-operative exploration of what behaviour means—the kind of exploration that we associate with psychotherapy, rather than with counselling (see Chapters 5 and 9).

Sometimes you may need to do more than simply ask, 'What does X mean to you?' If the client's response is 'heady' and seems unconnected with feelings, you may need to ask, '*What do you notice in yourself as you're talking about this?*' Such a question will often make it clearer to the client that she or he is 'blocking' something, or warding off some painful or uncomfortable feeling. For example,

Client: I guess I was probably one of those goody two shoes kids who always tried to please their parents. It was just what I did. So I suppose, thinking about it, um, pleasing other people was about being good and getting rewarded.

Counsellor: What are you noticing, as you're talking about this business of pleasing other people?

Client: What do you mean? I don't really understand what you want.

Counsellor: I mean, what's going on in your body as you're talking about this? Your breathing, or your muscle tension—stuff like that. You're talking about pleasing other people. What do you notice as you say that?

Client: Oh, um, nothing, really [pause]. I guess I'm focussed on you, not on me. I'm confused, because I want to do this right, you know, I want to answer your questions properly.

Counsellor: You're focussed on me—that's right. You're probably looking for little signs of whether I'm reacting well, or if I'm irritated or something … is that right?

Client: It is right. I always watch to see how the other person's reacting to what I say. I'm worried that they might disapprove of me.

Counsellor: It sounds like you get pretty tense, and when you concentrate on trying to please someone else—right now, that's me, isn't it!—you sort of lose touch with what you're feeling. All your energy is going into 'scanning' the other person and trying to figure out what they want, what's going to please them. Maybe you're scared that if you don't get it right, they might be angry with you?

Client: [long pause] Mm. I hadn't thought about it in here, but I suppose I do actually worry that you might be mad at me. I always used to worry about Mum getting mad. I had all these ways of making sure she didn't. Like sussing out what she wanted me to do, and doing it before she even asked—that kind of thing.

Counsellor: Sounds like you put an awful lot of energy into making sure she didn't get mad at you. It must've been awful, when she got mad at you.

[Here the exploration of the client's in-the-room experience leads to her identifying a quite different explanation of her 'pleasing' behaviour to the one she offered earlier. Her 'pleasing' was actually designed to avoid her Mum's anger, not to get rewards or praise—as the client's original answer suggested. By focussing on awareness, the client has 'dropped down' to a deeper and more authentic level. Implicit in this exploration is another choice point: the counsellor has opted to ask about how the client felt being the target of her mother's anger, rather than asking about the client's fear of doing the wrong thing in counselling. In Chapter 6, we'll look at examples of counsellors choosing to explore the client's feelings towards the counsellor.]

WHY NOT ASK 'WHY?'

In the 1960s and 1970s, with the popularity of 'cathartic' approaches like Gestalt Therapy, Psychodrama and Primal Therapy, it was an axiom of many training programs that counsellors ought not to ask 'Why?' questions. Trainees were told that asking 'Why?' took clients 'into their heads' instead of helping them 'get in touch with their feelings', which at the time was widely believed to be the ultimate goal of all therapeutic endeavour. Therefore, a good counsellor was allowed to ask 'How?', 'When?' and 'What?', but not 'Why?' (although illogically, 'How come?', which means much the same as 'Why?', was acceptable!) It is perfectly true that asking clients why they do something often does produce shallow rationalisations. Parents frequently say 'Why did you do that?' in an accusing tone to their children, when what they actually mean is 'You shouldn't have done that!' There often is a disconnection between how we feel and act, and why we *believe* we do so—a disconnection that has its origins in the different functions of different parts of the brain, which roughly corresponds with Freud's distinction between the 'conscious' and the 'unconscious'. There is a distinct difference between the left *hemisphere*, which thinks in words, and makes logical connections between things, and the right hemisphere, which 'thinks' by association between one image or feeling and another. Most of the time, in practice, the two hemispheres work together to make sense of what people experience—but sometimes, this process can lead us astray, as when the right hemisphere in a depressed person presents strong feelings which seem intuitively 'true'. The left hemisphere then attempts to make 'explain' these feelings, by connecting them with something else that is happening in the person's life: If I feel this awful, there must be a reason for it. And the reason must be that my family think I'm a complete waste of space. My wife's critical of everything I do, so she must believe that I'm hopeless. This may be partly true, or it may not be true at all, but the strength of the person's feelings will convince him that they must be soundly based.

Think about it

It is perfectly possible for a client to *talk about* feelings without 'being in touch with' those same feelings. This is compounded by the fact that in conversational speech, people often say 'I feel that...' when in fact they mean, 'I think ...'. A statement that begins, 'I feel that...' (as opposed to 'I feel', followed by the naming of some feeling or other) is almost certainly going to describe a thought or belief, not an emotion. 'I'm feeling puzzled' or 'I'm feeling confused' actually describe cognitive states, rather than feeling states—although there may be a feeling state associated with 'confusion' or 'puzzlement'—a feeling such as 'frustration' or 'irritation'. A counsellor taking part in a training workshop repeatedly claimed, 'I'm confused'. Eventually, it turned out that when she said this, she actually meant, 'I'm feeling angry'. Presumably anger had been something she'd not been allowed to feel as a child, and suppressing it again and again had led to its being out of awareness: all she was left with was a cognitive state—'confusion'.

It's not necessarily 'wrong' or 'bad' to talk about a feeling without actually experiencing that feeling. In fact, we all need to do it at times. But sometimes, when you have come to know your client well, you may realise that she consistently avoids experiencing a feeling, and instead talks *about* it. In this case, a good first step is to draw her attention to this, and ask her what might be going on. You will be dealing with an unconscious defence against feelings, and there will be a good reason for that defence. She may indeed need to 'experience her pain' or 'feel her anger', but she will need to feel safe enough to do so. Your job is to help her feel that sense of safety, not to crash through her defences and put her in a situation where she may be overwhelmed by the strength of her own emotions, without adequate preparation or warning. One reason why many professionals came to doubt the value of expressive-cathartic approaches to therapy was precisely this: inexperienced therapists could easily attack their client's defences, and leave her at the mercy of powerful emotions that she felt overwhelmed by.

What this complex business boils down to is that when we ask a person why they do what they do, or why feel what they feel, their answers, emanating from the left hemisphere, may be out of touch with the true motivations, which are often 'known' only to the right hemisphere, or even to more primitive parts of the brain, buried below the cerebral cortex, and cannot readily be expressed in words or logical connections. This is precisely why Freud devised the technique he called 'free association'. If patients relax enough to talk about anything that comes into their minds, Freud reasoned, then it is likely that their free flow of talk will indicate some of the 'unconscious' associations that can make sense of their conduct—but usually only with the help of the therapist, and this kind of guidance goes well beyond 'exploration' as we are considering it in this chapter.

On the other hand, there are some times when it is quite useful to ask clients 'Why?' questions. For example, if we are asking them about someone else's motivation, rather than their own, a 'why' question can often provoke the client to realise, perhaps for the first time, that the other person might have genuine and compelling reasons for acting as she/he does. This is particularly the case when we are asking a young person about his/her parents, or a parent about his/her child—between close relatives, a great deal is often unexamined, taken for granted.

Client: He treats me like I just don't matter to him.

Counsellor: Why might your son act as if you don't matter to him?

Client: I don't know, I've never thought about it. He just does ... I suppose, I don't know, I suppose he might be mad at me.

Counsellor: Why might he be mad at you?

Client: Maybe because he thinks I don't let him do what he wants all the time?

Counsellor: And why would he think that?

Client: Because a lot of the time, I don't. I can be a bit hard on him, I suppose. I hadn't realised that he might actually be angry with me—he doesn't really show it much.

Counsellor: It's a new thought that he might be angry with you. It's a bit surprising! And it's surprising that he gives you so little indication that he's angry. I wonder if he does it by treating you like you don't matter to him?

Client: Mmm. I guess so. I hadn't thought about that.

And even when clients are asked why they themselves might act in a certain way, they can occasionally produce a sudden flash of 'right brain' intuition:

Counsellor: Why would you automatically say 'no' to him? Wouldn't you sometimes be thinking, 'Well, he's got a point, maybe I should agree with him?'

Client: That's right, I just say 'No' without thinking about the rights or wrongs of it. It just happens, it just comes out of my mouth. Maybe … I don't want him to have all the things he wants, because I missed out on what I wanted when I was his age?

Here the client herself makes a connection with a feeling of resentment that she associates with her own growing-up years. Being asked to think about the other person's motivation has resulted in a connection between her past and her son's present, an insight that broadens her understanding of her own motivation.

FROM EXPLORATION TO INTERVENTION

You will probably have noticed that although each of our examples of exploration starts as a quest for more information without a predetermined direction or goal, most of them end at a point where an underlying issue is uncovered—a potential point for intervention now, or at a later stage of the counselling process. This is one of the key points we want to make. If you let your client and your own sensitivity guide you in exploring the client's presenting problem, you won't need to be busily deciding what the client's 'real problem' is, or what his 'underlying issues' are (using questions to establish whether or not your assumptions are correct). Trainers and supervisors often say, 'Trust the process'. That's exactly what we're talking about here—the process of exploration, in itself, will take you where you need to go. Relax and go with the energy. Gestalt therapists used to say, 'Don't push the river—it flows by itself'. It's another way of saying the same thing.

In this chapter, we've mentioned 'diagnostic questioning' or 'assessment questioning', and distinguished it from 'exploration'. But there is another form of questioning which is different again. This is the deliberate use of carefully chosen questions to shift clients' focus, or to manoeuvre them into a different mindset with regard to their problem. Such questioning techniques have in the past been associated with some forms of 'strategic therapy' (see Chapter 5), and are now employed extensively in Narrative therapy, Strengths-based therapy and the variants of Brief Solution-Focussed therapy. These questions do not 'follow the client's lead', at least, not in a way which would be obvious to the client. Instead, they re-focus the client, with the intention of disrupting a pervasive pattern that the therapist judges to be unhelpful (e.g. relentless blaming, or a consistent negativity), and keeping the client's attention on aspects of his or her life that are more hopeful, and more affirming of their strengths, resources, and hopefulness. Sequences of questions of this type certainly do have an 'exploration' function, but it is more akin to the kind of exploration that asks clients to fill in 'missing' aspects of their stories and 'gaps' in their accounts. (Michael White's final publication, *Maps of Narrative Therapy*, (Norton, 2007) offers many examples of such questioning. He is patient, persistent and unrelenting in the face of clients' tendency to cling to negative and self-blaming interpretations of their own behaviour.) For example, faced with the client's distress at her son's refusal to comply with her requests, a Narrative or Strengths-based counsellor might proceed as follows:

Counsellor: So clearly, there are lots of times when your son refuses to do what you ask. And you end up feeling pretty bad about that. Could you tell me about the times when you have no difficulty at all in getting your son's co-operation?

Client: He hardly ever does what I ask. I'd have to go back years ...I can't remember ...

Counsellor: It doesn't matter how small the example is, or how long ago it was. Maybe you can remember just one time when your son seemed delighted to accept your suggestion, or keen to assist you in some way?

Client: Well, I guess there was the time that I wanted him to ...[gives details of the incident.]

Counsellor: OK, so on that occasion, your request met with instant, enthusiastic agreement. What do you think made it possible for you to gain his co-operation in that way?

Client: I don't know. Just a fluke, I guess.

Counsellor: I'd be interested in hearing your ideas about what it was *in you* might have made it possible for your son to co-operate so readily. What personal strength or resource did you bring to the conversation with your son, that seemed to produce such a wonderful outcome—one that you've never forgotten?

Client: I don't think it was anything in me. I think he was just easier to deal with then.

Counsellor: I notice that you've held onto that memory for all those years. It must mean a lot to you. What do you think it might show about what you value in life and relationships, that you've held onto that memory so long, and prize it so highly?

Client: I'm not sure what you mean.

Counsellor: You wouldn't have held onto that memory so tenaciously if it hadn't said something to you about a quality that you value—maybe it was some aspect of relationship, or a mother–son relationship, that you really hold dear?

Client: Mmm. I suppose it might be that there should be times when mothers just know what their son needs, and their son is really grateful, because they couldn't have done it for themselves.

Counsellor: What word would you put on that quality? How would you describe what you've just told me?

Client: I suppose I could call it' intuition'. 'Loving intuition', maybe.

Counsellor: How might it affect your relationship with your son in the future, if you were to call on that 'loving intuition' in your dealings with him? [and so on.]

We hope that this example has demonstrated what we tried to explain earlier in more abstract terms. This is questioning, and powerful questioning, but it goes well beyond 'exploration'. It is, in fact, a form of intervention.

CHAPTER SUMMARY

- Exploring is the logical next step after holding. In early sessions, you will typically be *both* holding your clients, *and* exploring with them. Exploring may occur at any stage in the developing therapeutic relationship, because new things will be constantly emerging.

- Exploring is *not* about verifying your pre-existing ideas about your client and their problem. It is about opening up areas that are potentially relevant to them.

- In questioning, your first guideline is to *follow the client's lead.*

- In general, ask questions that open up (*open questions*) rather than ones which close off options (as in *diagnostic questioning*).

- *Closed questions are not always 'wrong'*, but they come into their own as you (and your client) become clearer about what is most important.

- *Questions tend to weaken the client's connection with the counsellor* and engage them in a left-hemisphere 'search for answers' that may not be useful.

- Following the client includes asking about areas that are 'in the shade', things that the client may have ignored or de-emphasised, where common sense would demand some more information.

- *In any exploration, there will be choice points.* At times it may be vital to explore clients' experience, including (but not limited to) their feelings. At other times you may choose to focus on getting a detailed 'factual' account of the scenario that the client is presenting— who said what, when, and how things played out. The account may not be the literal 'truth', but it will still be useful in widening the client's initial account of the scenario.

- *Asking 'Why?' questions is not always inappropriate, but it often leads to 'intellectualising'*— rationalisation and defensiveness. On the other hand, it can sometimes be very useful to ask clients why they think a significant other person is doing what he/she is doing, because such questions may encourage empathy and greater understanding of the other.

- Sometimes clients use words which seem to mean something important to them, but fail to spell out what that meaning is. It is useful to ask them directly what a particular word means to them, and it can also be important to ask them *what they experience* as they talk about that meaning. This may assist them to connect out-of-awareness feelings to intellectualised understandings.

- Questions that help you and your client explore are quite different from strategic questioning techniques deliberately designed to help clients re-focus their attention in a more helpful direction. *Exploration, as we have described it, is an open-ended process, in which neither you nor your client necessarily know what you are going to discover.* It may lead to intervention, depending on where the exploration ends up. Strategic questioning is an intervention in its own right, designed to shift a dysfunctional orientation (e.g. a sense of self as victim; a sense of self as a failure) in a more functional direction.

Chapter 4

The Elephant In The Room: The First Three Sessions

INTRODUCTION

When you see a client for the first time, you do not know what to expect. The rules of counselling and therapy in our society dictate that clients will, mostly, be people that you do not know.[1] You do not know why they are seeking help, what they are hoping for, what sort of individuals they are, or how they will relate to you. Even if you have already spoken with them by telephone, and have some preliminary impressions as a result, a great deal will remain uncertain. In the course of the first few sessions, much will become clearer. But at first, there will be a certain amount of anxiety involved. Even experienced counsellors and therapists can still feel that slight sense of apprehension when they meet for the first time with a new client, especially if they have reason to expect that the client may not be a straightforward one. This apprehension can contain a tinge of excitement, as with any unknown. You never know who might come in the door.

As we mentioned in the preceding chapter, many mental health professionals are trained to conduct an assessment in the first session (or the first couple of sessions), asking structured questions designed to clarify the nature of the problem, the resources available to the client, and how well the client is functioning in life. Making an assessment removes much of the anxiety that inexperienced counsellors feel. It also provides much useful information. However, conducting a structured assessment may also obscure or inhibit a process that will naturally unfold if the client is allowed to present his or her situation in his or her own way.

Encouraging clients to present their concerns in their own way, and being sensitive to their emphasis, can provide a different kind of information—about the client as an individual personality, and about the client as she or he relates to you. (It can also answer many of the 'assessment questions' you might otherwise have asked.) If you do not conduct a formal assessment, then you are going to learn about your new clients not just from the answers they provide in response to your questions, but from the (largely unconscious) way that they present themselves to you. For example, if you ask a series of questions, and clients simply answer them, then *you* will have determined the order in which things are talked about. If you allow clients to talk unprompted, then the *clients* will have determined the order—and that order will show you something of how their minds work—as well as what is *on* their minds! This is the principle behind 'free association', which we glimpsed in the last chapter. How much, or how little, they say about particular topics will show you how important they consider those topics—or how safe they feel to expose themselves around them. Remember the title of this book: your aim is to create *a safe place for change*. If it is not safe, there will be no change.

If you allow your client to take the initiative in this way, what happens in the first three sessions will have a degree of predictability to it—although curiously, this seems not to have been much thought about by practitioners[2]. In the first session, clients typically 'tell their story'—that is, lay out some of their problems and sometimes, the 'backstory' that lies behind them. If the counsellor listens well and demonstrates (through holding skills) that they can understand and empathise, then the client typically feels relieved and often appears more hopeful or at least more settled by the end of the session.

In the second session, the client typically goes over the problem presentation again, often filling gaps that were left in the first version, or telling more of the backstory. As we saw in the last chapter, you may play a more active role in this session, exploring aspects that are clearly important to the client, perhaps being more overt in your empathic responding. By the end of the second session, however, there are often hints that the client expects that by now, 'something' should have 'happened'. There will be signs of disappointment or frustration, although these may be very slight, and easy to miss unless you know to watch for them. Clients in the first couple of sessions are typically polite (see later in this chapter). They will act in accordance with social norms. Anger and disappointment will normally be veiled, if expressed at all.

But it is impossible to miss the change that frequently occurs between the second session and the third. Some clients cancel the third session, offering an excuse (plausible or implausible) and saying that they will call back later to reschedule (they rarely do). Others simply fail to show up. These are often described as 'psychologically unsophisticated'—which in practice usually means less educated, poorly paid, or unemployed. But even those clients who do return for their third session often do so in a markedly different mood. Typically, they show more obvious signs of anger or disappointment than at the end of the second session, as if these feelings have gained ground since you saw them last. Depending on how the counsellor handles this, clients will either commit to ongoing counselling, or drop out. Thus, although some drop-outs occur *after* the third session, just as many occur after two sessions, and *prior to* the third session.

Our experience is that the three-session sequence is likely to occur pretty much *regardless of what you, as counsellor, do or fail to do*. Poor counselling skills will increase the likelihood of early drop-out, but even good counselling skills will not prevent a substantial number of clients dropping out around the three session mark. Conducting a formal assessment—even a three-session one—may delay the 'crisis' but it will not prevent its happening. The only exceptions are when your clients have already had counselling or therapy in the past, can acknowledge where their real difficulties lie, and are prepared to get straight to work. These are 'psychologically sophisticated' clients—which doesn't mean those who have picked up some professional language and use self-diagnosis to give the impression that they have 'figured themselves out'! And even psychologically sophisticated clients will often seem a little less hopeful, and more frustrated and disappointed, after a couple of sessions, despite their commitment to continuing to see you.

Why does this three-session process happen? And what does it mean? We'll argue in this chapter that in the first few sessions there is an 'elephant in the room', a presence which is invisible, but which nevertheless exerts a very real influence on what happens between you and your client. This 'elephant' is your clients' unconscious, or barely conscious, awareness of what the 'real problem' is—of what it is in them that creates difficulties in their lives. But at the start of the counselling process, very few clients can actually 'see' the elephant. Many simply know that 'something' is there, something that they feel profoundly uncomfortable about. They want to avoid talking about it—even thinking about it. Despite this, they will still be influenced by it.

Whatever problem they report will be presented as if it is insoluble. Whatever situation they describe, it will seem that they are trapped, that there is 'nothing they can do'. Their sense of being 'locked in', unable to act, at the mercy of someone or something, may be extreme, or it may only be mild. But their 'stuckness' will transmit itself to you, the counsellor. You, too, will start to be affected by the presence of the invisible 'elephant'. You, too, may become anxious, frustrated and confused. Like the client, you will start to feel that there must be an answer which (if you are like many beginning counsellors) you will believe it is up to you to supply. Yet you will be unable to locate this answer. Thus, your client's anxiety will become your anxiety, and both of you will circle warily around the 'elephant'. Here is where you can play an important role—not by figuring out what the 'real problem' is, or knowing better than the client what he is 'avoiding', but by enabling your client to name his own experience of stuckness and desperation, and by providing a calm assurance that you will stay with him for as long as it takes for the nature of the elephant to be discovered—or for him to describe an elephant he already sees, but does not yet feel safe enough to talk about.

Clients typically tell you about problems in a 'defended' way: they tell you about the external forces (the things outside of themselves) that prevent them being happy or fulfilled, they tell you about the things that they can't control, the things they don't understand. They don't usually tell you about the way their own behaviour torpedoes their relationships, the way their own attitudes and habits of thought may contribute to maintaining their sense of misery or dissatisfaction. The problems they will present, initially, will seem insoluble because their own contribution will be out of their awareness. It is your job as a counsellor or therapist to help them feel safe enough to reach the point where they can 'see' the 'elephant'—face up to the real problems within them. With time, patience and sensitivity, it will be possible for you to help many clients to see the elephant in this way. As soon as they begin to do so, the problems and dilemmas that seemed so impossible begin to seem less 'elephant-like', more manageable.

Sometimes, the 'elephant' will not simply be the client's denied awareness of his/her own responsibility for the problem. It will be complicated by the way *you* have responded to the client. If, for example, she has begun to sense that you are judging her, or are 'freaked out' by what she has told you, then those perceptions will make the 'elephant' harder to see—in fact her perceptions of you will become part of the 'elephant'. Acknowledging the unexpressed here-and-now feelings both you and your client are aware of is called the capacity for *immediacy*. Addressing what is in the room but unspoken provides the 'breakthrough event'. It can get you and your client past the initial impasse in the counselling relationship— the impasse that we have called the 'third session phenomenon'. And it will greatly enhance your clients' trust in you—their sense that you will be able to stay with them on the journey they are embarking upon, wherever it may go.

Now, let's take a look at the first three sessions in more detail, looking at what typically happens, briefly mentioning some exceptions to the generalisations that we've just made, and discussing how you need to be with your clients in order to bring about the best possible outcome at this very early stage of the counselling relationship.

THE FIRST SESSION: TELLING THE STORY

Gerard Egan, in his widely-used textbook *The Skilled Helper*, sees a counsellor's primary aim in the opening phase of a counselling relationship as 'helping clients tell their story'. The word 'story' is now so loosely used that perhaps we need to clarify what it means in this context. Many clients do not 'tell a story' in the original sense of that word. There is no 'narrative'. Instead they may describe symptoms that are troubling them, complain about the behaviour of someone else in their world, or talk about feelings of dissatisfaction, anxiety or confusion. An initial presentation to a counsellor may not sound much like the sort of 'story' you read in a novel, or watch in a movie. Other clients do seem to come along to the first session prepared to 'tell a story' (often, these are clients who have already gone through a formal history-taking with other professionals). Such clients begin, perhaps, with childhood experiences that they see as significant, and then explain how their problems have unfolded over their lives, noting key events and turning points in the history of the problem. Here is an example:

Client A: Well I suppose what I want help with is these feelings that I have…I call them my 'slowed down' feelings. Where do I start? See, I never knew my mother when I was growing up. I didn't know anything about her. I never felt like I belonged there.

[Where is 'there?' Wait, and probably the client will make it clearer later.]

> But they did look after me quite well, I think.

[Who are 'they'? Is she talking about her biological family, or step-parents, or even foster-parents? And what does she mean by 'quite well'?]

> Only I never felt that I belonged, I didn't fit. So when I was a teenager I sort of rebelled, I ran away a lot, I didn't really know why, I just wasn't happy. I had a boyfriend, well, a few boyfriends, and I used to go off and stay with them for a while, and then I'd get sick of it, and I'd go home. Then I got a job, and I moved out. That was when I noticed that I was starting to feel …something wasn't right. You know, sort of slowed down, like everything was an effort, not much energy. I didn't think much about it at the time, I was going out drinking most nights and having a good time, or I thought I was. But after I had my first, she's seven now, that's when I really got affected by those slowed down feelings, I realised I might be depressed. I went to the medical centre, and he gave me a script for Prozac. Well, it gave me a bit of a lift, and since then I've been OK most of the time, until just this last couple of months

[So what's been happening that might have triggered the symptoms again?]

A relatively organised story like this one, with a beginning, a middle and an end, tells us a lot—but it also leaves out a lot. We have put in square brackets some of the questions that might have occurred to you while listening to this 'story'. When we come to discuss the second session, we'll look at how you as a counsellor might want to explore aspects of an account like this one, by asking those questions, or others like them. But if you simply listen, you may find that the client answers many of them anyway, over the course of the first two sessions. Others you may need to ask eventually, but there is no need to do so straightway. But for now, let's contrast this client's 'story' with a very different kind of presentation of a somewhat similar-sounding problem:

Client B: I don't know where to start, really. What do you want to know? Um, well, it's this sort of heavy feeling. I can't seem to shake it off. I've been to the doctors about it, but they can't help, they just tell you to take a holiday and unwind, well, you know, that's out of the question isn't it—I can't afford not to have money coming in. If I go off for a holiday, there's mouths to feed, and nothing to feed them with, right? Um [pause] I was hoping you'd ask me questions, that's what they usually do.

[Who are 'they'? Other professionals?]

Counsellor: Well, tell me a bit more about the 'heavy feeling' that you mentioned

[The counsellor responds to the client's challenge/request.]

Client B: I don't know, it's just, it's just…it's hard to put into words, um…you know, there's so much on our plate right now, there's the repayments and there's the school and the uniforms and all of that, there's the kids getting into strife, there's Rob hanging around…

[Who is 'Rob'—a previous partner? A grown-up son?]

> and I don't know what he really wants, he seems happy enough to stay over, but when you ask him to chip in and help out a bit, I mean financially, he's like, 'What is this?' Like I did the wrong thing to ask him.

This client has 'rolled' from one issue to another, and even when the counsellor asks her to say more about one of the problems, she seems unable to stick to that topic for more than a few seconds. Again, her disjointed, disorganised way of talking is worth paying attention to—not *what* she says but *how* she says it (not '*content*' but '*process*'). Before we jump in and start trying to find out what the 'real' issue is, it is very valuable to listen to her talk unprompted, so that we get a sense of the chaotic way that she experiences her life, and her difficulty in organising or prioritising her various difficulties. What she says may not sound like a 'story', but it does contain a possible theme—the theme of a person who feels overwhelmed by how to handle life, looks to others to help her, and is constantly disappointed.

Whereas client A gives indications of having 'grown up' to some extent (she can look back on her earlier life in an objective way, from a vantage point of greater wisdom or self-knowledge), client B still handles life as the child she once was—small, helpless, and overwhelmed by experiences that she cannot control. On the other hand, client A's relatively clear, chronological account is lacking in many specific details. It is too well organised. Things that perhaps do not fit the story have been neatly tidied away, and everything comes out as if rehearsed. We are hearing, not the reality of the client's life, but a highly selective, 'processed' summary of it, with much of the complexity and the subtlety left out.

But whatever form a client's initial presentation takes, we would normally expect, from a new client, a flow of information and (sometimes) feelings—as if some pressure has built up, and when the 'tap' is turned on, the flow will continue unabated for a while. This is why we talked, in Chapter 2, about 'staying out of the client's way'—not interrupting unnecessarily, but letting clients tell us about their concerns at their own pace, in their own order. If, like client A, they do, in fact, recount a 'story', it is easy enough to let them go ahead, and simply listen attentively. But if clients seem 'all over the place', sliding from one problem to another, switching from past to present, and back to past, talking about a whole range of different relationships and people without identifying them, then it is, obviously, much harder to stay out of the way. The natural temptation is to intervene in some way, to bring order out of chaos. By all means do what seems necessary (as the counsellor does with client B above) but do it is sparingly as possible, so as to give the client space.

Some clients enter counselling with a clear idea of what they want help with. They immediately select one main problem and talk about it. Others simply talk, in a seemingly aimless way. Some present apparently quite trivial situations as 'the problem'. Others, without preamble, start straight into an account of deeply painful experiences, often from the past, as if they need to talk about these experiences, but without connecting them in any obvious way with their present difficulties. *Even when there does not appear to be much logic in a client's initial presentation, you can normally afford to relax and listen. It may not make total sense now, but most of it will be repeated in the next session, and probably many times after that.* As we said in Chapter 2, your task in most first sessions is to employ holding skills just enough for the client to sense your interest and involvement.

WHAT IF YOU CAN'T GET A WORD IN?

A minority of clients would probably talk for an entire hour without stopping if you permitted them to do so. There might be several different reasons for this behaviour—they might be extremely anxious; they might be afraid of what they think you are going to say (and so fill all the space with their own talk); they might be traumatised, and need to 'pour it all out'. They may be so unused to being listened to that they can't even tell you are there. It is rarely a good idea to allow a client to speak uninterrupted for an entire session because counselling is an interpersonal process and we know that the benefit for the client lies in feeling the beginning of a connection with us. After about 15-20 minutes we would usually offer some verbal response (a reflection or a statement of empathy is usually the safest), partly to show the client that we really are listening to them, and partly to test their readiness to allow our participation. We may even have to interrupt our client (*Do you mind if I make a comment here? Would it be OK for me to come in here?*) to make a space for our own contribution. When we 'test the water' in this way, the client's response will probably give us some tentative information about her needs. If the behaviour continues past the initial session (usually it doesn't) a mild confrontation may be in order to explore what might be happening for her as she talks compulsively in the room (see Chapter 6).

WHAT IF CLIENTS DON'T WANT TO TELL THEIR STORY?

Wanting to 'tell their story' is the norm for most clients. However, there are some clients for whom Egan's model does not fit very well at all. Some of these are 'involuntary' or mandated clients, that is, those who have been instructed or ordered to see a counsellor. Many of them will feel resentful or angry at having been compelled to seek 'help' that they do not believe they need (or know they need, but are terrified of encountering). Initially, such clients may refuse to say much at all, and may respond to your questions with surly, one-word answers. Don't assume that such clients don't have any problems. They almost certainly do. But before they begin to acknowledge any of what is going on for them, these clients are going to make you pass a test—prove that you are patient, and genuinely interested in them. Sometimes, as well, you may have to be prepared (at a far earlier stage than you would with voluntary clients) to confront their evasions or to challenge their claims that they feel 'fine' and have no need of assistance.

Counsellor: You've told me that you don't want to be here, and that you're only here because the Department says you have to have twelve sessions of counselling. Fair enough. I can't force you to talk about stuff. We can sit here in silence for twelve sessions if you like. But maybe it would make more sense for you to talk about something that you actually do need to talk about. It doesn't have to be the stuff they sent you here about. That way, you might get something out of this, instead of just wasting your time. What do you think?

Some *voluntary clients* behave in a rather similar way, and we will consider them shortly. These clients may be very clear about their need for help. However, they are highly guarded individuals, for whom self expression does not come easily. They, too, will give away as little as possible until you have proved your trustworthiness. So at a fundamental level, the two types of client have much in common. With both, you will need to 'work harder', and take a more active stance, but this does not mean you necessarily have to ask heaps of questions!

THE FIRST SESSION: FORMING AN ATTACHMENT

Whether clients talk freely in their first session or hold back, there will be something else going on. They will be 'trying out' the counselling relationship, often offering you relatively superficial or minor problems, reserving more serious and painful issues until they are sure that they will not be judged or criticised. At the same time, they may be covertly seeking information about you. *Is this the sort of person that I can talk to? Does she/he seem to share my values and priorities? Will she/he jump down my throat and give me advice that I don't want?* (Or conversely, *Will he/she have the answers, or sit there and refuse to tell me?* Many new clients do not understand why counsellors might refrain from giving advice, but there are times when giving advice will be appropriate, and we will be discussing these in Chapter 7).

In other words, *clients will be entering into relationship with the counsellor, or, if you like, attempting to form a connection with him or her.* As we shall shortly see, most clients are likely to bring to this process the strategies they have learned in the past to rely upon when forming an attachment. For example, if they have generally found that smiling and agreeing with the other person smooths the path towards a relationship (personal or even professional) they will tend to do so now, even if secretly, they do not agree with what the counsellor has just said. They will not consciously decide to do this, they will simply do it, because it is what they are used to doing. It is automatic. Something called procedural (or 'implicit') memory governs such automatic patterns—the same mechanism that enables us to drive a car, or ride a bike. Once learned (often long ago in childhood), such behaviour patterns become second nature, and are activated in appropriate situations, without our having to think about them.

Alternatively, if clients have generally tended to get into arguments with anyone who does not seem to agree with them, then this pattern, too, may display itself—although perhaps only in a mild form, at such an early stage of the counselling relationship. As the counsellor, you might notice a tiny frown, a hesitation, and indrawn breath, or a sudden body movement, signalling the client's discomfort or dissatisfaction. In more extreme cases, clients will openly challenge or disagree, even in the first session, saying things like:

- *How can you say that? You don't even know anything about me yet!*
- *You say you can understand—but I don't think you do!*
- *Hey, let me finish, please, this is important!*

These clients act almost as if they expect that you will fail them. Where the first category (smiling, compliant) treat you as if you are automatically trustworthy and well-disposed towards them, this second category (reactive and rebellious) seem to make contact with you through struggle and opposition. This need not mean that they are not *capable* of trusting you. It may simply mean that you need to 'pass the test' first—a bit like the involuntary clients that we talked about a short time back. If you have watched the first series of *In Treatment*[3], you will notice that in their first sessions, the young gymnast, Sophie, and the Navy pilot, Alex, both fall into this category. Both seem to settle down a bit within a couple of sessions, once Paul, the therapist, shows that he is not intimidated or offended by their aggression. He is prepared to engage with them, and (up to a point) to give as good as he gets. He 'passes the test' and they begin to trust him with more of their vulnerability. (Later, however, they will again become furiously angry with him, make threats, and even, in Alex' case, intimidate him.)

Other clients will display a still more puzzling pattern of behaviour. Faced with the process of forming a relationship with a new person, they may retreat into a relatively passive position, making only brief, guarded statements, and waiting to see what the counsellor says. Such clients are difficult to respond to. They say so little that there are awkward gaps, tempting counsellors to rush in and fill the spaces with questions, or with comments on what the client has already said. However, the questions that counsellors ask, at this early stage, will not make things all that much better, because the client will answer them as minimally as possible—almost like sullen teenagers being cross-examined by their worried parents (*'Where did you go?'* *'Out'. 'What did you do?' 'Nothing!'*) The voluntary, but reluctant, clients we described earlier in this chapter are probably examples of this category.

Such clients may be hinting to us that they feel naked and exposed in a situation where they are expected to speak of intimate and personal things with a virtual stranger. Rather than try to win the counsellor's trust with smiling compliance, and rather than arguing or debating with the counsellor, these clients seem frozen, unable to take much initiative. It's as if you have to come to them, only they give away so little that it is not easy to work out how to approach them in a way that they will find acceptable. Most of us proceed by 'trial and error', feeling awkward and stilted as we do so. But if it doesn't get any easier after a couple of sessions, it may be important to 'name' what has been going on:

Counsellor: Sarah, I think we need to stop for a minute and talk about what might be happening here. I can see that you're a bit reluctant to talk, and I'm sure there's a good reason for that. People nearly always have reasons for what they do, or don't do. What seems to be happening is that you say nothing, and then I ask you a question, and you answer it. Only you don't say a lot, so it's hard to get a conversation going. I probably sound pretty awkward and forced, don't I! I wonder if maybe this is very hard for you, only you don't feel able to tell me about it. Could that be right?

Again, statements like this one demonstrate the skill of immediacy. When normal communication breaks down, and something seems to 'get in the way' of the counselling process, it is this skill which every competent counsellor or therapist will need to use. *Immediacy puts into words what both you and the client are aware of—but aren't talking about.* The relief that comes from this acknowledgment is often palpable.

Think about it

How your clients behave is not solely a product of their own style of relating. If *your* responses to them are awkward, unempathic, or intrusive—in other words, if you fail to employ good 'holding' skills—then even clients who would otherwise be quite willing to talk may retreat into silence or produce minimal answers to your questions!

Many trainee counsellors, engaging with their first 'real' clients in an internship or placement, report that their clients are 'resistant' or 'won't talk'. Instead of leaping to the conclusion that there is something badly wrong with these clients, wise supervisors consider the possibility that the fledgling counsellor's lack of skill and sensitivity may be part of the problem. Anxious beginners often struggle to be good listeners, but as they settle down and relax into the relationship, they find their clients reciprocate by 'opening up' more readily. A 'positive feedback loop' has been created (this is a concept from systems theory—see Chapter 5).

THREE WAYS OF ATTACHING

Seventy years ago, in a book called *Our Inner Conflicts*, psychoanalyst Karen Horney famously described three categories of people: those who 'move towards' others in a confident, trusting way; those who 'move against' others, as if expecting a fight or a disagreement; and those who 'move away', trying to guard against intrusion. The type of client we have just been describing is definitely a 'mover away'. The type of client who seems to expect a 'fight' or a 'struggle' is definitely a 'mover against'. The type who smiles and seems to trust you from the beginning is clearly a 'mover towards'. In fact, these three categories correspond to some degree with the principal 'attachment strategies' empirically identified by the Attachment research of Mary Ainsworth and Mary Main.[4] One seems generally trusting of others, and the other two, in distinct ways, indicate their lack of trust.

Read more

Freud talked about a phenomenon he called *transference* (see Sigmund Freud, *Introductory Lectures on Psychoanalysis* (Penguin Freud Library, Vol. 1, Penguin Books, 1974: 482500. The lectures were first delivered and published in 191617) Patients, he said, act towards therapists, doctors and other authority figures as if those figures were their mother, their father, their older sister, their feared schoolteacher, or whatever—*transferring* the behaviour they displayed in the distant past onto professionals in the present. Vastly elaborated, this concept became a keystone of the psychodynamic approach. It boils down to this: If a therapist displays a neutral attitude to clients, showing neither approval nor disapproval, and being equally interested in everything the clients say, they will almost automatically start to act towards the therapist in the same ways—both functional and dysfunctional—as they have displayed in the past with those individuals with whom they have formed their earliest significant relationships. Transference does not have to take dramatic or obvious forms. If client and counsellor are sitting facing each other, with their eyes open, then obviously, the 'transference relationship' will usually be much less intense than if the client lies on a couch with eyes closed. The more actively the counsellor engages with the client, the more of the therapist's personality and individuality is 'on display', the less 'transference' will manifest itself—at least, in obvious ways. That is why psychoanalysts emphasised 'neutrality'—to give the transference the best chance to develop and flourish.

Modern research into the way we form our earliest relationships has substantially confirmed what Freud theorised, although scholars of human development use different language to describe it. We do, as infants, evolve distinct, recognisable patterns of behaviour towards significant others—designed to ensure that we get the love and attention we need from our primary caregiver. Following the pioneer work of Bowlby, Ainsworth and Main, we now call this process 'attachment'. The patterns that we learn will differ, depending on the way that our mother (or other primary caregiver) behaves towards us. The formation of an 'attachment strategy' is thus an interactive process, in which two people adapt to one another, not a one-way process in which a baby is driven solely by instinct. An infant needs ways of ensuring its carer's attention in order to survive: it is that simple—and that important. An individual child's attachment strategy becomes lodged in its brain as 'procedural memory'—Attachment theorists call this the child's internal working model—and is automatically activated whenever, later in life, it finds itself in a situation which seems similar to the situation in which the strategy was originally learned.

Coming to see a counsellor or therapist is, for many people, an anxiety-provoking thing. Clients are in distress, sometimes acute distress, and they desperately hope for something to change so that they can feel better. They are in a very vulnerable position. They must trust a supposedly qualified expert, whom they do not know, with their innermost secrets. They have, initially, no particular reason to expect that they will be understood, or treated with care and respect, or even that what they say will be kept confidential. And in some cases, they are paying quite a lot of money to the professional they have chosen to consult. Is it any wonder that, in this novel situation, clients revert to behaviour patterns first learned in infancy, when they needed to gain the attention, nurturing and protection of an all-powerful parent?

Sitting opposite the counsellor for the first time, clients will often, on the surface, act as if they are fully in control, rational beings, speaking to the counsellor as an equal. But underneath that surface, other dynamics will be played out. Parts in their brains like the amygdala will have preserved implicit (unconscious, non-verbal) memories of their earliest infant experiences. Although the clients will not consciously remember these experiences (how their mother behaved, and how they behaved in response to her) they will nevertheless by guided by those memories in how they now approach their counsellor. So attachment theory, and the research that supports it, has actually converged with Freud's original ideas about 'transference'.

If you want to know more about attachment theory, probably the best place to start is with Robert Karen's *Becoming Attached* (Oxford University Press, 1998). Karen gives a readable account of how ideas about attachment evolved over half a century, including the fierce debates and controversies that surround the 'nature/nurture' question. He provides pen-portraits of some of the leading attachment researchers, so that we sense what sort of people they were, not just what ideas they stood for. It's also well worth while reading at least some of John Bowlby's major trilogy (*Attachment*, Hogarth Press, 1969; *Separation: Anxiety and Anger*, Hogarth Press, 1973; *Loss, Sadness and Depression*, Basic Books, 1980), to get a sense of the wide field of research and observation he drew upon in formulating his theory. Important elaborations of Attachment Theory have more recently been made by Patricia Crittenden, who has evolved what she calls the 'Dynamic-Maturational Model' of attachment. Her controversial publication *Raising Parents: Attachment, Parenting and Child Safety* (Willan Publishing, 2008; Routledge 2012) offers a readable account of her theory, with particular reference to what goes wrong when parents abuse, or fail to protect, their children.

ANXIETY AND POLITENESS IN THE FIRST SESSION

Transference does not always 'kick in' immediately, in the way that it does with Alex and Sophie in *In Treatment*. There are also clients who, as they come to feel safer and more comfortable with you, will display a fuller 'transference'—that is, more aspects of their early behaviour and feelings towards attachment figures will probably be on show.

In Chapter 2, we urged you to listen carefully and speculate tentatively in your earliest contacts with a new client, instead of rushing in with specific questions or comments on what they have just said. One reason for our advice is the one just referred to in the text box about transference: clients will typically be nervous to some degree when they first come to see you, although this may not always be obvious. So what you see in a first session—even a first few sessions—may not be a completely accurate guide to what sort of person you are dealing with. Anxiety may cause some clients to act more 'together' or 'sorted' than they actually feel; it may induce others to act more dependent and 'helpless' than they actually are. Remember, you are an 'authority figure' to your clients, no matter how warm, human and accepting you may be. It is natural to think of yourself as 'safe' to talk to, and so you may forget that your client may not 'know' this yet. It can be very tempting to tell your clients things like, '*this is a safe place*' or '*you can trust me*'. In fact clients need to learn this though *experiencing* our trustworthiness and ability to create a 'safe haven' for them. *Verbal reassurances will not do it.*

In laying out a few broad patterns of relating, as they typically manifest themselves in the first few sessions, we are not encouraging you to 'categorise' or 'diagnose' your clients, or to predict how they may act in the future. We're merely making you aware of some of the many things that you might be aware of in a first meeting with a new client, and what they might mean. Noticing things—without necessarily assuming you know what they 'mean'—is one of the keys to successful rapport-building with a new client. It is also important for the client, because it shows them that you are wanting to know *all of who they are*, not just the one or two bits that happen to be of most interest to you!

There is one further aspect of all this that we return to briefly, and that is the way that you, the counsellor, may 'feed into' the way the client responds to you. In the counselling room, you are in a professional role, but you are still a person! Traditional psychodynamic 'neutrality' was designed, in part, to reduce the amount of 'person' present, but even if we sit with a poker face and say very little, we will still be who we are, and our feelings towards our clients will in part be influenced by the attachment strategies that we, too, formed very early in our lives. The smiling, 'helpful' counsellor may feel upset when her client seems unresponsive to her pleasant attitude, or rejects her 'help'. The counsellor who has learned to defend himself by attacking may be tempted to be too confrontational, too early in the process. The counsellor who as a child learned to keep all her feelings to herself and remain silent may struggle to cope with a client who clearly needs some warmth and nurturing. And so on.

As counsellors, we may even come to realise that *our behaviour in the room actually reproduces the way that our client's mother or father, or elder sibling, behaved* in our client's childhood. Counsellors also report sessions where clients discuss situations that are very close to what may be happening in the counsellors' own lives at the time. Such things probably happen because two human beings in an intense relationship like counselling 'pull' each other into a shared interpersonal field which both forge unconsciously by the way they react to one another, moment by moment. Remember that a great deal of the communication between two people happens at a level below conscious awareness, and is not contained in words. We will be returning to this subject throughout this book (see Chapter 8).

THE SECOND SESSION

As we said earlier, your own anxieties may get in the way of your ability to listen in a relaxed, open way to a client in the first session. The second session gives you another chance to listen—and a better chance, because now the client will no longer be a totally unknown quantity, and you will probably be less on edge. You may have missed many of the details, but you will have gained some impressions of your client, and picked up on what seems important to him/her. Most of all, you will have had a chance to reflect on what your client has already told you (or not told you). Thus, you can usually begin the second session with greater confidence, and perhaps have a mental list of some things that you would like to find out more about. There is nothing wrong with coming to a second session with an actual list—provided that you don't read it aloud, or use it in a rigid way to control the session. Instead, you'll find that you'll be able to work some of your questions in naturally, as you listen to the client cover ground that has already been traversed last time. The 'right' time for your interest will present itself, if you just listen, think, and wait to see what unfolds. Here is an example of a counsellor 'working in' a couple of questions that she had formulated in the first session:

Client: So anyway, I think I told you last time, my Dad isn't interested in me, we don't have much of a relationship, and so I've told my kids that "we don't visit Pa", "he has his own life", that sort of thing. I think they're a bit disappointed but you know, it won't mean much to them really because they haven't had much contact with him, and even when there was, he couldn't be bothered with them much.

Counsellor: Your Dad doesn't show much interest in your kids, or in you either....I wonder how that started? When you talked about it last time you didn't mention whether it was something that's only happened in the last few years, or whether it goes back a lot longer than that.

Client: Oh, well, it's not recent. Not recent at all....I mean, with the kids it's recent, because they're little, but with me it goes way back. I can't ever remember Dad being that interested in me. I'm kind of used to it really [looking away and fidgeting]. I suppose once I probably felt disappointed or rejected or something, but now it's just the way things are, you know—it is what it is [sounding resigned].

Counsellor: So it's....you've never felt that your Dad cared about you, is that right?

Client: Yes, that's right No, no, wait a minute... I think I did hang onto him a lot when I was really little [more animated], maybe we were close then, I don't remember, but from around six or seven, that all changed.

Counsellor: Things changed quite a lot when you were around six or seven...so what was happening in your family around that time? Apart from you going to school, I mean.

Client: Oh, well that's when they split up. My Mum and him. I think I was around six, I can't remember.

In this example, you can see how the counsellor is able to introduce things that he wants to know more about, by waiting until the client is again talking about that subject. Thus, the counsellor's questions indicate his interest and curiosity, rather than cutting across the client's preoccupations and introducing an agenda that is his own. The counsellor also gains credibility and trust because he has accurately remembered what the client said in the previous session, and uses that information to build a bridge between the client's account, and what he himself wants to know. We have previously talked about how exploring can actually be combined with assessment, without the need for a formal set of 'assessment questions'. In the example we've just quoted, you can see this combination happening.

ATTACHMENT IS A TWO-WAY THING

By the second meeting, you will also have had time to notice and think about your own feelings during the first session. As we remarked earlier, it is not just that new clients attempt to form a relationship with you, employing the strategies that they have commonly used in the past. *You* will have been trying to form a relationship with *them*, and you, too, will have been using strategies that have served you well in the past. Of course, your learned behaviour as a counsellor may disguise your underlying attachment strategies to some extent. Nevertheless, your behaviour will supply small clues as to your preferred way of relating to a new person in a situation of anxiety and vulnerability. Unless you are a naturally impassive person, your facial expressions will give some indication of warmth or reserve, acceptance or judgement. If you want your clients to like you, that will probably be evident to some degree. If you expect them to be 'difficult' and expect to have to struggle, that too will probably be evident, at least in small ways. For example, you might move restlessly in your chair, or sit there with your arms crossed. A degree of warmth and obvious interest usually works well with new clients. There is no need to suppress your natural personality completely—but you do need to pay close attention to how your client responds to it.

What parts of your 'natural helping style' seem to work for the client, make him or her feel safe? What aspects seem to be off-putting, or to 'shut the client down'? For example, if you naturally have an expressive face, which indicates your emotions as you listen, some clients will feel reassured by your interest and involvement with them. Others, however, may be dismayed at your vivid reactions, and withdraw into themselves, perhaps thinking that you are 'judging' them, or feeling overwhelmed and intruded upon by your obvious 'joining in' with their feelings. Any strong reaction clients have to your attachment style can provide important information about their developing relationship with you, and can, later, become a vehicle for learning.

THE ICEBERG AND ITS TIP

As we have already anticipated, what clients choose to talk about in the initial session (or sessions) of a counselling consultation is not necessarily the thing that they are most concerned about. They do not fully trust you yet (indeed, they may not trust you at all!) and there is nothing unreasonable about that. In fact, if a client seems to trust you immediately and totally, plunging into deep self-revelation as if he has known you all his life, then this may mean that he lacks appropriate boundaries and for some reason or another, has not learned to keep himself 'safe' in social situations. By the same token, cultural differences can produce the appearance of 'pathology' (damage, dysfunction) when in fact individuals are simply doing what their culture has socialised them to do. Even within English-speaking societies, the 'reserve' of the typical Englishman or woman is proverbial, while Americans are often described as willing to tell you their entire life story within minutes of meeting you. Both of these are of course cultural stereotypes—there will always be individuals within every culture who fail to follow the norms of their fellows—but the norms do contain a measure of truth, nonetheless.

When clients begin by discussing something that sounds trivial, or present superficial problems that appear to be easily resolvable, it is important to allow them to do so. Don't assume that they are 'avoiding the real problem' or that they are wasting your time. In fact, don't assume anything. Take them seriously—but not too seriously (in other words, don't feel that you must enter into an in-depth exploration of the issue the client initially presents). Be interested and involved, but be prepared to wait until your client has had a chance to settle in to the relationship, and show you more of what he or she is really struggling with. Of course, holding skills will be crucial to facilitating this. You will be responding as a good parent might do to a troubled child—'being there' for them, while not overreacting to their distress, feeling for them, while not entering so intensely into their pain and confusion that you sink in over your head (as it were); helping them find words to convey what might be going on. Remember, with many clients, good holding skills alone will be enough to assist them to reveal more of their real concerns in the second and third sessions.

Often, there is a relationship (symbolic rather than literal) between what clients choose to talk about initially, and the more central issues they later focus on. For many years, therapists have been advised to pay attention to the first things a client says as well as what she or he say as they are leaving the room, because in such 'off the record' remarks may lie clues to concerns that the client is not yet safe enough to voice. In a more general way, the 'presenting problem' may be the tip of an iceberg, most of which will initially lie below the surface of the water. For example, a nineteen year old may start by explaining to a counsellor that he has a problem at work: his boss treats him as untrustworthy. The client does not feel confident enough to be assertive with his boss and tackle the issue head on. Instead, he feels resentful at the unfairness, and reacts by feeling little enthusiasm for the job. But he needs the money, so he feels trapped. It would be a plausible guess that this problem, though real enough, is presented initially because it is 'safe' (not too personal, not too painful). The client is 'testing the water' a bit. However, it may be that several sessions later, the client starts talking about his feelings towards his father (who is living separately from his mother, and from the client). As the client talks about this complicated and difficult relationship, it becomes clear that it contains similarities to the work problem. His father, too, seems not to trust him. Just as he does with his boss, he feels unable to speak out and name what he thinks is going on, because he fears losing his relationship with his father entirely if he does. The client's fears may or may not be realistic. But either way, he feels 'trapped' and helpless, in exactly the same way as he does in the work scenario.

Now of course, this young client did not *decide* to talk about the work situation because it mirrored his painful relationship with his Dad. He was not conscious of the similarity. But, if you like, his unconscious 'chose for him' an issue that closely reflected his family conflicts, one with a similar theme. He, the client, plays a similar role in relation to a man in authority, a man on whom he feels dependent, and thus unable to speak out. The client's initial problem is not his most significant problem, but it is nevertheless quite 'real' in the issues it embodies— and they are core issues for him. A therapist of a psychoanalytic persuasion might already be wondering whether the client will sooner or later display the same passive, helpless, 'trapped' behaviour towards her. She will be alert for signs that she herself may start to distrust him in some way, because she knows that individuals tend to behave in ways that *elicit* (call out, invite) from a significant other person (including a therapist!) the same behaviour that they complain of in others.

Relax! As a beginning counsellor, you're not expected to 'get' such deep-level connections between clients' presenting problems and their underlying issues. Even experienced therapists sometimes fail to get them. Try seeing it this way: *clients will continue to present their concerns to us until we start to grasp what they are trying to convey.* If we fail to understand the concerns correctly, they will repeat the message, in slightly different forms, until we do understand. What is crucial is that they sense that we are interested in understanding. Beginning counsellors tend to assume that clients are desperate to have their problems solved. In fact most clients are as keen to be *understood* as they are to resolve their problems. And as a counsellor, you need to understand fully, before you can start to help with problem-resolution. If you rush into 'solving' or 'fixing' without a true understanding of where the problem is coming from, you will simply miss the point, and the client will ignore your suggestions and re-present the problem, as if to say, 'You haven't got it yet!' Of course, there are clients for whom problem-solving takes precedence over being understood, who may not be interested in the latter at all, except, of course, that they want the counsellor to understand the problem in the same way as they do! Chapter 5 shows how the difference between these two types of clients is reflected in the tension between 'problem-solving' and 'relational' concepts of counselling and therapy throughout their history.

So, as early as the second session (as your client tells you again, but perhaps in more detail, about her presenting problem) you may begin to notice that something is missing, or something doesn't quite add up. If this problem is so superficial, why hasn't your client solved it already? Can this be all that has motivated your client to seek professional help—surely there's something more? Why does your client seem to be 'spinning her wheels' instead of getting down to 'deeper stuff'? Why do you get a sense that something is being withheld, that there is more, but the client seems unable to reveal what this 'more' actually is? Any, or all, of these realisations can point you in the direction of the 'elephant in the room'. There is something here that cannot be talked about, and both of you know that, yet neither of you is actually acknowledging it.

Here is possibly the first of many places in the unfolding counselling process where you need to be braver than your client. And for counsellors, being 'brave' often involves asking questions without knowing in advance what the answer 'should' be, or frankly admitting that you aren't sure what's going on, but trusting your own instinct, which tells you that something is going on. This is what 'immediacy' is all about. How do you do it? We'll come to that shortly.

THE THIRD SESSION: CHALLENGE AND RESPONSE

Typically, clients enter counselling with a mixture of anxiety and hope. As we said earlier, if the counsellor does a reasonable job of listening and empathising in the first session, most clients will go away feeling somewhat better ('relieved' might be a more accurate word. They often report feeling 'lighter', as if a burden has lifted). Nothing has changed in their situation, but they feel they have made a start: the counsellor is no longer a totally unknown quantity. They return to the second session with a renewal of hope. But however well the counsellor listens, empathises and understands what they are presenting, the pressure seems to return. Nothing is being solved. They are just talking, repeating the story of their distress, but feeling just as bad as before. Some clients will give little hint of this in the second session itself, others will (certainly by the end) begin to voice their concerns, although often in 'safe' ways, which may not be fully conscious. Here are some of the ways in which clients hint that something is 'not working':

- *Can you suggest something that I could read?*
- *Are you going to give me some homework, you know, some exercise or something?*
- *I guess I'm still wondering what strategies there are that could help me cope with this… is there anything you think would help me?*
- *Should I be seeing a psychologist? They're supposed to be the experts aren't they?*

All of these let the counsellor know that the client is uneasy about something, though clients themselves may not be aware that this is what they are communicating. Beginning counsellors typically respond to these sorts of questions in two ways—neither of them very useful. First (and this is what most beginners do) they comply with the client's apparent request—suggesting self-help books to read, homework exercises, or 'strategies'. These things may eventually have their place in counselling, and we will say more about them in Chapter 7. However, if you offer such practical help at this too-early stage, clients will be unable to embrace it. For example, if you set a homework task to be done before the third session, clients will typically not have done it, have done it only half-heartedly, or have done it, but are no longer interested in talking about it. Some may even have completely forgotten that you gave them such a task! There could be no clearer indication that their original request was not for this kind of practical help, but for a different kind of assistance from you, the counsellor.

The second way that beginning counsellors may respond to client requests for 'extra help' is less common, but equally unhelpful. These counsellors ignore the request, or fob off the clients by saying, 'No, it's too early for that yet'. These counsellors recognise that the clients' requests for extra help are inappropriate, but they fail to see that the client isn't asking for practical help, but for assistance with acknowledging the 'elephant in the room'. The only truly useful response you can make to such requests would be something like,

Counsellor: I wonder whether you're starting to feel that nothing is changing, and that you need something more from me, something that I'm not giving you. Would that be right?

Or,

Counsellor: You're asking me for strategies....and you know, I could suggest some things, but I don't feel sure that they'd help all that much. Maybe what you're feeling is that there's something about your situation that I don't understand yet, something that I don't understand yet, and, if I understood it better, I could help you more?

Statements like these initiate a shift into immediacy. The counsellor is beginning to acknowledge the uneasiness that both feel.

If client dissatisfactions do not come out by the end of the second session, they will come at the beginning of the third—but more usually, by the time the third session rolls around, clients have gone beyond polite requests of an Oliver Twist type ('Please sir, I want some more!') Instead, they are clearly irritated, frustrated, or despondent. They seem to be 'giving up'. Characteristically, clients either appear gloomy and lacklustre, or else agitated, frustrated and angry. Many clients have been too well brought up to voice their frustration with you openly. Instead, they will talk about *other causes of anger or disappointment* in their lives:

Client with relationship problems: Well, me and my boyfriend had a big fight last night. I'm so mad at him, and I've pretty much decided to break up with him!

Client with relationship problems: I don't know...I think over the past week we've actually got worse. She can't stand me, and I can't stand her. I don't think we have a future together, to be perfectly honest.

Some, however, will be more open in expressions of frustration or disappointment:

Client with anxiety symptoms: I talked to a clinical psychologist I know, and he said that I ought to go and see someone who really specialised in OCD, you know, an Anxiety Clinic, or something like that. Apparently there's training they can give you, you know, techniques that really help people. He said it's not about understanding why I do it, it's about training my mind to think differently.

Client with a psychotic daughter: What exactly are your qualifications? How much experience have you had in dealing with mental health issues?

Again, what you need to do in response to such challenges is to remain calm, and help your clients to voice their underlying feelings more openly and honestly. Here are two examples of ways that counsellors might invite a client to talk honestly in the 'here and now':

Counsellor: Well, it sounds like you're feeling upset and disappointed in your relationship. I guess I'm wondering whether there's some anger and disappointment with me, too. You know, you've come along a couple of times and told me about your difficulties, and yet nothing has changed yet. Maybe in a way that feels like my fault?

Or,

Counsellor: I think you might be letting me know that you feel pretty upset with me. You're wondering if I really know anything that could help you. Would that be right?

It is important that you acknowledge the clients' disappointed or aggressive feelings, without taking them personally. What clients say may sound like an attack on your competence or helpfulness, but it will not be helpful for you to respond as if attacked. It is important that you help clients to name their loss of hope, and the resulting despondency, or their angry search for someone to blame. Your clients will not necessarily agree with you, or even seem to hear what you have said, but the mood in the room will often alter, and the clients will settle, in the same way that a baby will settle when picked up gently by a caregiver who recognises the source of its distress. When Freud talked of *transference interpretations*—statements in which the therapist would acknowledge a meaning of which a client might be unaware—this is the kind of thing he meant, and the kind of impact it can have.

Most people have not been able to let others know when they have felt upset with them, or let down by them. This may be their first experience of being able to speak frankly about their anger or disappointment, and have their feelings received respectfully and thoughtfully—instead of defensively or aggressively. In itself, this can be a transformative experience, a powerful validation of their right to 'speak their truth'. Equally, a non-defensive response to such a confrontation can assist clients to moderate their stance, and start to see that what they are thinking may not be entirely reasonable. This realisation will be something the client spontaneously acknowledges, not something you point out to them.

There is no point in reassuring clients, or explaining that change takes time, and requires them to take responsibility, *until their feelings have first been recognised and taken seriously*. If you skip that step, your attempts to inform or comfort will fall on deaf ears. However, when clients feel that their disappointment and sense of let-down has been understood, they may be readier to adopt a more realistic perspective on how change occurs. Here is a counsellor acknowledging what is happening, actually naming the 'elephant in the room':

Counsellor: Is it OK with you if we just stop and talk for a few minutes about what's going on in here today? I'm noticing that you seem quite 'down', compared with last time. And I'm feeling something too, as if there's a disappointment in the room, or a sort of 'let down'. I've found myself wondering what it's about—perhaps I might be part of the reason for it? Would you be willing for us to think about that together?

This version does not put the whole responsibility on the client to self-disclose or 'name' his feelings. Instead, the counsellor shares the responsibility, acknowledging that she may be 'part of the picture'. How might such an 'immediacy dialogue' then develop? The example that follows is one where the client doesn't make it easy. The counsellor has to be both patient, and persistent, assisting the client to see how what he's feeling in the counselling session might resemble how he's felt in previous situations:

Counsellor: I'm wondering a bit about what's going on today. I'm getting the impression that you're feeling frustrated, and maybe part of that frustration is towards me. Maybe there's something I'm doing, or not doing, that's getting in the way for you? Could we talk about that for a while?

Client: I just feel that something should've happened by now. I've told you all the background. You know what the problem is. I can't tell you anything more, because there isn't anything more. We're just going round and round in circles. Is this all there is to counselling? How can going round and round in circles help anyone?

Counsellor: You're right. You have told me everything that you know is relevant. It feels like you've done your part, and now I should do my bit—only it seems that I'm not doing it. Is that right?

Client: Yeah. I mean, you're the expert, you're supposed to know about this sort of stuff. I don't know what questions to ask myself, or what topics we should talk about. I was hoping that'd come from you!

Counsellor: Well, I can understand that. You're probably a bit pissed off with me, because I'm just sitting here and not taking a lead, and asking questions like a doctor would.

Client: Correct. I've brought my problem to you, and it seems like you can't solve it. It's beginning to seem like the blind leading the blind! That makes me frustrated.

Counsellor: Well, I wonder if this is a familiar sort of situation for you...that you feel stuck and helpless with some situation, and yet when you turn to someone else, someone who's supposed to have the answers, you still seem to end up feeling you're on your own?

Client: Well I certainly haven't consulted any counsellor or psychologist or anything, if that's what you mean. This is the first time I've tried people like you, mate. To be perfectly honest, I've usually had to get through the hard bits on my own. You know, I learned a long time ago that nobody was really going to pick me up and kiss it better [bitter tone]—I had to do it myself.

Counsellor: Hmm. So you're saying you've become pretty good at fending for yourself, and a long time ago you sort of gave up on expecting people to help you. But it sounds like you still feel angry and disappointed with the people who were supposed to help. Maybe you haven't entirely given up. Perhaps you keep hoping, and you keep getting disappointed—and that's what's happening right now, with me. Could that be right?

Client: Well I'm certainly feeling let down in this situation [slowing down and sounding thoughtful]. And looking back, lots of people have let me down....But you know, you have to grow up and be an adult [sharper again]... you can't be a baby all your life.

Counsellor: And yet, part of being an adult is taking responsibility for our own difficulties, not blaming other people for them. Adults have to learn that problems take time to solve, and that we can't expect miracles, as much as we might like the idea of having everything fixed in two sessions—

Client: [breaking in] Fair enough. But I still want you to lead a bit, you know, start asking questions, or doing something.

Counsellor: OK. I think you've just shown me something very important about you: that you really long for someone to help you, and yet you've disciplined yourself not to expect much, and to feel that you have to cope on your own. I bet that's a kind of lonely place to be in.

Client: [softer voice]. I don't know about lonely. But I certainly feel I've been on my own for most of my life. There isn't anyone you can rely on.

[This is just the most recent of a series of statements in which the client gives clues to the way he has typically handled his life and relationships—'there isn't anyone you can rely on'. In such statements, this client may well be supplying evidence for an avoidant attachment style—Karen Horney's 'moving away' position—but the counsellor does not hasten to 'label' the client, and simply stores the information for possible future use.]

Counsellor: It must be pretty hard to trust me, when you don't feel that anyone is reliable. I wonder what I'd need to do, for you to start to think I might be reliable?

Client: I don't know. I guess I'm prepared to give it a go for a while longer, though. Maybe time will show whether I can trust you or not.

[Client does not answer the counsellor's question, but acknowledges it indirectly, by softening his stance, and expressing a more realistic view of the time-frame that might be required for counselling to 'work'.]

This dialogue begins with immediacy—the counsellor's acknowledgement of an 'in the room feeling'. At first the client is still hostile and mistrustful. But the counsellor is able to use the client's feelings to lead gradually into a productive discussion of his life in general, rather than staying stuck on his distrust of the counsellor. As a whole, this dialogue goes well beyond what is strictly required from a counsellor in most 'third session challenges'. But we hope it will show you what can happen when the 'elephant in the room' is acknowledged, and the real work of counselling begins.

HOW DO YOU LEARN TO 'DO IMMEDIACY'?

Like empathic reflecting, the capacity to voice present-but-unspoken feelings is not something most of us grow up knowing how to do. Preschool children notoriously blurt out things that adults know, but don't say—but they rarely acknowledge 'here and now' *feelings*, even though they may at some level be aware of them, because the ability to articulate feelings—one's own, and those of others—typically matures only in adolescence (younger children can do it if adults model and encourage it). And by adolescence, most young people have learned only too effectively that they need to keep some things private. They have learned social rules that inhibit them from saying things like, 'Hey, we're both treading on eggshells around each other, aren't we! What's going on? Why am I so scared of you? Why are you so scared of me?' Even in intimate, adult relationships, where partners trust one another (at least in the early stages), there is a strong tendency to avoid being too honest because both partners fear to lose the relationship if they venture onto this treacherous ground.

Hence, *the capacity to 'do immediacy' usually has to be learned.* Most trainee counsellors find immediacy harder to acquire than any other skill. In its purest and most powerful form, immediacy puts counsellor and client on the same level. In the lengthy example above, the counsellor had to acknowledge the client's angry, hostile feelings—that might seem simple when you see it written down, but to do it in a real-life situation, calmly and non-defensively, takes practice and willingness to take a risk. Counsellors must 'own up to' their own feelings of stuckness, puzzlement, or confusion, in the interests of assisting their clients to acknowledge corresponding (or different) feelings. And this must be done in a non-anxious way, so that the client is not scared off or tempted to think that the counsellor 'can't cope with me'.

So, how do you acquire this delicate balance? *How do you come to feel comfortable with making yourself vulnerable, while at the same time, keeping to yourself any feelings that might leave your client feeling unsafe? How do you use your own 'transparency' (self-disclosure) to assist the client to move to a similar level of transparency?* Of course it is possible to experiment with immediacy during skills practice with a student client. And of course your supervisor may coach you in what to say as you begin work with real clients in a placement or internship—

assuming, of course, that your supervisor actually possesses this skill, and understands its importance (in our experience, many do not). But by far the best way to grow comfortable with immediacy is in the give-and-take of an interactive group. Forty years ago, such groups were called 'encounter groups', and acquired a somewhat negative reputation (especially among those who had never actually participated in one). These days, we avoid that name, but Irvin Yalom's lifetime work on group therapy has kept alive the concept of a group that exists for the purpose of helping participants to learn by giving and receiving direct feedback about how they affect one another in the here and now (Yalom's major work—and a remarkably readable one, for all its length and comprehensiveness—is *The Theory and Practice of Group Psychotherapy*, 5th Edn, with Molyn Leszcz, Basic Books, 2005).

Conventional therapy groups expect that group members will learn vicariously, through hearing each other's stories (as in Twelve Step groups), and by realising that others have felt what they feel. In such groups, members encourage each other, share similar experiences, and give each other advice ('this worked for me'). All of these things can be valuable, but none of them is as powerful as the learning that comes when another group member actually tells you directly, in a way that would be impossible in most social situations, how you come across to her, how your behaviour affects her. In turn, you will be invited (not pressured, but invited) to offer feedback to her—and others: to tell them how *their* behaviour affects *you*. In a Here and Now group (sometimes called an Interaction Group, an Experiential Group, an Interpersonal Awareness Group or a Sensitivity Group) you will learn to do this with tact and respect—the very same qualities you will need when using immediacy with a client. Here-and-now encounter is not an exercise in 'pulling people to pieces', or 'breaking down their defences'. As well as developing your self-awareness, you will learn tact and respect because these are the qualities that you yourself will want to hear in someone else's feedback to you!

By now it will be becoming clear that Here and Now groups offer training not only in 'immediacy' but also in what counsellors call 'confrontation' and other skills of encountering—of which we'll say more in Chapter 6. Sometimes the two may seem identical. Both require honesty and tact, and 'immediacy' is a form of 'confrontation', but there are two main differences:

- Immediacy involves the acknowledgment of present ('here and now') feelings
- Immediacy involves the feelings, or perceptions, of *both* counsellor and client

Some students believe they are 'using immediacy' if they say something like, *I notice that you seem upset, and you're breathing faster. What are you feeling?* Or even if they ask, *How do you feel right now?* If the client then reveals what she/he is feeling, then for some textbook authors, this is 'immediacy'. To our way of thinking, however, this is a watered-down version of the concept. The counsellor is entirely in the 'expert' position. She has revealed nothing about herself, and has not made herself vulnerable along with the client. The 'here and now' feelings are entirely the client's, rather than feelings that are occurring *between* client and counsellor. The fuller and richer version of immediacy, which we prefer, might be expressed as follows:

Counsellor: I'm thinking that you seem to be breathing faster and you seem upset, and actually, I'm feeling a bit on edge myself. I've been aware for a while that things have been difficult between us, and I'm wondering what might be going on. Can we talk about it together, and see what it might be about?

The skill of immediacy involves *bounded self-disclosure*—not the counsellor talking openly about 'there and then' (his or her personal history, or his relationships and current difficulties) but talking openly about 'here and now' (what he experiences right now, in relation to this client). Similarly, in a Here and Now group, members will not be encouraged to tell long stories about the past (*then*) or their present life outside the group (*there*). They will not be encouraged to present 'problems' for other group members to respond to in a 'safe' way by giving advice or offering support. Instead they will be invited to talk about *how they feel* in the group (*here*) at this moment (*now*). Here are two contrasting examples of 'saying how you feel right now' in an interactive group:

Group member: Right now I suppose I feel quite unsure … unsure of what's expected of me …I feel like everyone's looking at me. I guess I feel a bit scared, actually.

Group member: I feel frustrated. I know what I want to get out of this group, I know what I want to say, but somehow I can't say it. Other people are participating and getting somewhere and I want that too, but I feel paralysed.

When people speak direct from their present feelings, without too much masking or censoring, the atmosphere becomes charged with meaning and purpose. At some level, human beings crave 'realness'—what Carl Rogers called 'congruence' or 'authenticity'. (Mind you, human beings also defend themselves against these things. T. S. Eliot memorably observed, 'Humankind cannot bear very much reality'[5], and often it is the *idea* of what such a real encounter might feel like that people recoil from. Once they actually experience it people often start to feel safer to be themselves.) Since people both desire and fear 'realness', one of the arts of helping is to sense how much realness a client seems ready to accept, and to offer a challenge that is within his or her capacity. We are not advocating that you would necessarily speak to your clients as you would do to a fellow member of a Here and Now group. But we're definitely advocating that being part of such a group is the most direct and effective way to master the skills of immediacy and confrontation.

The group leader's role is to encourage members to confront 'the elephant' instead of generalising, or storytelling; the leader also ensures that group members treat each other with respect, and she intervenes if necessary, so that interactions are productive experiences from which participants can learn. If you are prepared to enter into a group experience of this nature, you will gain practice in skills which will, in time, make the difference between your being simply a supportive 'good listener' and a real counsellor or therapist, who can assist clients make decisive changes in their lives—but without telling them what they need to do, or how they should do it. Some counselling and therapy trainers actually incorporate such a group experience into their programs, but because many institutions perceive such groups as 'risky' and fear potential litigation if the group 'blows up' and someone complains, groups on the Yalom model are not as common as they used to be in counsellor training.

Of course, it is not only in response to the 'third session challenge' that counsellors need to employ immediacy. The ability to pay attention to, and acknowledge, the 'here-and-now' of the therapeutic relationship is something that you may need at any point in the unfolding relationship. As Irvin Yalom points out in *The Gift of Therapy*, Piatkus, 2002: 46-51) it is when the 'here and now' becomes the focus of attention in a session that the session comes alive. There is an energy in the room, a sense that something is happening. It is these challenging, intense moments that clients remember afterwards—and learn from—because in those moments the relational right hemisphere of both the client and the therapist is fully engaged. Immediacy embodies a kind of dialogue that is rare in relationships outside of the therapy room. Once it is modelled, and clients have themselves participated in it, it often becomes possible for them to go out 'there' and use the same skill in dealing with problematic situations in their own lives. In our experience, this rarely happens in the short term, but in the longer term, when clients encounter immediacy on a regular basis, whether in a group or with their therapist, they begin to behave quite differently with others in their lives—ways that they have never been able to behave before. And friends and family begin to *notice* that they are different—which is one of the ways experienced counsellors can tell that therapy has 'worked' (see Chapters 8 and 9 for more on this topic).

THE THIRD SESSION PHENOMENON REVISITED

What exactly does 'the third session phenomenon' actually mean? The answers we provide can only be speculative. We think it points to how powerful the unconscious dimension of human life can be. Counselling is about a deliberate, conscious choice to resolve specific, real life problems. No doubt about that. But underneath that conscious decision, with its rational belief that if there is a problem, there must be a solution, is another layer, much more primitive and childlike. This unconscious, child part of every client *does* want Mummy to 'kiss it better'. For many of us, in the first few years of our lives, a powerful person seemed magically able to help us, however bad our problems were—she (or sometimes he) would comfort us, advise us, cure us, and if all else failed, at least hold us in her arms and make us feel safe. For others, that wonderful, healing presence always been 'missing' and the client is (unconsciously) on a quest to get what was needed so long ago. Adult clients bring those expectations to their initial encounters with professionals. Provided the counsellor acts appropriately, those hopes of 'magical cure' will be sustained for about two sessions. Somehow, by the time the third rolls around (usually a week later, in normal practice), something has changed. The client has shifted from hope to disappointment (or even despair). It seems as if, in an adult, the 'magical expectations' have a life of about two weeks or, more accurately, two sessions that happen to be spaced a week apart. In an intensive workshop or personal development group that meets for over one whole day, the 'hope' phase lasts about the first couple of hours, and the 'angry/disappointed' or 'run away' phase then kicks in, usually just before, or just after, lunch! If the workshop runs for a week, then the 'third session phenomenon will occur sometime on the second day. Ask any workshop facilitator!

Remember the ritual magic of fairy tales, where what scholars call the 'rule of three' prevails. The hero makes three attempts to succeed in the magical quest. He fails the first two times, but succeeds on the third. This seems like the exact opposite of the therapeutic sequence we've been talking about in this chapter, but in fact there is a parallel. Fairytale heroes and heroines succeed the third time *because they do something different*, something that distinguishes their third attempt from the previous two tries. And if a counselling relationship is to evolve productively, and offer real hope of significant change, something needs to change around the time of the third session. In fairy tales, the protagonist is often assisted by a 'magical helper' (a talking fox, a dwarf, a fairy godmother). Often, the fairy tale protagonist ignores the helper's advice initially, but on his or her third attempt, takes it more seriously, even when it seems to be contrary to common sense. In counselling, it is you, the counsellor, who must provide the magical help—only it is not the kind of magic that your clients unconsciously expect. You cannot wave a magic wand or utter a spell so that their problems suddenly dissolve, and their distress is replaced by joy (although some people hope that hypnotherapists can). But you are in a position to do what they can rarely do for themselves—acknowledge that their feelings of disappointment and frustration may be directed at you, and by so doing, help them to accept that they will need to take some responsibility in order for the desired change to come about. By being 'braver than your client', by acknowledging the 'elephant in the room', you will have done something different, and very often, this will begin to unlock the client's resources so that change will become possible.

Clients who are able to persist beyond the third session, and who (more to the point) can face the loss of their hopes of instant 'cure', are well on the way to a successful outcome—even though such an outcome is unlikely to take the shape they expected when they first turned up at the counsellor's door. The work of counselling means harnessing our rational minds (represented by the brain's left hemisphere) to the task of *finding out about* our feelings and actions (represented by the right hemisphere). You may hear this referred to by different professionals as 'developing self-awareness', 'reconnecting with self' or accessing 'wise mind'. (See how different 'schools' of therapy can actually be talking about the same thing despite using quite different terms?) When we start to listen to those parts of ourselves that we don't really 'know', that we are 'split off from', our 'blind spots' (all of these metaphors convey something of the quality of our 'unconscious' parts) then we are in a position to deal differently with them—and with others in our lives.

But what about the clients who pull out *before* the third session? The ones who phone up with some excuse, and say they'll make another appointment when the car is working again, or when their kids are well again, or whatever, but never do? Is there anything you can do to help them see the 'elephant in the room'? Unfortunately, in our experience, the answer is usually 'Not a whole lot'. Sometimes it is worth offering such clients a quick interpretation of their behaviour over the phone—'*I'm wondering if maybe you've been feeling that counselling isn't getting you anywhere...*'. Sometimes this may enable a client to actually return a third time. More often, though, these clients will simply deny that they have any dissatisfaction or disappointment, and pressing the matter will only alienate them. They have already made up their minds that there is nothing to be gained from persisting with the sessions, and there is little you can do about that. They may need to cling to their hope that there is someone out there who will provide the magical cure they expect. It is exactly the same process as rejecting one lover, while preserving the wonderful illusion that sooner or later, there will be another, who will be all-healing, all-loving, all-accepting (and probably stunningly sexy and good looking as well), and that that relationship will last forever. Unfortunately, 'happy ever after' is comparatively rare in human lives.

Is there always a three-session process? The short answer is, 'No'. What we have suggested is a template that fits a substantial proportion of new clients, but of course there are exceptions. As we have already mentioned, clients who have had previous experience of professional help enter therapy with more muted hopes, and a higher level of awareness of their own irrationality than those for whom it is the first time. Some clients do display the three-session process—but instead of dropping out, or displaying anger or disappointment, they actually *get* cured in three sessions—or at least, believe that they have. Freud described such early dropout as a 'flight into health'—that is, these people accept a superficial resolution instead of probing more deeply into the causes of their difficulties. However, there is no way of being sure of how 'superficial' an improvement has been unless we conduct follow up studies with such clients, a year, or several years, after counselling terminates, and it is not easy to gain the co-operation of clients who have 'moved on' from therapy, or even to contact them (they may well have relocated).

Sometimes the 'three sessions' may be protracted, with each 'phase' actually taking several sessions. It may be useful to think of the 'three session process' as saying something about movement from hope to despair, something which may continue to occur in the counselling relationship, not just at the beginning. In Chapter 7, we will see examples of this 'three steps forward, two steps back' process when clients are attempting to change problematic behaviour patterns. Overall, though, the three-session template remains a useful one. Handle the 'third session challenge' calmly, employ the skill of immediacy to tackle 'the elephant in the room', and many clients will drop down to a greater level of honesty, responsibility-taking, and realistic commitment. Those who drop out before the third session are probably never going to continue, no matter what you do.

Chapter Summary

- In the first session, clients will typically want to 'tell their story' and our most useful stance is to allow them to do so with minimal interference. In contrast to a formalised set of assessment questions, this will allow clients to tell us not only what they consciously consider important, but also information about them that questions will not elicit—how they experience their world, how they relate to us, and expect us to relate to them.

- The second session provides an opportunity for clients to re-tell the story, often in greater detail, and for the counsellor to participate somewhat more actively, either through increasingly sensitive and accurate reflections or by beginning to explore aspects of the client's initial presentation that the client has already signalled as important.

- In the course of the first few sessions, counsellor and client will normally form an attachment. In this process, both client and counsellor will display the strategy that they have evolved in the past to maintain the attention of a significant other person. The counsellor's own behaviour towards the client may feed back into the client's perceived 'resistance' within the helping interview.

- By the time the third session occurs, a distinct change in the client's mood is often observable. Clients seem to move from initial relief to disappointment and frustration, apparently at the realisation that their difficulties will not simply 'go away' in a magical manner.

- This movement from hope to despair will occur, intensely and overtly in some clients, mildly and implicitly in others, regardless of how the counsellor or therapist has behaved, and regardless of the interventions employed. Inadequate counselling skills will exacerbate it, good counselling skills may temper it, but in either case, it will still be there.

- Some clients will not stay beyond two or three sessions, regardless of the counsellor's skill. However, those 'on the knife edge' may be encouraged to stay if the professional is able to receive and validate their feelings in an open, non-defensive manner.

- The reason for this movement from brief hope to disillusionment or even despair is 'the elephant in the room'—the client's half-awareness of what his or her real problem is, a problem which he or she feels unready to face at this early stage in the development of the counselling relationship.

- The counsellor's use of immediacy challenges clients to acknowledge their own part in the frustration or disappointment they feel, while at the same time making it easier for them to do so by 'sharing the load' of responsibility. Immediacy also deepens the relationship and enhances trust between counsellor and client.

- Immediacy is a powerful tool, one of the 'skills of encountering' discussed in Chapter 6. However, it does not come naturally to most trainees, and participation in an ongoing 'Here and Now' group experience is recommended as the most direct and effective way to learn this, and other, skills of 'facing up' to the reality of 'difficult' feelings within a therapeutic relationship.

Chapter 5

Fix The Problem, Or Re-Parent The Person?
Alternative Paths In Therapy And Counselling

COUNSELLING VS. PSYCHOTHERAPHY

Up to this point, we have used the terms 'counselling' and 'therapy' interchangeably, something that has become increasingly common in the profession. For a long time, 'psychotherapy' and 'counselling' were understood as referring to two different (though related) kinds of interpersonal helping, and many textbooks still preserve a distinction. 'Counselling' is often described as addressing 'ordinary problems of living' in a range of ways, including providing information, exploring options, and helping people handle their difficulties more effectively. By contrast, 'therapy' (originally a shortened form of 'psychotherapy') is said to be about 'reconstructing the personality'. Psychotherapy is seen as more suitable for individuals whose difficulties reside in hidden aspects of self, which can only be discovered and modified in long-term work.

The implication is that therapy is for more 'damaged' or impaired individuals, whereas counselling is for the so-called 'worried well'. It does not take long to see that these distinctions tend to break down in practice.[1] Psychotherapists see the 'worried well' (including lots of trainee therapists!) for long-term self-exploration, and counsellors often find themselves working with individuals whose problems are entrenched and hard to shift. There are brief forms of psychotherapy (as little as twelve sessions) and much so-called counselling can extend over years. Despite their perceived differences in focus and intensity, however, counselling and therapy share a common understanding that many people can be best helped to change within the context of a helping relationship that is co-operative, and focussed on the help-seeker's goals, rather than on the helper's. In both, the professional's ability to create a trustworthy relationship with the client is seen as a vital element in securing a positive outcome. Counselling and psychotherapy are 'relational arts'.

Generations of counsellors have been trained on Gerard Egan's highly-regarded text, *The Skilled Helper*, which for many years described a three-phase counselling process that began with 'helping clients tell their stories', proceeded to 'explore clients' preferred scenarios' and then 'moved clients into action'. Such a model implies that clients want to resolve their problems—despite some degree of ambivalence—and can be assisted to do so with the active intervention of the counsellor. The counsellor's role shifts, as the process unfolds, from empathic listener to 'change coach' (see Chapter 7). Egan's book, as it is today, has been heavily shaped by the current expectation that treatment for emotional problems should be brief, lead to measurable behaviour changes, and employ 'evidence-based' interventions (those that deliver improvement that can be verified by controlled outcome studies). The subtitle of recent editions of *The Skilled Helper* (e.g. the ninth edition, Brooks-Cole, 2009) is *A Problem-Management and Opportunity-Focussed Approach to Helping*.

However, the earliest versions of Egan's text (published thirty years ago) reflected a very different concept of counselling—as an open-ended, developmental process in which clients were assisted to explore and understand themselves. Sounds a lot like 'psychotherapy' doesn't it! There was much less in those versions about 'moving clients into action'—the implication was that behavioural changes would follow automatically from acceptance and understanding. But the changes in Egan's understanding of counselling not only show how social values and priorities can shape theoretical models—they also exemplify a continuing tension within the counselling and therapy profession—the tension between a *problem focus* and a *relational focus*. It might also, in a sense, be described as the tension between a *content* understanding of helping and a *process* understanding. This tension has been there from the very beginning, as we'll see in this chapter.

WHERE WE STARTED: PSYCHOANALYSIS

'Psychoanalysis' was the name Freud gave to his approach to helping people with emotional problems. The ancient Greek word *psyche* literally meant 'breath' and by extension, 'spirit' or 'soul'. 'Soul' is not the same thing as 'mind', but in a more secular age, 'mind' might be considered a rough equivalent of psyche (and Freud, although an ethnic Jew, was an atheist). If the brain is the physical organ that permits 'mind' to exist, our minds *feel* independent of our brains (just as, in spiritual language, soul feels independent of body). The human mind recognises its own individuality, remembers the past, imagines the future, tells itself stories about itself, and hence (to a degree) makes itself miserable or happy. So, for Freud, to 'analyse' the 'psyche' is to tease out the dynamics that dominate the individual mind, with the aim of understanding it: *psycho-analysis*.

As a neurologist by original training (he dissected the brains of eels), Freud continued to think of himself as a scientist. Now he sought a different kind of evidence. He saw people saying things that embarrassed them (which they then claimed were just meaningless 'slips'); people claiming that they wanted to be happy, yet unwilling to do what would enhance their happiness; denying that they were angry, or sad, when others could see those emotions 'written all over their faces'. From these common pieces of observable behaviour, Freud developed a model which viewed the mind as a battleground between conscious, rational intentions, and other forces, of which humans were largely unaware. He called those forces 'unconscious'. He could not prove that the unconscious existed, except indirectly, and he did not actually 'discover' the unconscious mind, because the concept was already in existence[2]—but Freud elaborated the 'unconscious' vastly, and popularised it to the point where many people now take it for granted.

Read more:

Freud's early work *The Psychopathology of Everyday Life* remains a very readable introduction to his attempt to find evidence for unconscious forces in 'little things' like slips of the tongue and slips of the pen. *The Interpretation of Dreams* (1905) is longer and more technical in its language, but not forbiddingly so. And remember, many of the dreams that Freud analyses were actually his own—although he does not admit that. Recording and reflecting upon his dreams was a major part of Freud's 'self analysis'—since he was the first psychoanalyst, he could not very well seek help from someone else! Reading works like these will give you a much clearer idea of exactly what Freud stood for, and what sort of person he was. He had a sense of humour, and a sense of drama—and, yes, he did think sex was a vital driving force behind much human behaviour, but that is not the same thing as the popular misconception that Freud was 'a dirty old man'. When he wrote these books, incidentally, Freud was in the prime of life, and a devoted father to his children, one of whom (Anna) followed his path and became a renowned psychoanalyst herself.

As we have seen in previous chapters, advances in laboratory study of the brain have actually confirmed much of what Freud asserted. There *are* parts of the brain that can guide our conduct in ways that other parts are not aware of. Very early memories, from before we learn to talk, *can* be 'stored' in the brain, even though we are unable to retrieve them by deliberate acts of will. We *are* sensitive, tormented creatures, torn between biologically-programmed survival instincts and consciously learned social values which tell us that some of these instincts are 'wrong', 'bad' or 'shameful'. Though the terminology Freud used ('id', 'ego' and 'superego'; 'repression', 'transference' and 'projection') strikes us now as forbiddingly obscure, there are brain functions and mental processes that (roughly) correspond with most of these terms. Some aspects of Freud's theory have proved misleading, but its outlines are broadly correct. No longer should lecturers tell first year undergraduates in psychology or social work that Freud's work was 'an elaborate theory without a shred of evidence to back it', a 'myth' rather than a 'science'. There is a brain basis for at least some of Freud's most central teachings.

What Freud would have told you about psychoanalysis is that it meant learning, slowly (and usually painfully) to acknowledge the existence within you of wishes and fears that might embarrass you, understanding how these forces might propel you in certain directions despite your conscious intentions. He would have warned you that you would come to see your motives as more complex, and probably less admirable, than you might like. 'The truth shall set ye free—but first it shall make ye miserable' is the way one humorous saying put it. If the mind is a battlefield on which opposing forces push and pull at us (which is what the adjective 'psychodynamic' means) then your task as a patient in psychoanalysis is to learn about the tactics of both sides, to appreciate both the conscious and the unconscious equally, and to accept that you are what you are. Your wish for a perfect world, in which you yourself are also perfect, is never going to be gratified. Life isn't fair, and we humans simply create problems for ourselves by believing that it should be.

At its core, the ideology of psychoanalysis is not dissimilar from Buddhist teachings[3]: by ceasing to desire so keenly what we do not possess, we can learn to value what we do have, and to 'live in the moment' rather than in vain dreams of the future, or painful thoughts of the past. Psychoanalysis was, and still is, a tough self-discipline. It was never going to appeal to the majority of human beings—quite apart from the fact that it demanded a very considerable amount of time (four or five sessions weekly) and consequently cost a lot too. Even psychoanalytic psychotherapy, a scaled-down version of psychoanalysis requiring as few as two sessions per week, could be confrontingly different from any normal social relationship ('Is that the kind of relationship you want us to have?' said a New York psychotherapist when, at the first session, his new patient offered to shake his hand).

Therapy means 'cure' or 'healing'. Like psychoanalysis, psychotherapy was a 'talking cure'—as contrasted with a cure through medication or other physical treatment, which often addressed specific symptoms rather than the whole person. Speaking freely and honestly about yourself, your life and your problems, would assist you to feel better. And, if you could do that by talking with a person who had been specially trained to listen, and who could help you to see further into yourself, then you would, in time, begin to handle your difficulties more sensibly, and feel more comfortable with yourself. For Freud, and even more for some of his successors, the *therapeutic relationship* was the arena in which the most important learning took place. When patients acted towards their therapists in ways that did not 'fit', ways that seemed exaggerated, or out of touch with the reality in the room, then something unconscious must be occurring—'transference'. As we saw in our last chapter, 'transference' meant that individuals may act and feel towards their therapists as they once acted and felt towards significant figures, usually their parents. Acknowledging these 'transference behaviours' and 'working through' them as they came up again and again over many sessions, became the way that patients learned about themselves. In time, it would also change the way they acted outside the therapy session. Freud saw this as an example of the 'unconscious becoming conscious', with the therapist's help.

Psychoanalysis seemed, for a time, revolutionary. Freud himself, deeply distressed by the pointless slaughter of the First World War, died in exile in London in 1939, with Europe sliding inexorably into another devastating war. He had long since abandoned the idea that psychoanalysis would change the world, but twenty years earlier, some of his adherents had been 'true believers'. Both at the individual level, and at the level of governments and nations, they thought, humanity might finally learn about its own irrational impulses—its aggression, envy, grandiosity and paranoia. This painful knowledge would help people to turn away from their accustomed ways, and adopt more humane and realistic attitudes to self and others. Sadly, that did not happen.

As each therapeutic revolution has lost momentum and retreated into safe orthodoxy—rigidly following the 'rules' laid down by its founder—new therapeutic concepts and approaches have arisen to challenge it. In the case of psychoanalysis, there were twin challenges, the first from behaviourism, and the second from Carl Rogers' 'non-directive counselling' (as he originally called it). Of the two, behaviourism posed the more thoroughgoing challenge. Behaviourists claimed that the mind was unknowable and ultimately irrelevant, since problematic behaviour (in human beings, birds or animals) could be altered by a systematic, common sense process of rewarding desired behaviour, and 'extinguishing' undesirable patterns. Behaviourists called this process 'conditioning'. For example, a behaviourist would reason that if a patient repeatedly asked a psychoanalytic therapist personal questions, and the therapist repeatedly refused to answer them, the patient would eventually learn not to ask (the response would have been 'extinguished', or 'trained out of him'). The therapist, of course, would have hoped that the patient would come to question his unconscious motivation for asking the questions in the first place—a very different intention from simply getting rid of the patient's behaviour!

Behaviourism, originally associated with Ivan Pavlov in Russia and John Watson in America, was adopted by the United States as enthusiastically as psychoanalysis had been earlier. By the middle of the twentieth century, psychologist B.F. Skinner was claiming that 'operant conditioning' could teach pigeons to pilot guided missiles, and that a saner, happier human society could readily be built by simply applying these same principles to human beings—a proposition Skinner persuasively described in his Utopian novel *Walden Two* (Macmillan, 1948, and still well worth reading). But twenty years later, the behaviourist movement had begun to lose momentum. It had become clear that many complex human problems did not respond to straightforward behaviour modification techniques—largely because those problems involved the mind—the same mind which radical behaviourists had claimed could safely be ignored. If behaviourism was to survive, it must move away from its extreme position and acknowledge clients' thoughts and feelings, which so greatly influenced how they acted.

That shift did come, in the form of cognitive approaches (which we'll come to later), but by 1970 the 'behavioural revolution' had run the same course as psychoanalysis had done: early claims of a 'universal cure' were being replaced by more modest ones (behaviourist approaches had proved effective in addressing phobias, for example, but had failed to shift problems that seemed less obviously dependent on learned behaviour).

The second challenge to psychoanalysis, from Carl Rogers' 'client-centred' approach, was less radical. Rogers certainly did not ignore the mind. He maintained Freud's insistence that entrenched problematic behaviour and attitudes were symptoms of something deeper, something that could be shifted only by a significantly influential relationship. However, he also popularised a new term for that relationship—counselling—and in so doing, was responsible for much of our current confusion over what 'counselling' means and how it differs from 'therapy'.

Historically, the word 'counsel' meant 'advice' or 'wise guidance'. Royal counsellors told Kings what they should do—advice the King often ignored. Sultans and Khalifs had a *wazir* who stood close by, whispered in their ear, and often had greater influence over policy than the Commander of the Faithful himself. U.S. Presidents today have advisors and experts who prepare digests of information on key issues, and suggest what the President should do.

Nothing has changed: the West Wingers' advice may be either followed, or ignored. If the suggested course of action misfires badly, the advisor will be sacked, not the President. And in the United States, the word 'counselor' is still used to mean 'attorney'—a person with legal expertise. These common usages all shaped the common understanding that counselling relates to 'information provision' or 'expert guidance'.

In some forms of counselling today, particularly those related to medical and genetic conditions, that understanding may still be accurate[4]. To quote one academic sociologist, 'I know what counselling is! It's providing information to people about HIV-AIDS, and how they can manage it!' He had supervised a Ph.D. on that subject, but he still thought of counselling in terms of *content* (information that counsellors provided). Just as in medieval times, the natural assumption of most people is that advice and information will be provided by the professional to the person seeking help. This is the 'instrumental' concept that we drew your attention to in Chapter 1—the idea that the professional does something to the person who seeks help. 'Doing something to someone' and 'imparting information' seem to fit naturally together—after all, this is the paradigm that governs teaching, medicine, and many other professional endeavours today.

By contrast, Carl Rogers' contribution to the redefinition of counselling struck at the heart of both the instrumental and the 'content-driven' assumptions. He insisted that counselling was not about providing advice or information, but about creating a particular type of relationship in which clients would be free to find their own truth. Rogers did not like the apparent arrogance of the orthodox psychoanalytic practitioner of the first half of the twentieth century, who sometimes acted as if he knew his patients' inner worlds better than they did, and whose seemingly remote stance made many patients feel that he did not care about them. (It has to be said that the stony-faced comportment of many orthodox psychoanalysts at the time probably supported such misunderstandings.) In contrast to this, Rogers advocated that counsellors display non-possessive warmth and *unconditional positive regard* (acceptance of the client's value as a unique person, no matter how unappealing his or her behaviour). He saw counselling as a process of discovery, in which both counsellor and client explored new ground together, rather than the counsellor 'guiding' the client in a certain direction. Hence his original name for his approach was 'non-directive counselling', later modified into 'client-centred' and then 'person-centred' counselling—or therapy (for Rogers, confusingly, continued to use both terms)[5].

Adopting a new terminology is one key way that innovators in our field (or any other, for that matter) differentiate their approach from existing 'models', and often, the new term simply replaces a similar one that is already in existence, creating the impression of greater difference than is actually the case. Freud, too, would have agreed that psychotherapy was a process of discovery, in which the therapist did not know all the answers in advance (although he did assume that professionals should be equipped with expert knowledge that enabled them to actively assist their patients' self-understanding). And Freud himself was on occasion far less 'neutral', far less like a 'blank screen' than some of his followers became. He was not above shouting at a patient who obstinately refused to accept what he (Freud) was trying to get through to him. Our ideas about confrontation (see Chapter 6) have become more sophisticated since then!

However, Rogers' reformulation of 'therapeutic neutrality' as 'unconditional positive regard' would certainly prove a better fit for many help-seekers than Freud's model of detached intellectual enquiry. In the century since psychoanalysis was first popularised, its adherents have substantially modified their practice in directions that Rogers would have approved, to the point where Rogers' 'empathic paraphrase' (which in this book we have called 'reflection') has been reinvented by influential Self Psychologists like Heinz Kohut, under the label of 'vicarious introspection' or 'empathic immersion', and by proponents of the Conversational Model like Robert Hobson in England and Russell Meares in Australia.[6]

As well as 'rebelling' against the psychoanalytic model, Rogers also disliked behaviourist psychology, which ignored the inner life of clients, and (he thought) treated them almost as a set of reflexes that could be modified through simplistic reinforcement programs. Rogers, who had once started on a career as a minister of religion, valued the unique spirit of each human being, and objected to the behaviourist treatment of the mind as a 'black box' that had no relevance to the practical job of changing behaviour. Agreeing with Freud, Rogers asserted that it was not the counsellor's job to change the client's behaviour—that was the client's task. Instead, the counsellor must assist the client to discover what needed to be changed, and why. Behaviour change would follow once clients deeply accepted who they really were, and understood the causes of their behaviour. Freud's emphasis on self-understanding remained vital in Rogers' 'counselling', although Rogers placed more importance on self-acceptance.

Rogers employed the term 'counselling' because it seemed to him to be lower-keyed, less 'clinical' in its implications than 'psychoanalysis' or 'psychotherapy'. Psychoanalysts saw 'patients'—largely because their founder had qualified as a doctor—and for many years, Americans who wanted to become psychoanalysts had to qualify in medicine first, virtually confining the profession to the well-off. The word 'patient' literally meant 'one who suffers', and implied a passive role (a sick person in a bed). Orthodox Freudians' use of the couch probably helped to cement this image of passivity, although of course, lying down simply helped patients to relax and speak freely. Lay people associated doctors and psychiatrists with mental illness (*You think I should see a shrink? Do you think I'm crazy or something?*), even though in fact 'normal' people also sought their help. (This is one way that the textbook distinction between 'counselling' and 'psychotherapy' breaks down in practice).

Rogers wanted his new terminology to get away from all of this. His 'counsellors' saw 'clients'—he wanted to emphasise that seeking help with emotional and relational problems was no different from hiring a lawyer or an accountant. Fifty years after Rogers' 're-branding', his term 'client' had started to become contaminated by associations with the abnormal and the medical. So Solution-Focussed therapists adopted the word 'customer', renewing Rogers' original emphasis on someone 'purchasing a service', and social workers began speaking of 'mental health *consumers*' instead of 'clients with mental illness'. Even 'counselling' itself had begun to sound ominous to lay people, and so the term 'life coach' was coined to reassure clients that they were 'normal': seeking help with personal problems was much the same as hiring a 'personal trainer' at a gym—which, of course, is true of some current therapies, although wildly inaccurate as a guide to counselling and therapy in Freud's or Rogers' sense.

Rogers did not believe that one had to have a lengthy, demanding professional training in medicine or psychology in order to help people with a wide range of problems. Increasingly, training programs (in marriage and family counselling, for example, in pastoral counselling, or in drug-alcohol counselling) were prepared to take applicants without conventional psychology or social work backgrounds. Nurses, priests, youth workers and even teachers might all think of themselves as 'counsellors'. Rogers and his followers were enthusiasts, who sought to democratise psychotherapy. (Exactly the same impulse had motivated psychoanalysts in the 1920s to set up free or minimal-cost clinics for people on low incomes, but these had never really taken off in the same way that 'counselling' did in the USA from the 1950s onwards.[7])

For all Rogers' opposition to psychoanalysis and psychoanalytic psychotherapy, he and his followers hung on to some of their key features. Rogers may have come up with the buzzword 'non-directive', but psychoanalysis and its derivatives had always been non-directive. In other words, therapists (and now 'counsellors') did not tell people what to do; they did not give advice. So it came about that 'counsellor', a word historically associated with advice-giving, was redefined into something quite opposite. Mature decision-making came about, not by being told what to do by the counsellor, but through a dynamic interaction with the professional helper, focussing on *process* not content—in other words, clients would learn about themselves, grow, and change, as a result of *the relational connection between themselves and their counsellor.*

Rogers did not deny that seeing connections between past and present might offer clients an important pathway to change. However, he placed less emphasis than Freud on the client's childhood relationships, and much more on the direct impact of the therapist's (or counsellor's) attitude. Where psychoanalytic training had insisted that the therapist show as little of his/her personal feelings and attitudes as possible (in the interests of encouraging transference), Rogers taught that the professional's warmth, empathy and personal honesty were crucial to creating an environment in which change was possible for the client.[8] This would do away with the need to encourage transference, and with the need for the counsellor to 'interpret the transference' in the session. The relationship between professional and client, in Rogers' view, nurtured the client in the same way as rich soil, sun, and appropriate watering nourished a growing plant (Rogers had grown up on a farm, and another of his early, abortive career choices had been agricultural science).

Rogers insisted that the therapist be *congruent* (speak from true feelings) rather than *neutral* and self-concealing—although it is important to remember that the self-disclosure Rogers advocated was only in relation to the therapist's in-the-room feelings towards the client. He never advocated therapists disclosing the 'there-and-then' of their lives. Rogers always thought that the honesty of the therapeutic relationship was one of its most productive features—the therapist could be honest in a way, and to a degree, that most clients would never have previously experienced. Thus, the therapists' disclosure of carefully selected feelings in the here-and-now would assist clients to risk similar disclosure in return, and this transaction would become a change-producing experience, the 'powerhouse' of therapy, as Irvin Yalom describes it. We have already seen examples of this in Chapter 4. The difference between this kind of 'honest encounter' between client and therapist and what the psychoanalytic school called 'transference interpretation' seemed greater than it actually was: in practice, both could be confronting for clients—and yet curiously liberating as well.

When looked at carefully, much of what Rogers advocated was not a completely 'new model' of counselling/therapy, but a 'major revision' of Freud's psychoanalysis, ignoring the complexities of the unconscious (to which much of Freud's theory had been devoted) in favour of a concentration on the real relationship between client and helper. Rogers did not see himself as knowing better than his clients, but in practice, he went pretty close. Every time Rogers, or any Person-Centred therapist, offers the client a reflection that goes beyond what that client has actually said in words (see Chapter 2), he 'nudges the client towards self-awareness'. In some textbooks, such reflections are called *advanced accurate empathy*.

The 'relational' concept of helping, as first devised by Freud, revised by Rogers and more recently refined and elaborated by Yalom, is distinguished by the following features. Such a relationship is:

- *Non-reciprocal* (that is, it exists for the benefit of the client, not the professional)
- *Intimate* (it deals with highly personal material, which creates intensity between client and helper) *but not sexual or companionate* (that is, professionals do not expect the client to offer them affection, gratitude, admiration, or sexual intimacy)
- *Non-directive* (direct advice and material support are not normally provided)

- *Both nurturing and challenging* (the strength and resilience of the bond between client and professional enables respectful confrontation, and facilitates the client's growing realisation of his responsibility for his own life difficulties).

The therapeutic relationship is unlike any other relationship—except perhaps for that between a Christian and his or her spiritual director. This is what makes it so effective. Close friendships may offer both support and challenge, but they are normally two-way—each person seeks something back. Romantic relationships may offer intimacy, but in combination with a sexual element, and they too are reciprocal—each person expects something 'back' from the other. Some people can refrain from automatically giving advice to a person who shares a problem with them, but though friends can provide 'holding', fewer of them offer respectful challenge along with it. And so on. The therapeutic relationship, as manifested in both psychotherapy and counselling, thus becomes, potentially, a significantly different experience—a 'safe place for change'. What this amounts to, in longer-term work, is a kind of 're-parenting' of the client by the therapist or counsellor. While nobody can literally 're-parent' an adult but they can certainly perform for another person, over time, some of the key functions that a good parent would perform for a child. In certain key ways, the therapist or counsellor provides the client with a significantly different experience from the one she or he had while growing up. And this different experience, this 'safe space', permits the client a second chance at growing up—at least in some important areas of living and relating. What we have learned in recent years about neural plasticity—the capacity of the brain to develop new neuronal pathways as a result of significant new experiences—supports the idea that re-parenting is not the wild overstatement that it might once have seemed, especially if the re-parenting relationship extends over years.

While the client will provide the *content*—the subjects that are talked about—the role of the counsellor or therapist in this relationship is to be responsible for the *process*. That is, the counsellor or therapist must notice the things that the client fails to notice, draw attention to the things which are hovering just on the edge of consciousness, but which the client fails to put into words. The most crucial things that clients will fail to notice and acknowledge are how they actually behave in *this* relationship—their relationship with the professional. That in turn will suggest how they might behave in other key relationships that involve trust and vulnerability to hurt. By putting these aspects of clients' relational selves into words, and by inviting clients to be aware of them and think about them, counsellors and therapists offer a corrective to clients' almost inevitably defensive and partial view of themselves. The relational intimacy that results can support clients to make needed changes in their lives and to develop aspects of themselves that have previously lain dormant or been repressed. We will be exploring this 'gentle honesty' in a lot more depth and detail in Chapter 6.

Of course gentle honesty can happen within a romantic relationship too, but because lovers need something from each other, one partner's feedback to the other may at times be evasive, manipulative, or even (if things are going sour between them) deliberately hurtful. And often conversations are never completed, leaving an impasse that rapidly becomes 'too hard' to explore. By contrast, in a therapeutic relationship that works well, difficult conversations can be continued and brought to a resolution. The therapeutic relationship may become the one relationship in our lives where we can find out what we most need to know about ourselves. Many other things may happen in a counselling/therapy relationship, but this is the heart of it. This is the 'counsel' that counsellors and therapists provide—not *advice about what to do*, but sensitive, unbiased *feedback* that acts as a corrective to the implicit, even unconscious concept we have of ourselves.

In welfare services, the *case manager's* role is often to provide *resources that are external to the client*. These resources might include information about services that are available, advocacy, access to finance or material support, and so on. In the relational type of counselling and therapy, the 'resources' are internal to the client. These 'internal resources' might include hope for a better future, determination, self-confidence, and so on. Most importantly, however, the resource counsellors and therapists help clients access is self understanding—realising why they do what they do, what effects it has on others, comprehending why they choose to do some things, rather than taking alternative courses of action. Counselling and therapy focus clients on what happens inside of them, how they 'block' themselves from being happy, how they fail to notice their own success, how they unconsciously act in ways that make life difficult to navigate.

PROBLEM FOCUSSED MODELS

Up to this point, we have been dealing mainly with one model of helping—the 'relational' model, which began with Freud's psychoanalysis. But, as we saw at the beginning of this chapter, throughout the whole history of interpersonal helping, there has been a second model which has been equally influential, and which in many ways is the opposite of the relational model. In this second model, which we've called the 'problem-focussed model', the professional's role was to be well-informed—a good teacher, a good 'coach', providing high quality information—and to train the client how to change via proven, empirically-validated techniques. Behaviourism was the first twentieth century approach to human change to adopt this model, which focussed primarily on the problem and how to 'fix' it, rather than on the clients, their feelings and thoughts, and their relationships. Behaviourist intervention was usually short-term and active—the psychologist would work out what was wrong, and move rapidly into devising a plan to assist the client to change. That plan would involve the use of principles that science had tested in carefully designed experiments. Professional psychology today belongs firmly in this tradition. Psychologists are typically trained with an emphasis on learning change-producing techniques, which are then taught directly to clients. If the psychologist is well equipped with knowledge and skills, then (it is reasoned), his or her personal, relational qualities are of relatively minor importance—they have value in the gaining of rapport, and in keeping clients in treatment until results start to show. But they are 'means to an end'. The problem-focussed model works well—*provided that its clients want to change, and are prepared to participate actively in their own treatment. And provided that their wish to change is not being 'blocked' by out-of-awareness trauma.*

As we saw earlier, *radical behaviourism*—the model in which the mind was regarded as largely irrelevant to altering behaviour—eventually encountered impasses, because human problems are often sustained not simply by a pattern of learned actions, but also by long-established patterns of thinking and feeling. In other words, many clients are not single-mindedly intent upon changing—in fact, they are deeply ambivalent about it. Think of a typical alcoholic. She wants to give up drinking in order to retain her marriage, but part of her still hopes she can hold onto her partner and keep on drinking as well. Yes, it's illogical and contradictory, but didn't Freud and his followers argue that such contradictions arose from an inner tug-of-war between different parts of the mind? Psychologists like Aaron Beck and Albert Ellis realised that professionals need to acknowledge the mind in order to produce lasting change, and that clients' habits of thought needed to be modified, if optimal outcomes were to be achieved. But the principles on which *Cognitive Behavioural Therapy* (CBT) depended are not really different from those of the earlier radical behaviourist model: what had been learned could be unlearned; desirable thoughts should be reinforced, and unhelpful ones 'extinguished' (as in 'thought stopping'); habits of thinking and feeling could be carefully recorded in diaries, measured, and then systematically modified. Realistic goals could be set, and problematic behaviour could be altered in gradual, planned steps.

Moreover, the client's illogical beliefs needed to be challenged directly by the professional— 'unconditional positive regard' ought not to extend to delusional or self destructive thoughts. If a client assumes that she can keep drinking and still retain her relationship, the job of the counsellor is to help this client investigate how much actual evidence there is for her belief. Thus, most of the 'new' techniques of cognitive behavioural therapy were extensions or modifications of earlier behavioural ones. Indeed, in some ways CBT is more aligned with lay people's 'common sense' approach to helping (now sometimes called 'folk psychology') than radical behaviourism had been (more on this shortly).

While it was easy for most people to grasp the idea of 'rewarding desirable behaviour', the same people naturally think of 'punishment' as the appropriate response to undesirable behaviour. The radical behaviourist notion that undesirable behaviour should be *extinguished* (by ignoring it, or removing its 'audience') took much longer to catch on. 'You're grounded for two weeks' is widely viewed as a punishment rather than as extinction, and indeed, it is questionable whether it really functions as 'extinction' at all. As every parent knows, some children are adept at turning 'time out' into a stage for further 'performances of dissent' that escalate the challenge to parental authority ('*If you don't let me out I'm going to smash everything in this room!*')

By contrast, the mental furniture of CBT corresponds well with the kinds of pragmatic advice that human beings in our society have long given each other: '*You mustn't think that way, it's not doing you any good*', '*It doesn't make sense to believe that!*', '*You're going to feel really tired tomorrow and that's going to make your work less effective? Is that really the end of the world?*'—all of these broadly correspond with CBT techniques, although the language is different. 'Positive imagery', 'everyday miracles', 'imagine yourself as a winner', 'draw a line under the past', and other catch-phrases widely advocated in self help books, corporate training sessions, and sports psychology are all consistent with the general principle of 'Think positive and you'll feel a whole lot better'. Part of the reason CBT has been successful and well-accepted has been precisely because it corresponds so well to such attitudes—although psychologists would naturally prefer to believe that its widespread adoption has been due to its being scientifically validated. Less in tune with lay perceptions of how problems are solved, however, is cognitive psychologists' recent interest in the Buddhist concept of 'mindfulness'. For example, 'Acceptance and Commitment Therapy' (ACT for short) recognises that in order to change, clients first need to accept the way they are, instead of struggling against it. Hardly new, perhaps, but new to some professionals. This shift has brought cognitive-behavioural approaches a step closer to a philosophical position that both Person-Centred and Psychoanalytic models had earlier reached. And coaching clients to 'watch their thoughts pass through their minds' without beating themselves up for having such thoughts—surely this is not so far from Freud's 'free association'?

If Freud's 'radical idea' was to take seriously the idea of unconscious motivation as a force that could undermine conscious decisions, then Watson and Skinner's radical idea was to dismiss all motivation (conscious along with unconscious). CBT's innovation has been to reverse this dismissal, reinstating the mind as something that has to be reckoned with in the attempt to change human behaviour. This is how our field has always proceeded: circling round and round the same dilemmas, evolving counter-intuitive new ways of dealing with them, but then, inevitably, modifying or even abandoning those radical ideas when they proved 'too hard' for most people to embrace. No truly radical concept in the counselling/

therapy field has ever been able to capture the 'high ground' for very long. For a time, people join the new movement in droves, wanting the 'badge of belonging', adopting the new jargon, but not deeply accepting (or even fully understanding) the principles on which the movement was originally based. Then, as the movement loses momentum, and becomes 'just another therapy', these same people jump ship, and find a new leader, a new 'movement'. Others continue to wear the badge, but start to modify the radical force of the original ideas, combine them with other ideas and techniques, and generally return the movement to the mainstream of the way human beings think about change.

Even more disturbingly for the 'gurus'—the therapeutic celebrities who create 'new' approaches to helping—it is increasingly evident that clients who are highly motivated to change and prepared to persist in the face of initial difficulties are likely to experience some level of positive outcome *no matter what model of counselling or therapy they are exposed to.* Poorly motivated or profoundly disturbed clients, on the other hand, seem 'resistant' to almost any treatment model, although many new models may start off by claiming that they have found a 'cure for schizophrenia' and other severe disorders[9]. It is with these clients that the 'fit' between individual client and individual professional (regardless of the model she or he employs) is most likely to be crucial—a point to which we will come back shortly.

Several approaches to counselling and therapy that emerged to prominence in the last quarter of the twentieth century also belong in the problem-focussed category. All of them assume an active stance on the part of the professional, most claim to offer short-term solutions, instead of a long, 'two-steps-forward-one-step-back' change process. These more recent approaches include *strategic family therapy, brief solution-focussed therapy*, and *narrative therapy*. Most of them owe a debt (whether openly acknowledged or not) to the unique strategic approach devised by American psychiatrist Milton Erickson, who combined trance induction with storytelling, therapeutic metaphor, and paradoxical messages that 'tricked' the unconscious (an intriguing introduction to Erickson's unique approach can be found in Jay Haley's eye-opening and often very funny *Uncommon Therapy: The Psychiatric Techniques of Milton H. Erickson, MD*, Norton, 1973).

A strategic therapist (whether working with an individual, like Milton Erickson or with a family, like Jay Haley) was not greatly concerned about the therapeutic relationship—although like any other problem-focussed professionals, strategic therapists recognised that their first job was to connect sufficiently well with clients to earn them some credibility. A strategic therapist's goal was to *manoeuvre* clients into change, rather than coaching them in a direct, straightforward manner (as a behaviourist or cognitive-behaviourist might do). The 'manoeuvring' might take the form of the 'strategic questioning' which we mentioned at the end of Chapter 3. Strategic questions (like 'forced choice' questions in personality assessment questionnaires) require people to move in either one direction or another (thus they function in the opposite way to the open questions we talked about in Chapter 3). Many narrative therapy questions work by directing clients away from how they feel, and encourage them to *reshape how they think*, by asking them to engage with perspectives that they might find odd or baffling at first, but which ultimately could become liberating.

Similarly, though in a less complex way, brief and solution-focussed approaches direct clients to areas of strength, success and competence, rather than to the stories of failure that most clients automatically bring to therapy. (See Brian Cade and Bill O'Hanlon, *A Brief Guide to Brief Therapy*, Norton, 1993) Such approaches do not invite clients to engage in increasingly honest dialogue with the therapist, nor does the therapist offer direct feedback on clients' ways of relating (although the feedback is there by implication in the pattern of questioning). This recognises the unpalatable fact (for therapists) that many clients do not want to be told uncomfortable truths about themselves, or even to 'discover' them. Honesty and confrontation may be too brutal for some people, and there needs to be a subtler way of getting through to them.

These new 'strategic' approaches were all designed quite deliberately to tackle the continuing challenge of clients who seem so sunk in misery and perceived incompetence that they 'fail to learn from their own success' (as narrative therapist David Epston wittily put it). No existing approach—whether psychodynamic, person-centred, behavioural or cognitive—had seemed able to assist such clients to 'shift'. It seemed easier for most professionals simply to diagnose them as 'personality disordered' and doubt that they were capable of change at all. However, by taking a stance that was strikingly different from the one their clients expected, adherents of the strategic approaches avoided becoming bogged down in the clients' 'problem-saturated narratives' and 'failure stories'. As with Aikido and other martial arts, strategic therapists use their clients' habitual stance as leverage to overthrow their entrenched patterns of thought and action. When expertly and non-anxiously done (as by Milton Erikson, Jay Haley, Bill O'Hanlon, Michael White or David Epston) such approaches could be spectacularly successful. When employed by less expert, confident practitioners, strategic techniques could fail in an equally spectacular way, with clients angrily walking out of sessions, complaining that the professional had 'made fun of them' or 'completely missed the point'.

The 'radical idea' underlying strategic approaches was that drawing overt attention to clients' unconscious motivations and 'bringing them to the surface' (as both the psychoanalytic and the cognitive approaches would counsel) would actually terrify certain clients, who would then cling even more fiercely to their problematic behaviours and thought-patterns. Instead, what is 'unconscious' must be acknowledged at a symbolic, metaphorical level. The client's unconscious will 'know' that the therapist has recognised it, but the client's conscious awareness will be oblivious (here you can see the way that these approaches have been shaped by hypnotherapy, a key plank in Milton Erickson's practice). Change will then occur *despite* what the professional appears to be saying and doing, not *because* of it.

For example, a strategic therapist tells a fighting couple that they 'should have more fights' before they return for their next session, because the fights are actually doing their relationship a lot of good, and that they should be in no hurry to stop quarrelling and criticising, because if they did, their relationship might deteriorate. *Here the therapist is taking the role previously played by the clients' unconscious.* The couple, baffled and somewhat irritated, return in a week or two, reporting that they have had no fights at all, and that they have enjoyed the change (the therapist's intervention has enabled them to generate new behaviour, which they would not have been able to do if the therapist had counselled them to avoid fighting). The therapist responds to the couple's report, not by praising them for doing so well, but by worrying openly that they are doing something that sounds quite risky, and that he would be much happier if they could allow themselves to resume fighting. Again the couple are confused and angry, but again, they find themselves acting outside their accustomed pattern. By the time a month has gone by, they have experienced a sustained period of marital harmony, and getting on well has begun to seem like a viable option. If the therapist had worked straightforwardly to 'coach' them towards 'better communication' or 'effective conflict resolution', the couple would have resisted at every step of the way. If the therapist had sought to expose the murky depths of their unconscious motivations for lacerating each other, they might have quit therapy, and never returned.

Constructivist approaches like narrative therapy and solution-focussed therapy are, at base, strategic too—although that element is often obscured in the way they are presented to trainees and to clients. Post-modern theory asserts that there is no fixed 'truth', there is no 'reality'—what we treat as 'truth' or 'reality' is simply a social construct—an unspoken 'agreement' to perceive the world in a certain way. Children grow up being told 'X is true—Y is not' or 'You've got a bad problem, we'll have to take you to see a psychologist', and they take these linguistic expressions for a 'hard reality'. Our socially-constructed 'reality' depends almost entirely upon language. For example, it is customary in our society for people to believe that problems are located within individuals ('I've *got* depression'; 'she's *got* an eating disorder', '*my bipolar* is playing up again'), which naturally leaves them feeling that any perceived problem 'must be their fault'. If we change the way we talk about something, then, constructivist therapists assert, we change the thing itself. In the above example, the therapist advised the clients to fight more, thus tacitly suggesting to them that 'fighting is good'. The couple then unites to 'fight against' this idea, which seems nonsensical to them. The change in language (with its associated reversal of the socially-agreed understanding that 'fighting is a bad thing') has resulted in a change of behaviour. Similarly, if a solution-focussed therapist asks a series of questions designed to manoeuvre a client into recognising that she has actually succeeded at something, despite her entrenched view of herself as a failure, then that therapist has used language purposefully to achieve a change in thinking and feeling around the client's stated problem.

When family therapy began, it was seen as revolutionary and different because it involved more than one client simultaneously. In reality, however, the result of working with several people in the room (some of whom might well be children) was that family therapists tended to focus more on behaviour than on relationship, more on the perceived problem than on the need for re-parenting of the client. Families would not usually tolerate a long-term, exploratory approach: they wanted the problem solved. As every family therapist knows, you cannot reflect back, with deep empathy, everything that every family member says; if you do, your session will lose focus. And if you start to invite individual family members to explore their relationship with you (as might happen in individual psychotherapy), the family may well turn into a set of 'siblings', rivals for your attention and vying for your 'love'.

No, working with conjoint clients pulled most of the professionals who embraced it inexorably in the direction of standing back from the system, seeing the 'whole' rather than the individual parts, and on this basis, formulating interventions that challenged the system's 'habits'—the entrenched patterns that have come to govern their behaviour towards one another. Thus early family therapists often intervened in ways consistent with behaviourism and, like the strategic school, ignored the *meaning* of behaviour, in favour of seemingly powerful, active methods of inducing change.

Because they considered the therapeutic relationship less important than Freud or Rogers had thought, most family therapy approaches placed less emphasis on the professional's own personal awareness than the 'relational' approaches did. Indeed, Jay Hayley famously maintained that it was quite unnecessary for the strategic family therapist to undertake any personal therapy at all—he or she simply needed thorough training in the techniques, and 'live' supervision from an experienced strategic therapist via a one way mirror into the actual therapy room (Jay Haley, *Learning and Teaching Therapy*, NY, Guilford, 1996). While this is a debate that may never finally be settled, our own view is that self-awareness and personal work are prerequisites for any counsellor or therapist, regardless of what approach she or he adopts. This is, in part, because the ability accurately to 'read' others, and be sensitive to their feedback is heavily dependent on accurate knowledge of oneself—including 'hidden' or sensitive parts of the self.

If a problem-focussed professional fails to recognise that her client's lack of enthusiasm for 'change strategies' may indicate an underlying wish for deeper understanding and empathy, then that professional will be handicapped in her attempts to help that client, who will probably drop out, because the therapist doesn't 'get' what he really needs. That client needs to experience being understood before he will be ready to practise change. Why would the professional have such a 'blind spot' in relation to the client's needs? Because the professional herself has not recognised her own needs for relationship, has failed to see how her enthusiasm for 'solutions' has sometimes been a way of avoiding vague feelings of discontent or dissatisfaction in relationships.

In the same way, a relationally-focussed psychotherapist who is so fixated on the transference that she fails to recognise that a client wants some hints to help her change—if only as a step on her way towards self-understanding—is letting her client down too. This client may need to experience change before he can feel understood. That psychotherapist will fail to respond to his hints because she does not recognise that a part of her, too, might benefit from a 'just do it' approach at times, despite her conviction that change only comes as a result of a deep, intense, ongoing relational work, and must always be 'owned' by the client, never suggested by the counsellor. Neither approach is the 'correct' one for all clients, and neither approach absolves the counsellor/therapist from the journey of personal awareness.

Is THE RIGHT MODEL FOR YOU THE RIGHT MODEL FOR YOUR CLIENT?

As we said at the start of this chapter, the two terms, 'counselling' and 'therapy' are now loosely and interchangeably used by many people in the field. Rogers and his followers referred to 'counselling', but what they were advocating was in many ways identical with what Freud would call 'therapy'. The relationship, in these models, becomes the vehicle by which clients learn about themselves and others, in direct interaction with the therapist or counsellor. By contrast, many approaches that class themselves as 'therapy' are in fact problem-focussed, more or less didactic, and emphasise the practising of new skills and strategies by the client. As we have seen, these include mainstream behaviourist approaches, the newer cognitive behavioural and 'mindfulness' approaches, and the majority of family therapy approaches. Many of these approaches could be regarded as counselling—if counselling had retained its original sense of the provision of expert guidance, insight and advice. And if 'therapy' had not been widely perceived as indicating something more prestigious than mere 'counselling'!

What we have done in this chapter is to focus on the distinction between *problem-focussed approaches* and *relational approaches*. This might in fact be a better basis for a clear distinction between 'counselling' and 'therapy'—as long as we remember that with any given client, both might be involved. The problem-focussed approach, perhaps, might be regarded as more 'pragmatic', more in keeping with a secular, materialist approach to life; the relationship-focussed might have more in common with spiritual teachings—with the idea that 'the journey, not the arrival, matters'. This concept of helping converges broadly with the idea of 're-parenting'—it is the relationship with the helper that makes the key difference—usually, but not only, over a considerable period of time. By contrast, in the problem-focussed concept, the helper is far less intimately involved with the 're-growing' of the client, and confines herself to a more 'teacherly' role, normally over a shorter time period.

In fact, the problem-solving model of counselling/therapy seems to have been evolved by individuals whose own preference has been for problem-solving rather than relationship, and it suits clients with a similar preference[10]. These are the priorities of the left hemisphere. The relational model seems to have been evolved by those who care deeply about relationships in general, and perhaps have a degree of right hemispheric dominance. Relationally-focussed therapists trust that problem-solving can occur without the provision of advice or strategies—and it suits clients with a similar preference. While change is certainly possible in both models, what is very clear is that if there is not a reasonable match between the model you offer, and the preference of the particular client, then you are unlikely to get very far. To a problem-focussed individual, the relational approach, slow, quiet and often non-directive (at least at first) seems to be 'going nowhere'. Furthermore it is threatening, because the therapist does not rapidly join the client's left hemisphere-led hunt for solutions, and hints that there are deeper issues to be explored. To the relationship-oriented client, the problem-focussed model is going to seem crude, superficial, and beside the point.

Think about it

Believe it or not, Freud's psychoanalysis actually began as an attempt at 'behaviour modification' via hypnosis! When Freud switched from experimental neurology to trying to cure emotional problems, he first tried cocaine as a 'quick fix' (like LSD a century later, cocaine was then seen as a wonder-drug rather than as a potentially dangerous substance). When he realised that cocaine could become addictive, he began to look into the possibilities of hypnosis. Free association began in this way, with the doctor inducing an actual hypnotic trance. When Freud realised that the 'induction' was not necessary, and that patients would talk freely without it if encouraged to do so, the 'talking cure' was born. Even so, psychoanalysis began life as a relatively short-term affair. As some patients' problems remained unchanged, Freud began to see them for much longer (years instead of months), reckoning that it would take many more sessions, and deeper probing, to get past their entrenched resistance. Freud's successors carried on analyses for even longer than Freud himself had done, maintaining that failure to gain rapid improvement—or any improvement—must be because treatment had been too brief. Eventually, psychoanalysis became so protracted that it lost credibility. Some analysts began to develop shorter-term models (e.g. twelve session 'time limited psychotherapy'), as if in response to the challenge from the problem-focussed approaches. And so the wheel came almost full circle.

What happened within the psychoanalytic world can also be observed within other major therapeutic paradigms—a pendulum-swing between long-term and short-term, relational and problem-focussed, non-directive and interventionist, 'mindful' and behavioural. Both models have been with us from the very beginning.

SO WHAT ARE THE IMPLICATIONS FOR YOU?

Hopefully, by the time you have reached this point in the chapter, you will already have been asking yourself 'Where do I fit on this continuum of approaches?' Some of you will be clear that you are drawn to the 'problem-focussed' end of the spectrum. Some of you will be equally sure that the 'relational' end is the one where you belong. In thinking about how you might develop as a counsellor in the next few years (see Chapter 8), you need to know what is a 'safe place' for you to operate within this profession—what is the model of change which allows you to use your own personal qualities to their best advantage. But as we have already anticipated, you will inevitably encounter some clients who will not feel comfortable with what feels most comfortable for you. As you and your clients move into the 'working phase' of counselling/therapy, as you begin to engage more overtly with the client's difficulties in living and relating, you will come to appreciate the 'choice points' that you will encounter—points at which you will need to decide whether the needs of your client are best met by the 'relational model' (key skills involved are described in Chapter 6) or by the 'problem focussed model' (key skills of which are described in Chapter 7). Sometimes, you may be able to move flexibly between the two, at other times you will not have this flexibility. How this process evolves will have as much to do with your client as it does with you. It is not something that you 'impose upon' him or her—it is something that he or she 'negotiates' with you, not explicitly, but in the give-and-take of the relationship. Successful negotiation depends heavily on the very same sensitivity to your client's reactions that we have emphasised throughout this book. Watch and listen as clients take in what you have just said. Ask yourself what their reaction means. If you're not sure, ask them! *Be guided by your client, not by your theoretical model.*

At the beginning of this chapter, we pointed out that the textbook distinction between 'counselling' and 'therapy' is often hard to maintain in practice. In working with any one client, you may operate as either a 'counsellor' or a 'therapist', depending on the client's own agenda, on the stage that the therapeutic process has reached, and so on. In Chapters 1 to 4 we used both words, to indicate that the skills and capacities those chapters deal with are those that are fundamental to both counselling and therapy. But from now on it will be different. In Chapter 6, we will consistently refer to 'the therapist', because the skills and capacities involved in 'encountering' are those which (to our way of thinking) belong to the relational concept of interpersonal helping, as described earlier in this chapter, and the more you as professionals focus on the relationship as the vehicle of change, the more you will be operating in the realm of psychotherapy.

In Chapter 7, by contrast, we have used the term 'counsellor', even though the skills involved are those that many professionals today would consider part of 'therapy'—whether behavioural, cognitive, or strategic. We class these skills as belonging to counselling rather than therapy because they relate to the problem-focussed concept of helping, as detailed earlier in this chapter. What distinguishes them from the 'therapeutic' skills and capacities dealt with in Chapter 6 is that they address clients' conscious motivations and goals, and do so by direct 'coaching' towards change, rather than by using the therapist-client relationship to catalyse shifts in awareness and behaviour.

Of course, such a distinction will not appeal to everyone, and those who are accustomed to thinking of themselves as 'family therapists' or 'cognitive therapists' will probably feel uneasy at seeing their skills categorised as 'counselling'. They may even see us as 'devaluing' their work. Far from it! We reject the notion that therapy is somehow superior to counselling, or that it requires less skill. Rather, our whole point in this chapter has been to emphasise that both sets of skills are important, that we may need to deploy both, depending on what our clients need—while accepting that our own personal styles will 'pull' us towards one end of the continuum, or the other.

One concern that is often raised by professionals is the 'risk' of training lower-tier helpers in skills considered more appropriate to more highly qualified helpers. The risk expressed is that well meaning but inadequately trained counsellors may unwisely attempt to 'do therapy', opening up areas which may overwhelm the client, and which the counsellor does not 'know what to do with'. Our whole emphasis in this book has been on paying close attention to how your client responds to what you say and do, and on following the client's lead as a default setting. With good skills in holding, exploring and immediacy, and with the capacity for honesty and humility, it is unlikely that 'risky' situations will develop at all, because clients will feel safe to voice their concerns, and counsellors will take them seriously. In our experience, potentially dangerous situations are far more likely to develop when helpers (whether they call themselves 'counsellors', 'therapists' or 'psychologists') focus primarily on their own power and therapeutic 'magic' rather than on what is happening to their clients. That way, indeed, lies the possibility of 'retraumatising' clients and doing lasting damage.

CHAPTER SUMMARY

- For a variety of reasons, the terms 'counselling' and 'therapy' have become almost interchangeable in clinical practice, and the distinction has come close to losing its meaning.

- The more meaningful distinction, by now, is between approaches that focus on the problem and those that focus on the therapeutic relationship.

- The 'relational' approach usually assumes that lasting change involves a kind of 're-parenting' of the client by the professional. Normally, this would imply a long term relationship. The relational approach (whether psychoanalytic (Freud), person-centred (Rogers) or existentialist (Yalom) tends to be non-directive, and emphasises the client's developing ability to understand and accept self.

- The 'problem-focussed' approach places the responsibility for change on the professional, who takes an active, interventionist and (often) didactic role. It tends to be of shorter duration, and de-emphasises the therapeutic relationship and client self-understanding, in favour of measurable behaviour change.

- This distinction is not a hierarchy of worth: both counselling and therapy are valuable and necessary. In practice, therapists may give direct advice and coaching to their long term patients, and counsellors may use the exploration of the client's way of acting towards them to promote insight and behaviour change.

- As a future counsellor/therapist, you will most likely choose the approach that fits most comfortably with your own personality and your own assumptions about change.

- However, if your client's theory of change makes your model a less comfortable fit, you will need to vary your approach in response to your client's needs

- Thus, a competent counsellor/therapist should ideally possess skills in both the relational and the problem-focussed approach, and be prepared to shift flexibly between the two, thus paying attention to both right- and left-hemisphere priorities and where possible, helping clients to integrate them.

Chapter 6

Gentle Honesty: Skills Of 'Encountering'

'TERRIBLE TWOS' AND REBELLIOUS TEENS

Infants need reliable, non-anxious holding at the very beginning of their journey into life. Toddlers, as we saw in Chapter 3, need our help to explore their environment in a safe and productive way, although by now, they can make an active, energetic contribution to the process. By the third year of life, small children have also begun to challenge their caregivers, and to define a sense of themselves as separate, with minds and wills of their own. Although they may be tiny, toddlers can pose a formidable challenge to the adults who care for them. In our culture, parents often refer to this period of child development as the 'terrible twos'. Typically, toddlers refuse to co-operate with perfectly reasonable parental requests, with which they would previously have complied. Or they may stamp and scream, instead of calmly accepting a parent's 'No.' These seemingly irrational and arbitrary behaviours are best understood as children's attempts to find out what they can achieve by asserting their independence of caregivers, and what limits they must accept. The fact that toddlers oppose their parents in this way is strong evidence that they are now more aware of themselves as separate beings, with needs that are 'theirs'.

Parents who can respond calmly to these tantrums seem to do the best. The small child needs the assurance that he will still be loved, no matter what he does. But he also needs to know that his parents will not allow him to run unrestrained into danger, or to treat others with disrespect. By setting clear limits with our toddlers, we teach them to set limits for themselves when they are older, and to enjoy the self-respect that comes from doing so. By the same token, parents who are sensitive to their children's individual personalities show flexibility in how they respond. There might be times when it is appropriate to accept the toddler's 'No!' There may be times when genuine heartbreak may result from a firm restraint, and the child needs extra comforting in order to deal with feelings that are overwhelming, rather than just a crisp, 'Now settle down or you'll have to go to your room!'

In doing some of the 'good parenting' described above, what sensitive parents are actually doing is helping their child to *regulate* its own urgent feelings. This regulation comes from outside the child, but through this young children gradually learn to do it for themselves, that is *self-regulate*. When a parent says, 'It's really hard when I say "no" to that ice cream, isn't it' she is speaking out of empathy. She is acknowledging what her child is feeling, and how powerful and overwhelming that feeling may be. At the same time, however, she is sticking by the limit that she has set. 'No, you can't have an ice cream right now.' Unfortunately, many parents (perhaps most) don't go through this step. They sail right into outright confrontation (*'I said no and I mean no!'*) or 'punishment' for the child's 'bad behaviour'. Language like 'tantrums' and 'terrible twos' does not help us to be sensitive to our child—it makes us readier to 'judge' our child. It is often hard for parents not to see their toddler's behaviour as deliberate, 'wilful'. But it is not. The child's behaviour is generated by the older parts of her brain, and feel 'right' to her.

In early adolescence parents encounter a similar phase of 'rebellion' or 'self-assertion' in their growing children. Like toddlers, adolescents often take risks and get themselves into unsafe situations—partly because their brains are not yet developed sufficiently to envisage the likely consequences. They need to be restrained from taking risks that are too great, while at the same time, their caregivers must show flexibility and empathy in enforcing these boundaries. The big difference between the adolescence and the 'terrible twos' is that adolescents are by now far advanced towards adulthood. They can speak fluently and express their feelings in words—though some of them may find it hard to be completely honest about those feelings. It is possible to have a meaningful conversation with them, even if it involves argument and conflict. It is also possible for an adult caregiver to be more open about her own feelings and needs, because most adolescents have a greater capacity for empathy than they did as toddlers. A confrontation between an adult caregiver and an adolescent is much more like an encounter of equals than a confrontation with a toddler. Yet in both cases, adults must respond with a mixture of two seemingly contradictory attitudes, varyingly described as 'good authority', 'tough love' and (more recently) 'loving firmness'. In self-help books, Rogers' principle of 'unconditional positive regard' is rephrased as 'I love you, but I don't like your behaviour'. It is not a balance that many parents and caregivers find easy to learn. Their natural tendency is to react to an irresponsible young person either by offering criticism and punishment, or by caving in to the child's demands. Both are equally damaging and oscillating arbitrarily between the two is just as unhelpful.

It is very important to realise that when some adolescents *act out* (becoming abusive, taking serious risks, failing to value their own emotional or physical health) they do so because when they were small children they were not offered the patient, understanding listening that would have helped them to feel that their anxieties and frustrations were manageable, and that their fears would pass. Instead their parents told them to be quiet, tried to distract them with sweets, toys (or these days, iPads!) yelled at them or hit them—anything but treating them as small people with legitimate concerns. Thus they were unable to realise that distressing feelings could be talked about and worked through. They had to find ways of indirectly communicating the frightened, out of control or angry feelings they were experiencing. Under stress, these adolescents are still emotionally two years old.

In counselling, an adult client sometimes crosses the boundaries of the therapeutic relationship in a way that resembles a toddler's—by arriving late for sessions, by cancelling appointments at short notice, by assuming his right to answer an intrusive call on his mobile phone (which he has forgotten to switch off), by assuming that of course he can pay for the session later. Any of these things may be trivial and excusable if they occur only once in a while. We all forget things and make mistakes. But if they happen too often, we are entitled to ask what such events might mean. Of course this is only possible if all of the rules of the counselling relationship have been discussed the client at the beginning—thus setting up the 'frame' that psychodynamic therapists refer to (the arrangements for how often sessions will occur, how long they will last, what they will cost, preservation of confidentiality, turning off of phones, etc). These rules are designed to safeguard both the client and the counsellor, and they generally help clients to feel secure and cared about.

Like an egocentric small child, a client may need to be alerted to the fact that he is disrespecting others by following his own impulses without regard for their needs. Conversely, a client may (also like a small child) be wanting to assert her autonomy by 'bucking the rules'. She might feel a deep fear of becoming dependent on someone else—in this case, the counsellor—and perhaps being 'swallowed up', or 'used'. Some clients need to find out whether their counsellor is capable of being firm with them (as perhaps their own parents were not). Whatever the behaviour means, a more in-depth discussion may need to be held, one that helps the client to explore the possible reasons for his actions. Trivial though they appear, behaviours like these are often clues to longstanding habits of thought and action in the client, habits that may later need to be addressed in the context of the client's other relationships.

Some of your adult clients, like adolescents, are in the business of discovering who they are, and part of doing this is testing you out, and energetically resisting what they may see as your wish to 'tell them what to do'—even if you are, wisely, refraining from doing that! But before they will be prepared to modify some of their deep convictions about themselves, and to consider changing the way they behave, they may need to struggle with you. In that process, they will also be struggling with parts of themselves—parts that they feel ashamed of, afraid of, or angry about. Often, these will be child parts—parts that may even, in fact, correspond to the oppositional-yet-vulnerable toddler they once were or the oppositional-yet-vulnerable adolescent they later became. As your relationship with your clients strengthens and deepens, these 'young' parts are likely to emerge from hiding.

And so the adult client struggles when a therapist invites him to consider uncomfortable truths about himself, or invites him to see that he could behave differently in order to achieve the outcomes he claims he desires. There is 'resistance', not just to the therapist—whose words may sound 'critical' or 'judgemental'—but to that part of client that clings to what he knows, the part that fears shame and self-doubt. We met this in Chapter 4—clients' uncomfortable perception that *they* might need to change if their *situation* is to change for the better, their painful realisation that they cannot blame other people for everything that has happened to them, or expect their counsellor to perform miracles and solve their problems in a couple of sessions. In this chapter we shall discuss the various ways in which you, as a therapist, can assist your clients to face the uncomfortable truths about themselves. How you handle this struggle will be crucial to achieving a good outcome. But this time, although your client may react to you as a critical or controlling parent—and indeed, you may actually find yourself acting in that way—the reality is that you and your client are both adults. You cannot stop your client from acting in ways that you consider stupid, or even dangerous. And if you start to think you should be able to do that, then you are unlikely to be very helpful. You will need to develop the capacity to remain non-anxious in the face of your clients' distress, confusion, or impulsivity. It isn't easy, but it can make all the difference.

Many parents of adolescents struggle with strong feelings of disempowerment. Both toddlers and teenagers, in their different ways, often send a loud, clear message to their parents: 'You're getting it wrong. You haven't understood me. You're not treating me right'. In response, parents often feel confused. Some give up the struggle, and retreat into inaction and permissiveness—allowing the young person to get away with unacceptable behaviour, blaming themselves for the fact that their child has 'turned out bad', and creating within the child a deep sense of unsafety. Others react with anger, in a rigid, punitive way, attacking the child, and often inadvertently confirming the child's inner conviction that she is 'bad' and does not deserve love or understanding. Despite the publicity our society gives to assertive communication and good listening, the reality is that most of us—as young people or as parents—do not expect to be listened to in an open-minded, non-judgemental and curious manner. Parents send their kids to an 'expert' (school counsellor, therapist, psychologist) to be 'fixed', instead of opening themselves to the hard work and patience demanded by genuine dialogue. But you as a therapist need to be in a position to model meaningful, respectful communication. '*It must be so hard to have to behave that way in order to be understood!*' might get you a lot further than '*Get real! This behaviour is completely unacceptable*'. We need to have faced our own 'shadow side' in order to say the non-blaming first statement with conviction.

Faced with clients who attack or blame (*'You don't get it!', 'You're not helping me—this isn't what I need!'*) some therapists are so invested in preserving a pleasant relationship that they are unwilling to risk a confrontation. Other therapists interpret their clients' behaviour as a 'power struggle', which they (the therapists) must 'win'. They react with confrontations that sound as if they think the client is to blame for everything, and result in mutual defensiveness instead of mutual responsibility-taking. They are honest—up to a point—but do not balance their honesty with empathy, or display a wish to understand the real reasons for the client's behaviour.

REDEFINING 'CONFRONTATION': GENTLE HONESTY

In contrast to these two unhelpful types of response, this chapter will introduce the possibility of 'therapeutic encounter'—a dialogue informed by *gentle honesty*, in which the therapist neither gives in to the client nor attacks her, neither 'flees' nor 'fights'. When the elephant in the room has been acknowledged, and some commitment on the client's part to staying the course has been established, you will have a space to operate in—sometimes referred to as the 'working phase' of therapy. In this space, as your clients trust you with a fuller and more honest account of themselves, it will become apparent to you, sooner or later, how their own behaviour is getting in the way of their achieving happiness or satisfaction. In the skill of reflecting, we hold up a mirror to what clients have said, enabling them to 'see' and 'hear' themselves more clearly, and in the process, validating their own thoughts, feelings and beliefs. Sensitively-conducted exploring will assist clients to open up areas of experience that are 'there', but not always recognised or understood by them. With immediacy, we use our own awareness, our own feelings, in the service of the client, and hence create an 'encounter' in which both of us must put into words what has hitherto gone unspoken. The skills we will be describing in this chapter also fall into the category of encounter. Either our clients are encountering us, or they are encountering themselves (coming face to face with sensitive parts of themselves). Often both occur simultaneously. But in either case, clients are grappling with an awareness that is potentially distressing, painful, or even frightening, something that they have previously kept well to the back of their minds—or out of their minds—for very good reasons.

In the microskills approach to counsellor training, this is the territory normally labelled 'confrontation'. We prefer 'encounter', for several reasons. First, because to many people, 'confrontation' suggests something tough, harsh and conflictual. Trainers struggle to reassure their students that the actual *practice* of 'confrontation' needs to be respectful and gentle—what is in question is not a kind of combat—but despite their efforts, confrontation is often thought of by trainees as something scary or risky. Second, because confrontation (often defined quite narrowly in the microskills approach[1] is only *one* of the things that need to happen in the working phase of the counselling process. In this chapter, we will consider not only confrontation, but allied skills—pointing out a theme in what clients are presenting; offering feedback in the here-and-now (as in the skill of immediacy), and 'interpretation' (drawing attention to meanings which the client may not be conscious of).

All of these interventions involve the counsellor or therapist taking the initiative, rather than simply following the client's lead. In employing the skills of encounter, a therapist still follows the client—but not all the time. At key moments, she may choose to 'intervene' (the word originally meant to 'come between') and introduce a challenge. All the skills we've just listed involve the client coming face to face with something new, unexpected—something that may sometimes come as a relief or a reassurance, as well as being surprising or disturbing. In the language of humanistic and existentialist therapy, 'encounter' is a 'meeting of minds' in which both parties are 'authentic'—true to themselves—and honest with the other. In the therapeutic context, of course, authenticity and honesty must always be tempered with respect for the client's sensitivities, and recognition of how much of the 'painful truth' he or she is ready to hear right now. Hence 'gentle honesty', not 'brutal honesty'.

GENTLE HONESTY IN PRACTICE

In the first session with a couple, the man stood up, said something angrily to his wife, and seemed about to leave the room. The counsellor said, *'It must be awful to have to get so mad to make yourself understood'*. He sat down. With tears in his eyes, he said *'Yes, I hate myself when I do this'*.

In their fifth session, a different couple, who were deeply committed to each other, were exploring how the wife had been affected by the way her husband had reacted to a situation that was traumatic for her. She spoke, with tears in her eyes, of her longing for connection with him at that time. He became stony, and said she was overreacting to the trauma and shouldn't have been affected in this way. This was devastating for the wife to hear. The therapist commented on the impact of what he'd said, and challenged him (gently) by saying *'I wonder what you were feeling while you were listening to her pain?'* The man couldn't identify what he had felt, but mentioned that when he was growing up, his family hadn't believed in 'indulging' feelings because that would 'make them get bigger'. He had been able to connect his current behaviour with something from the past, and his wife would have had more understanding of why he had been so seemingly unable to empathise with her in the way she needed.

In order to employ the skills of encountering, you will need some capacities beyond those required by the skills of holding and exploring. First, you will need courage. *Once again, you will need to be braver than your client.* You must take that step into the unknown which your client is instinctively avoiding. You need to 'lead the way', and show by example that fear can be faced, and the unknown embraced ('Feel the fear, and do it anyway', as the well-known self help book advises us![2] The second resource you will need is *an accurate knowledge of your client* (her strengths and weaknesses, her 'tender spots'). It is rare for any inexperienced therapist to possess such knowledge early in the counselling process. You may think that you 'know exactly what is going on' for your client, or that you have 'seen her before'. And in some respects, you may be right—but to *assume* that you are right, and to move into 'encountering' on the strength of your assumption, is arrogant and risky. You will learn much about your client in the first half dozen sessions, but there will still be a lot you do not know. Some clients will only start to let down their defences after a prolonged period—months, even years. Typically, the 'healthier' and less damaged the client, the sooner he or she will permit real challenge from you. Rigidly-organised and profoundly damaged clients may take far longer to be ready for challenge. *Patience* is a capacity that is rarely mentioned in relation to counselling and therapy, and yet it is vital. If you cannot tolerate a slow progression via 'two steps forward, one step back', you probably are not well fitted for this profession.

The skills of encounter belong to the stage where the therapeutic relationship has been tested, and where the alliance between you and your client is now sufficiently robust to withstand the stress of a confrontation. Beginners sometimes think, 'Why do I have to wait so long before pointing out to my clients what they need to know? Isn't it just a waste of my time and theirs?' These trainees are still thinking of counselling or therapy in an instrumental way, as 'doing something to someone'. They see themselves as the agents of change, surgeons operating on a patient. It might be more accurate and more useful if they thought of themselves as monitors of the client's change process—watching closely so they can be aware of the client's level of readiness for the next step, and then timing their intervention sensitively, so that it comes at the point where the client can accept it and make use of it, rather than simply pushing it away. To do otherwise is simply to invite resistance—which has sometimes been described as the client's reasonable response to mistimed and insensitive intervention!

Thus *timing* is the third capacity you will need in order to employ the skills of encountering. Unless you choose your time wisely, your challenge may risk alienating your client, even causing him to flee from the whole therapeutic process. Timing cannot be taught through precepts and 'rules', it can only be learned from experience, and most of us learn it the hard way—by failing to get it right on many occasions, until we gradually build up a better sense of how much *this* client is likely to hear *now*. In Chapter 2, we saw how an inadequate or insensitive reflection usually generates a client response that shows us we were wide of the mark. In the same way, if you challenge a client prematurely, the client's response will normally show you that you have mistimed the challenge. The client will offer a minimal acknowledgement and then change the subject, or become defensive and start to argue with you. More passive clients will appear to agree, or accept, but cancel the next session, make excuses to postpone it, or simply refuse to answer your calls. We've already considered one exception to the 'don't challenge early' rule—in Chapter 4, where we saw how involuntary or extremely reluctant clients may need to be 'called' on their attitude at a very early stage, perhaps even in the very first session. But this is not the norm. Most clients do not respond well to too-early confrontation.

If you do mistime a challenge and realise it straight away, you will need to fall back on your holding skills—finding a way of connecting empathically with the client's feelings of dismay, affront or shock, and thus assisting him or her to voice these feelings directly to you. Even a mistimed confrontation can be turned into a meaningful experience of immediacy, in which the client is able to tell you directly how she responded to the encounter with you, and you are able to 'hold' her reaction without becoming defensive or critical. In some cases, you may need (after some careful thought) to back down, and even apologise to your client. There is a school of thought that follows the famous principle, 'Never apologise, never explain'—much beloved of today's managers and administrators—but we think such a stance is inappropriate for a therapeutic setting. Effective acknowledgment and 'repair' can lead to deepening trust from your client. An apology should be brief, sincere and say no more than is necessary. In the following example, the therapist apologises for the *manner* in which she offered the intervention, but does not retract the *meaning* of her earlier statement:

Therapist: You're letting me know that what I said really upset you. Thinking about it now, I can see that I may have spoken too strongly. After all, you've been telling me for months how hard you try with your Dad, and how much you want to reach out to him. I think it sounded like I didn't appreciate that. I'm sorry. And maybe I didn't fully realise how hard you'd tried.

Of course, good timing will depend heavily on the nature of each individual client and his/her situation. That is why we cannot give you 'rules' like 'Always wait until the twentieth session before you confront your client'. Some clients may be ready for an honest encounter with you quite early—those who can voice their feelings in the 'third session challenge' may be among them. Others may not be ready for a year or more. Psychoanalysts in the past spoke of 'ego strength' as the quality that enabled clients to survive and learn from the vicissitudes of their lives, and which also enabled them to respond constructively to a therapeutic encounter, rather than fall to pieces and withdraw from therapy. These days the buzzword is 'resilience', but the basic concept is not all that different. Clients who demonstrate ego strength or resilience early on will be more likely to cope with, and use, a challenge from you, then or later.

Another way of looking at it is to distinguish 'solid self'—the ability to maintain a thought-through position in the face of others' pressure or anxious neediness—from a 'fragile self'. A solid self is capable of bending under pressure, like steel. A fragile self is like that older building material, cast iron. It seems strong but it is rigid, and if the pressure on it is too great, it will fracture. Some clients have selves so fragile that any confrontation, however gentle, is going to sweep them away like an earthquake or a tsunami. They will flee from therapy rather than endure the feeling of disintegration caused by a simple request or reasonable rule ('I'm afraid you can't smoke in here'), which they experience as a profound attack on their selfhood.

Practice task

Although you may not work with clients with so little 'solid self', you still need to develop ways of saying things so your clients are able to hear them. Such skills will be a reflection of your understanding of clients' individual sensitivities, and your willingness to treat them with respect and care. Most counsellors and therapists have, over time, collected or invented forms of words that achieve this. For example, you might say, *'So a part of you feels so angry that you imagine yourself punching him over and over'*. Some people react to any criticism as meaning that they are 'all bad', so if their therapist locates the 'bad' in *one part* of the client (not the whole of the client) this usually allows the client to begin connecting with anger, pain, and other feelings that she has, understandably, been using lots of energy to avoid. The phrasing 'One part of you ... another part of you ...' is typical of psychodynamic approaches. Narrative therapists have popularised the idea of 'externalising the problem' (*'How long has Depression controlled your life?'* When Anxiety is in the driving seat, what's it like for you as a passenger?*) so that clients do not feel that the problem 'belongs to them' or is 'identical with them'. Some of these ways of phrasing difficult statements will be more comfortable for you than others. You may come up with your own, too, for particular clients, because if you listen carefully to how they talk, you may well learn the kind of phrasing they themselves use to acknowledge their 'bad bits'.

It is particularly useful, as you approach the skills of encountering, to equip yourself with phrasing that 'softens' otherwise confronting statements, phrasing that is tentative and value-neutral. Therapists with sensitive clients (which is a fairly high proportion of clients!) soon learn the value of such ways of speaking (*I'm wondering if maybe ...'; 'Could it be that ...'; 'It's as if you ...'; 'Perhaps you felt a little bit upset'*, and so on).

It can be a most useful exercise to imagine the most confronting thing anyone could say to you—drawing on your own knowledge of your 'sensitive spots'—and then ask a fellow student to express that statement to you, first in a very direct way, with no softening, and then in a more tentative way that respects your vulnerabilities. What do you notice about yourself, as you react to the two 'versions'? What sort of feelings or thoughts are aroused? You can then reverse roles, and go through the same exercise with him or her as the 'client'. This activity becomes even more realistic if your 'counsellor' persists with the original confrontation and expands upon it, as if she/he is really invested in offering you this 'feedback'. See also the Practice Task later in this chapter, on 'Bad Therapy'.

Clients who in their lives outside the therapy room demonstrate that they can take, and use, respectful feedback from a friend or a family member, or who have made good use of feedback in an earlier experience of counselling, are more likely to be candidates for early confrontation than those who spend session after session telling you how they were 'devastated' by a friend's challenge, or who say evasively that they 'only saw that counsellor for a few sessions' because 'she didn't understand me' (which often translates as, 'She didn't respect my defences, and introduced stuff I wasn't ready to hear'). You can also calibrate your clients' 'solid self' by observing how they respond to the micro-challenges posed by holding and exploring. Does your client reject your empathic reflections time after time, telling you, 'No, that's not the right word, you haven't got my point'? Does your client take offence at a carefully worded question directly related to something she has previously mentioned? (*'What's to say? I've told you I don't get on with him! End of story!'*) If the answer is yes, and you have actually done a good job of following your client's lead, then you are probably safe in assuming that she will respond in a similar, but more intense, way to an attempt on your part to help her 'face up' to some uncomfortable truth about herself.

There is one final capacity that you will need in order to craft productive encounters with your clients, and this is perhaps the most controversial of all. What you will need is *a clear sense of what constitutes healthy, functional human behaviour in our society*. For sooner or later you are going to have to be honest with your clients, and tell them how their behaviour affects you—and appears to be affecting others in their lives. In doing this, you will step over that line that separates 'unconditional positive regard' from 'taking a value position'. When a therapist confronts a client with words like, 'This sort of conduct is not acceptable', 'Your attitude is creating real problems for you', then they are most certainly taking a value position, acting as a moral arbiter or agent of social control, and needless to say, clients may react strongly to such wording.

It sounds like an ethical minefield, doesn't it! No wonder that Rogers and his followers insisted on the importance of being 'non-directive', no wonder that today's Narrative therapists constantly talk about being 'respectful' of their clients' cultures-of-origin and their individual values. In very different ways, both these practices allow practitioners to avoid seeming 'judgemental' or 'morally superior'. But if followed to the letter (which in reality they rarely are), these rules would prevent us from ever offering what our clients might need most from us: an honest reaction to their conduct, from someone who is disinterested (which in its true sense means 'unbiased', not 'uninterested'), who is motivated by the client's well being, not their own, and who is prepared to say to them what their parents, partners or even best friends may never have been willing to say.

Offering this sort of feedback seems like an awesome responsibility. How can we possibly set ourselves up as authorities on what makes a human being in our society 'happy' or 'normal'? Even concepts of what is 'destructive' or 'inappropriate' conduct will vary considerably from one culture to another—and from one family to another, within a culture. The helping professions are full of individuals who are only too happy to voice their prejudices and judgements in response to their hapless clients—telling parents that they are 'abusive', telling couples that 'they should separate because their relationship is 'unhealthy', telling adult children that their parents were 'toxic' and so on. How is this different from what we're talking about here? Well, there is a difference, and it is a very important one.

Good therapists or counsellors have done their personal work. They recognise their own wish to 'rescue' others in order to make themselves feel good, or their wish to 'read the riot act' to others in order to make themselves feel powerful. (Remember Chapter 1, where we asked you to think about the underlying reasons you might have for wanting to be a counsellor?) They know where, in their own personal histories, the impulses to attack or appease come from, and they know how to 'take a step back' when these impulses (regarded as aspects of 'countertransference' in the psychodynamic tradition) arise in a session. They have become aware of the unexamined values of the families in which they grew up and of the taken-for-granted values of the culture of which they are a product.

Of course counsellors will not always get it right—but those who have never explored their own inner worlds, who have never honestly considered the impact of their behaviour on others, will get it wrong as often as they get it right. Most of us are perfectly capable of offering sensitive, non-judgemental feedback on how this client affects us, and how others in the client's life seem to be being affected by his conduct. We can do this accurately and appropriately, working directly from the client's own stated concerns, *provided only that we understand and monitor our own motives in doing so*.

Here is a simple example of such an 'honest reaction':

Therapist: You know, Tim, I've listened to you talk about this relationship over quite a few sessions now, and I've found myself wondering whether perhaps you're missing something. You've given me a very clear idea of how badly this young woman let you down, and how hurtful she was to you. I can appreciate how you must have felt, with her seeming to come so close, and then, when you said you were starting to love her, she seemed to back away and suddenly accused you of being 'making her feel like a prisoner'. But in all of this, you never say anything about what *you* might have done. It's like what happened had nothing to do with you. I guess I'm struggling a bit to see it that way. In every relationship breakdown that I know, each partner always plays a part in the breakdown. Of course often they don't realise how they might be contributing to what's going wrong. But they are. Without meaning to, they're actually inviting their partner to feel more distant from them, or to get angry with them, or to feel misunderstood, or whatever. I suppose I'm thinking, 'Surely Tim must have done something. It just doesn't quite add up, unless he has.' What do you think?

Quoting a statement like this without a broader context (what came before it, what triggered it, what followed after the therapist intervened in this way) is of limited usefulness. Later in the chapter, we'll be supplying some of the context for the above statement, so that you can develop a clearer understanding of when it might be appropriate to offer a client this kind of 'encounter with self'. But we hope that this brief example may indicate to you what kind of thing we mean when we talk about offering a client 'gentle honesty', informed by a sense of what usually happens between people. The therapist is certainly measuring the client's behaviour against a norm—and a judgement of a sort is implied—but we hope the statement will not strike you as 'judgemental'. It is simply calling attention to a 'telling gap'[3] in the client's account, and suggesting to him that his truth may not be the only truth.

Again this highlights the vital importance of having done your own personal work before, or concurrently with, your work with clients. There is no substitute for knowing how it feels to be vulnerable in the face of someone else's judgement, no substitute for the personal experience of being told an unpalatable truth by someone you have learned to trust. Yes, you may feel hurt, or angry, or shamed—but part of you also knows that your therapist is not telling you this truth in order to hurt you, shame you, or make you angry. She, or he, is exposing you to the cold wind of truth, but tempered with a sensitive awareness of your defences, your needs, and your vulnerabilities. Your therapist has had the courage to help you face what you cannot face alone, and if you are devastated, she or he will stay with you, and support you with empathy and warmth, as you struggle to let in what you need to know.

The skills of encountering require you to be more than simply a compassionate professional, motivated by a concern for your client's best interests. Encountering requires you to step beyond the safety of 'professional neutrality' into a place of vulnerability—as one human being to another. This is the spirit that Carl Rogers described as 'congruence'— being true to our own feelings, experiences and accumulated wisdom, not hiding behind 'expertise' or 'professional objectivity'. In Chapter 4, we saw how the skill of immediacy requires this kind of congruence—the counsellor's willingness to open up about his own sense of 'stuckness', not simply requiring the client to talk about *her* sense of 'stuckness'. Most of the skills of encountering require something similar from you: willingness to take a risk, and be open about your own experience of the client—but combined with your continuing 'non-anxious presence'. You cannot offer a confrontation, and then run away from it. You must face up to what you have said, just like your client must. In the remainder of this chapter, we've described the skills of encountering in sequence, from the least 'confronting' to the most, from the ones which simply build on what the client has been saying, to those that cut across the client's agenda, or offer a radical change of direction in a therapeutic process that has become 'bogged down'.

Pointing out a 'theme'

In 'pointing out a theme', the counsellor or therapist is simply connecting some parts of the client's ongoing story with other parts—but in so doing, may be inviting the client to notice something about his or her own life and relationships that may previously have been out of their awareness. In many ways, pointing out a theme is a logical extension of the skills of exploring that we outlined in Chapter 3. If you have listened well, you will be starting to see themes in your clients' stories, and patterns in the way that clients present those stories, too. The following dialogue is an example of what we mean, and in following the story of this particular client—the one to whom the therapist was responding in the brief example given earlier—we will help you to see how you need to build up to offering a client an 'encounter with self', first establishing a secure base with your client, and then proceeding step by step, checking frequently to ensure that your understanding of your client is accurate.

Therapist: So, Tim, you've told me about how this relationship ended, and how painful that was. Is this the first time that sort of thing has happened to you? With a relationship, I mean—what about earlier girlfriends? How have those relationships gone?

[The therapist asks an 'exploring' question, to open up a potential new area. She is aware that there is often a pattern to an individual's relationship history, and she wants a sense of how this client perceives his relationships generally.]

Client: Oh, they were totally different.

[He proceeds to describe two previous relationships where he eventually realised that the woman was 'not what he was looking for', and so brought the relationship to a close, although keen to emphasise that they have remained 'good friends' and still talk from time to time. The client's focus is on who was responsible for ending the relationship, and he sees his earlier relationships as 'different' *because it was he who ended them*, whereas in his most recent relationship, the woman 'dumped' him abruptly and painfully. The client's initial response dismisses the implication that there might be any similarities between the course of the three relationships. He does, however, provide a clue to his own contribution to the breakdown in stating that earlier girlfriends were 'not what he was looking for'. The therapist makes a mental note of this to explore later.]

Therapist: OK, so what made this recent experience so different was that this time it was her who ended it, whereas before, it had always been you who made the decision that the relationship was over?

[The therapist reflects the client's understanding of the events, and keeps on hold her own sense that something else might be involved, which the client is failing to notice.]

Client: That's right. Of course I felt a bit 'down' that those relationships didn't work out.

[Upbeat tone, indicating that he isn't connecting with any pain as he tells the story.]

But at least I knew why, and I could do something about it. It's not fair, to keep a woman dangling, you know, when inside you already know that it's not going anywhere. So I just tackled it, all out in the open, because that's my way. I just said to them, 'Hey, we both realise that this isn't working. There've been some really good times together, but overall, it's not what we want. So we need to call it quits'. That's the way I like to do it.

[The therapist wonders whether when the client says, 'It's not what *we* want', he actually means, 'It's not what *I* want', which is what he said earlier. The therapist decides to expand the picture by asking how the earlier girlfriends reacted.]

Therapist: You like to be open with your partner, make it plain how you see things. You see yourself as someone who isn't scared to face up to reality?

Client: That's exactly right. I think it's better for all concerned if it's out in the open. If it's not working, it's better to admit that it's not working, and make an end.

Therapist: OK, so when you did that...tackled the issue with them...how did they respond?

Client: Oh, well, they were pretty upset. Jan in particular, she was gutted for a while, said she'd thought we were going pretty good. But, you know, it was time for her to face the facts.

Therapist: Sounds like you were very clear about where you stood in the relationship with Jan. Only she wasn't standing in the same place?

[The therapist subtly introduces the possibility that Tim's partner might have seen things very differently from the way he did.]

Client: Yeah, well, I suppose so. But hey, someone has to do it, right? She was just hiding her head in the sand. I realised what was going on, and I took action. Someone needed to do something, it was just dragging on, and the end result is that she just would've got hurt even more if I hadn't said anything.

Therapist: Hmm. You wanted to spare her the hurt, and you also wanted to act decisively, so that it didn't 'drag on'. Sounds like you'd made up your mind, and when you make up your mind, you go straight in there, and do something about it, because then the situation's resolved?

Client: That's right, I don't like things that are murky and sort of ... you know, you don't know where you stand. She's clinging on, but it's for the wrong reasons, and I don't want to be living with that.

Therapist: You like things to be clear, and you don't like things to be ambiguous, or, you know, messy. Is that right? [client nods agreement] And that's how you have been in all your adult relationships. You know what you want, you know when it's not happening. There's no room for being unsure, or having a bet both ways.

[Again, the therapist's wording hints that perhaps the client's belief excludes any possibilities other than the ones he feels comfortable with.]

Client: No, that's right. I always know what I want. I'm the same at work. I don't beat about the bush ... if a job's not what I need, I just hand in my notice, and find something better. I don't like staying around where I'm not wanted.

Therapist: That sounds a bit painful...to be working with people who don't want you.

Client: Well I wouldn't say 'painful', I'd say, 'unsatisfactory'.

[Client rejects a word that speaks directly to feelings that he cannot yet connect with.]

Therapist: Unsatisfactory, OK. But what you're telling me is that 'murky' situations are hard for you.

['Hard for you' implies feelings, but does not name them. This sort of language is going to be easier for the client to hear than words like 'painful', which he backs away from.]

You don't like them at work, and you don't like them in your personal relationships either. You want to cut to the chase, and get out of those situations. It's difficult for

> you to hang in there when there's a conflict between what you want and what other people want.

[Here, finally, is the 'theme', stated unequivocally. The therapist could have gone a step further and re-stated this theme more strongly: *When someone else doesn't see it your way, you don't feel safe any more and you want to get out. You don't even consider the possibility that the difference might be talked through or resolved.* The therapist doesn't do this, because she realises that right now, the client would reject such an explicit statement or see it as an unfair criticism.]

Client: That's exactly right.

At this point, some of you are probably wondering how pointing out a theme is any different from simply offering a summary of what the client has been saying. And that's a fair comment. Skills can be distinguished from one another only up to a point. Despite the neat categories that textbooks set up, it is probably most useful to see the various skills as existing on a continuum, where one skill may 'shade into' the next one. Drawing clients' attention to a theme is somewhat similar to offering an illuminating summary. Perhaps the 'edge of difference' is that when you point out a theme, you are concentrating on one single strand in what the client has been saying, and stating it in such a way that it emerges unmistakably as a distinct aspect of the client's way of seeing the world, way of relating, way of thinking about him/herself.

Thus 'stating a theme' begins to merge into 'offering feedback'. It can even be viewed as a mild form of confrontation—which is why it appears in this chapter. But (as we emphasised earlier) statements of a theme cannot be offered without careful preparation, and in the above example, you will have noticed how much ground the therapist covers first, and how careful she is to 'feel into' her client before she explicitly states to him the pattern she has noticed in his accounts of both his personal and his work life.

CONNECTING PAST AND PRESENT: SUGGESTING A MEANING

In Chapter 3, we introduced the skill of connecting present experience with past experience as part of 'exploring'. But this, too, can go beyond exploration into an 'encounter with self'. To begin with, it is important not to assume that clients have failed to notice such connections. It can be useful to ask, 'How would you connect X with Y?', where 'X' is something in the present or recent past, and 'Y' is something in the past (often, the client's childhood). This gives clients the opportunity to make the connection for themselves. Here is an example, again using the male client you have met in earlier dialogues in this chapter.

Therapist: You've agreed that you don't like things to be unclear and unresolved. I think 'murky' was the word you used for that feeling. I wonder how that might connect with what you experienced when your Mum left your Dad, and you said you 'felt very confused'? I think you were around six years old at the time, is that right?

Client: Right, I was six, or maybe seven, I can't remember now. It isn't really that clear-cut, because I think they'd been fighting a lot before that, well, really I can't remember a time when they weren't shouting, and Mum wasn't walking out the door and saying she wasn't coming back.

Therapist: Can you recall what it was like for you after they actually split up? Can you remember what you thought?

Client: I don't know. It was a helluva long time ago. [pause] I know that when I was living with Dad, he used to blame Mum a lot, say she broke up the family, that sort of thing. And when I was living with Mum, she used to say I didn't understand how hard it was to live with a drinker. It was like they were still fighting, only sort of at a distance, you know? I didn't know what I was supposed to say. Mum seemed to need me to agree with her, so I'd agree, and then when I'd be with Dad, he'd say the opposite, and I'd feel kind of bad, for believing Mum. I ended up just not saying anything.

Therapist: Here were these two big people, the most important people in your life, and they both seemed to be right, and you were caught between them, and there wasn't a thing you could do about it. I'm guessing that you hated feeling so helpless, so out of control?

[The therapist's use of 'big people' speaks direct to the child part of the client, inviting him to re-enter the way he felt at that time. In fact, he accepts the therapist's statement only in a distanced, cognitive way, probably because the therapist has used the word 'helpless'. He doesn't want to feel helpless—in fact his whole adult life has been designed to avoid that feeling.]

Client: Yep. Well, I can't remember, but that's probably how I felt, yeah.

Therapist: So looking backwards to how you felt then, and forwards to now—how you behave in your adult relationships—what do you think?

[The therapist persists in asking the client to make the connection.]

Client: Ah … well actually, it's not the same at all. As a kid, you don't get to have any say. But when you're an adult, you do, and that makes things a lot more bearable.

Therapist: So what you're saying is that as a child you had no say, no control over what happened to you, but now you do, and the position you've taken is that if you're in a relationship with a woman, and things have gotten difficult or unclear, it's up to you to make a decision one way or the other?

Client: That's pretty right.

Therapist: Maybe you need to be in control now, because back then you couldn't be?

[Here the therapist actually makes an 'interpretation'—see below—which goes well beyond the client's own understanding at this point.]

Client: That's a bit over the top, isn't it? I mean, why does everything you do as an adult have to be related to what happened when you were a kid? Aren't we free to do what we choose, once we're grown up? Isn't that the whole point?

[The client is becoming defensive—scared at the implication that in some way his past experience might be 'influencing' his present behaviour. The therapist chooses not to enter into an intellectualised argument, but returns to the central theme of the client's strong need for control.]

Therapist: It's hard to contemplate that idea...that you might be being controlled by what happened to you in the past? Nobody wants to think that they're not free to choose.

Client: No, that's right. And now that you put it that way, I'm thinking that I've built my whole life since I left home around being free to be me, and do what's right for me. That's always seemed the most important thing, in my career … in my personal life too. Every decision I've made, I've always thought, 'What do I need to do here, so I don't get screwed around? What do I need to do to protect myself?'

[Here, the client finally begins to take on board some of the therapist's interpretation of his behaviour.]

119

Therapist: What do you need to do, to not feel helpless ever again? Perhaps like you've made a promise to yourself not to feel that way ever again?

Client: [long silence].

Maybe he is pondering the validity of what the therapist has just said, or maybe he has retreated from the pain of the feeling. There are no words to tell us. However, the client's body language is eloquent. He hunches down into himself, and his eyes are fixed and distant. Eventually, the therapist asks directly.]

Therapist: What's been going on? What's been happening for you there?

Client: I don't want to feel at anybody's mercy. It's horrible. I hate it, and I suppose I do pull out of relationships because of that. I guess I think that if I stay there and it keeps getting murkier, I'll...I don't know, lose my freedom, or something? Like, if I don't get out then and there, I'll *never* get out!

[The client has started to 'work' on the issue. He is thinking for himself, making his own connections, entering into his feelings.]

In the dialogue you've just read, you can see how helping clients to connect present and past is not necessarily simple or easy. The dialogue has touched on the client's need to be in control of 'murky' or ambiguous or conflicted situations, but as yet, he is not able to acknowledge just how strong his need to control others has been, and still is. You can also see, in the above example, how connecting past and present has involved making an 'interpretation'. In focussing on the client's helplessness as a child (something he has not stated, and perhaps is not fully aware of), and linking it with his powerful need to be 'in control' (i.e. not helpless) in adult relationships, the therapist has gone beyond acknowledging a theme, and beyond the simple connection of past and present. She is, essentially, inviting the client to view his current adult behaviour in a new light—as a reflection of his strong (and understandable) response to childhood feelings of helplessness at the hands of powerful, 'controlling' others. This kind of insight, whether self-generated by clients, or 'assisted into birth' by professionals, is part of the territory of psychotherapy. You can see, from the examples of 'limited' interpretation we have given here, that from time to time, if you work intensively in a relational way with your clients, you will inevitably make some use of interpretation.

ACKNOWLEDGING CONTRADICTIONS AND DISCREPANCIES

In Chapter 3, we saw how part of exploring was drawing attention to omissions in the client's account, and asking directly about them. Pointing out contradictions in the client's self-presentation is similar, but goes a step further. Now, as counsellors, you are helping your clients to notice the discrepancies between what they say and what they do, or between what they say on one occasion, and what they say on another. Here is an example, this time with a different client:

Therapist: So, Janine, you're telling me that you're really upset at how little help you get from your Mum. You feel all alone with your kids, and she's not offering to help. But then last week you said that she actually minds your son for one day every week. I'm having a bit of difficulty understanding what's going on here. From what you've told me, it looks like she is willing to help out. But you don't feel like she's interested in helping you. Can we talk about what's happening for you here?

Client: Well, yeah, I suppose she does help. And she loves having him. But I hate having to ask her. I don't feel like I can approach her to ask her to mind Kerry as well as Tim.

Therapist:	OK, so it's not that she isn't willing to help, it's more that you feel this block to asking her [sympathetically]. The thought of asking her to help again…that's really difficult for you. Can you say a bit more about that?
Client:	Oh, I don't know [sighs]. It's just all too hard. Why does it have to be so hard? Why can't she just offer … Why do I have to come to her, and kind of beg on my knees, when she's there living her own life, enjoying her freedom, you know, and spending her money…and I'm really struggling!
Therapist:	It feels quite unfair. She's got her life together, and you haven't, yet you have to beg her to help. And maybe too, it sounds like you're quite angry that it has to be this way?

[The counsellor is picking up on the sigh, and 'It's all too hard'.]

Client:	[long pause]. Yes, I am angry. I don't want to ask her. I'm too angry to ask her.
Therapist:	Maybe asking her would sort of put you in her power, and you don't want to feel in her power? You're too angry to make yourself vulnerable in that way?
Client:	That's exactly how it feels. She wasn't there for me when I was growing up, and she should've been. It really goes against the grain, to be asking her to help me now!

In that example, the counsellor's pointing out of an apparent contradiction in the client's account leads to the client revealing more clearly the anger that underlies her 'stuckness'. The counsellor draws attention to that anger, which the client has not explicitly acknowledged, but only hinted at, in part, non-verbally. This intervention is what the followers of Rogers called 'advanced accurate empathy'—putting into words a feeling that seems to hover in the air, without actually being voiced. Again this moves towards what psychodynamic therapists would regard as 'interpretation'. In the counsellor's final intervention in the above dialogue, we can see interpretation 'out in the open'. The counsellor has stepped beyond the client, suggesting a possible explanation for the client's seemingly self-defeating behaviour. This explanation depends upon a tension, an inner conflict, of which the client seems to be unaware. In this case, the client immediately embraces the interpretation. It 'fits' for her, she has a small moment of revelation, as a missing piece is supplied that fits the 'gap' in the jigsaw puzzle of her own actions and feelings.

It is important that a contradiction or discrepancy be pointed out in a factual way, so that it does not sound like an accusation that the client is lying, concealing the truth, or incapable of logical thought. As we saw earlier, the word 'disinterested' originally meant 'neutral' or 'free of bias' (although today, people mostly use it to mean 'bored'). We need to be *disinterested*, in this original sense, when we confront a client with an apparent contradiction. Our client should feel that we are a committed observer of what they have said, keen to understand what is going on. *Curiosity* is the term that has been employed by family therapists to describe this stance, and more recently the favoured term has been a 'not knowing' attitude. In many ways, all of these correspond with what psychodynamic therapists call 'evenly hovering attention' (that is, being equally 'interested' in everything the client says). Often, as a counsellor, you might start your 'confrontation' by saying, 'I'm interested that …' or 'I'm curious about …' This frames the rest of the statement as about exploration—finding out something new— rather than accusation (*'You've just said the exact opposite of what you said a minute ago! What's wrong with you?'*) If you point out a contradiction or discrepancy in a spirit of judgement, your client will most likely 'close down', and lock into defending themselves against your accusation, when what you hoped for is for them to realise something about themselves.

Of course it is also possible to say 'I'm curious to know …' in a way that sounds 'superior' and 'expert'. It all depends on your tone of voice, and in turn, your tone of voice depends on how you actually feel towards your client. If you feel superior and judgemental, then that will probably come across in your tone, and you will need to look at what is going on for you. If you feel angry and frustrated with your client, then that, too, will colour the way you frame your statement.

Practice task

Melbourne psychologist and family therapist Moshe Lang devised an excellent experiment around confrontation, which he called 'Bad Therapy'. It is used in supervision situations when therapists report being 'stuck' with clients, often because the therapist feels angry, disappointed or judgemental—feelings that she or he knows 'should not be expressed'. The therapist is convinced that stating those feelings would only do harm, and destroy the client's trust. Some therapists are overwhelmed by guilt that they actually feel such responses. Yet the feelings are there, and they get in the way of doing good, productive work with the clients. The therapist is 'blocked', and cannot help the clients to work through their own 'blocks'.

In this situation, Moshe would have the therapist participate in a role-played 'session', in which other counsellors (members of a supervision or training group) would take the parts of the client, or clients. Once it was clear what was going on, the therapist would be instructed to say, in the role play, exactly what he or she would most like to say, in the most 'untherapeutic' language. In other words, to *deliberately do 'bad therapy'*. The effect of this is very freeing. Typically, therapists feel relief and exhilaration at having openly acknowledged their 'real feelings'. Typically, those who played the roles of clients respond far less negatively than the therapist expected they would. A variety of possibilities then opens up, described in full in Lang's article 'Bad Therapy: A Training Technique', (*Australian Journal of Family Therapy*, 1, 3 (1980): 102-109). The usual outcome was that the previously 'stuck' therapists would report going into their next session with the real client, and offering a confrontation which 'really worked', surprising themselves with how honest they could be, without alienating their clients.

Our own guess about this technique is that when the therapists were given permission to say what they honestly felt towards their clients in a safe setting of the supervision group, the experience of acknowledging their 'destructive' opinions enabled them to go back to their real clients with greater confidence to be honest—although their wording was probably rendered more tactful by the presence of the clients themselves. We suggest that Lang's exercise is just as applicable in training contexts. For example, you might, in class, use the psychodramatic method, where one student first takes the counsellor's chair and makes their 'harmful' or 'blaming' statement, and then shifts to occupy the empty chair, and, taking the role of the client, responds as that client. The roles are then reversed again, and the student, as counsellor, offers the 'revised version', and then takes the client's role to respond to the modified confrontation.

We have also noticed time and again how *simply discussing a 'stuck' therapeutic situation with a supervisor or trainer, and acknowledging the feelings involved, can itself result in an 'unsticking' without the therapist needing to actually say anything to the client.* At the very next session after the supervision consultation, the therapist finds that the clients themselves seem to have 'shifted': they come in acknowledging something they have previously denied, willing to accept more responsibility for their situations. It is almost as if the therapist's 'unblocking' in supervision has somehow affected the clients—even though the latter have no knowledge that the supervision discussion has taken place! Here is 'parallel process' in action (see further below).

BEYOND TRANSFERENCE INTERPRETATION:

OFFERING FEEDBACK IN THE HERE AND NOW

The topic of 'feedback in the here and now' has already been discussed in Chapter 4, where we introduced the skill of 'immediacy'. And earlier in the chapter you are now reading, we gave an example of how a therapist might confront a client, drawing on the therapist's own sense that something in the client's account 'doesn't add up'. Now it's time to return to the therapist–client 'encounter' in its purest form; offering clients here and now feedback, based on sensitive awareness of their strengths and weaknesses, combined with compassionate understanding of the earlier experiences that have shaped how they now they act and feel.

As you know, traditional psychoanalytic therapy places a lot of emphasis on something called 'transference interpretation'. Transference interpretation connects the patient's behaviour towards the therapist with his/her relationship to a parent, or other significant authority figure, in childhood. For example:

Therapist: You seem very deferential to me, and you seem reluctant to disagree with anything I say. I wonder if you might have felt the same towards your Mum? From what you've told me, you expected her to criticise you whenever you opened your mouth. Perhaps it feels like I'm going to do the same?

In offering this sort of interpretation, psychoanalytic therapists traditionally remained detached, revealing little of themselves, apart from stating how the patient's behaviour has struck them. However, such interpretations can also serve as a kind of feedback to clients, surprising them with the awareness of how their current behaviour might actually affect another person (in this case, their therapist, but by extension, other important people in their world). If the patient feels safe to be really honest within the therapeutic relationship, information that the therapist did not anticipate might emerge from such a transference interpretation. This involves both parties in a person-to-person encounter, in which the therapist must be both disciplined and spontaneous, both tactful and honest. That is not an easy assignment, and that is why, towards the end of Chapter 4, we recommended participation in 'Here and Now' group experiences as an important training-ground for such person-to-person encounters.

Let's look at how an intervention like the one we just quoted might lead to an 'authentic encounter', in which the therapist has to be more of a person, and less of an 'objective commentator':

Client: Well, um—I suppose I am scared that you'll criticise me. Sometimes your voice sounds kind of, I don't know, sort of cold or something, as if you're going to tell me about something I've done that's wrong. Every time you say, 'I'm interested that you use that word', I start to feel tense, because I know you're going to disapprove of something about me.

[At this point, the therapist could choose to continue exploring the 'transference dimension' of the client's statement, focussing on the 'child' part of her, which expects criticism at the hands of a judgemental parent. But there is an alternative pathway, where the therapist can choose to become engaged at a more personal level, as Yalom would advocate, offering 'here and now' feedback.]

Therapist: You're telling me that you feel sort of in awe of me, as if you've somehow got to please me, because otherwise I'm going to criticise you and tell you all the things you've done wrong. Well, I suppose that in response, I often find myself feeling kind of on a pedestal, as if I have all this power over you. Really, you know, I don't—and the fact that you're trying so hard to please me—you know, that's an uncomfortable feeling for me.

Client: You know, when you said that, I suddenly felt a surge of anger towards you. Like, what right do you have to be on a pedestal? And how come I put you there in the first place? I guess it's me that's doing it, isn't it!

Therapist: Well, that's right. I didn't ask to be on a pedestal, and it does feel like you're putting me there. Maybe that's something we could talk about together, and try to find out more about it?

Such a sudden burst of authentic feeling may be 'news' to both the therapist and the client. In this case, it triggers a revelation for the client—the realisation that instead of something being done to her by the therapist, it is she who is 'doing it' to herself. It is a moment she will not likely forget, and it has provided new insight into how she comes across to a significant person in her life. Yalom, whose own original training had been psychoanalytic, taught students to 'forget the transference', and to focus on the real therapist–client relationship unfolding in the room—using the 'here and now' feelings of both parties as a vehicle for the client's growth and self-awareness. Carl Rogers had described such interactions as 'authentic encounters' between two human beings, in which the client or patient would trust the therapist enough to share honest reactions, and the therapist would be 'congruent' enough to recognise what he/she was feeling towards the client, and share it appropriately, in a spirit of equality and dialogue.

'Here and now' dialogue between client and therapist is normally initiated by the therapist, because it represents a departure from the norms of social conversation, and most clients would not risk expressing such feelings towards a 'professional' even if they were fully aware of them in the first place. However, the therapist does not initiate such a dialogue in order to teach the client something that the therapist already knows. The therapist initiates it in response to his or her own sense of discomfort or lack of fit: something is not quite right in the way the two of them are relating, that something is getting in the way of the client's ability to freely express thoughts and feelings, This 'something' may turn out to be 'transference' (in the classic psychoanalytic sense) or it may turn out to be partly a result of the way the therapist is behaving (perhaps the result of his or her own prior interpersonal experiences and schemas—'counter transference'). By opening up a space to talk about the process between them, the therapist allows the possibility for something new to be discovered. Both parties will 'discover' it, not just the client.

When such a discovery occurs, there will be a palpable shift in the feeling in the room. After some minutes of heightened arousal (rapid heart beat, a rush of adrenaline—the body's sign that something important is happening), both client and therapist may feel more relaxed, less anxious. Feelings flow more freely. The therapist can feel more empathy for the client, and the client can feel more trust in the therapist. Often, the client's level of self disclosure deepens, or the initial focus shifts to something more central to the client's self. Just as with any form of 'immediacy', an impasse has been dissolved. As we have noted several times earlier in this book, the kind of self-disclosure that a therapist would use in such encounters is limited to how he or she feels in the room (here and now). The therapist will not normally go on to talk about his or her own past experiences, or the source of his/her feelings of discomfort at being 'put on a pedestal'. These things would invite the client to focus on the therapist, and distract from the possibility of the client exploring the personal learning that the encounter opens up. It might also invite the client to think that the therapist needs help, and that she, the client, should offer it—which would of course undermine the special *non-reciprocal* relationship (see Chapter 5) that makes therapy a 'safe place for change'.

While it is perfectly possible for therapists to offer clients feedback at any time after a sound relational basis is established, such feedback has more impact and more chance of promoting lasting learning and change if it comes in relation to a 'real event' in the therapy room. Again, this is something that Irvin Yalom talks about persuasively in the book that distils a lifetime's wisdom, *The Gift of Therapy*. If the client comes late, forgets to turn off the mobile phone, or seems unduly preoccupied with the fact that the therapist's door is hard to close—any behaviour that signals that 'something may be going on'—that is the time for the therapist to open up a discussion of the event in relation to how the client may be feeling towards the therapist.

Client: Something I really hate…I know this is going to sound silly, but…I really hate sitting in the waiting room until my session time. There's all these other people around, and I see people coming out [from the corridor where the therapist has her consulting room] and I wonder if one of them is your last client, and I look at them and think about what they might have been talking to you about, and whether they might be really frustrating or difficult for you to deal with. I know I shouldn't think like that, but I do.

Therapist: Maybe it's hard to share me with other people? You know I have other clients, but you don't see them and you don't know who they are. But you think about them, and you wonder about them. Maybe you wonder if you might be difficult for me to deal with, too? Maybe you wonder if I might prefer some of my other clients to you?

Client: Well, um, yes, I do, actually, but it's so embarrassing having, you know, this... [Covers her eyes. A long pause follows.] Well, I guess I don't feel like I'm a very interesting person, and I feel very stuck, and I haven't got any big changes to tell you about, so I guess I start to worry that you might be getting bored with me.

WHEN THE CHALLENGE COMES FROM THE CLIENT

While many 'immediacy' dialogues are initiated by therapists, some are initiated by clients. Here we return to something we mentioned briefly near the beginning of this chapter: the situation of parents whose adolescent son or daughter confronts them with, 'You don't understand me!' or 'You're making it worse for me!' Such challenges, as we saw earlier, are painful for parents who are genuinely trying to do their best, and they can easily leave the parents, in turn, feeling 'misunderstood', as if their love and care are being attacked or dismissed in a blaming or judgemental way. It is much the same when clients come in (much later than the third session, when therapy is well under way and things appear to be going reasonably well) and launch into an open or veiled attack on the therapist:

Client: Look, I've been thinking about our sessions, and you know, I have to tell you that I'm not sure that things aren't actually getting worse since I started coming here. I'm not saying it's your fault or anything

['But who else's fault could it really be?' thinks the therapist.]

I'm sure you're doing your job in a very professional way. Maybe that's the trouble, though. I just feel that you're so professional, so clinical, that you don't really relate to me and my problems. What you say sounds like it comes out of a textbook ... like that big red one on your shelf over there, what's it called ... *Problem Personalities in Clinical Practice*! I wonder if that's how you see me, you know, as a kind of 'case study' or something. Are you planning to write a thesis on me?

Obviously, it is not easy to be confronted in this way, but it does sometimes happen. However, such an 'attack' can sometimes open up a pathway to authentic dialogue in much the same way as we have described above:

Therapist: Well, what you've said has really taken me aback. I wasn't expecting you to say that. But if that's how you're feeling about our sessions, then we need to talk about it, and I'm glad you've been prepared to bring it out in the open.

[Notice that, although the therapist feels some anger and shock, he acknowledges only the surface of his feelings, and directs the ball back into the client's court. However, he neither angrily accuses the client of being 'unfair', nor starts into, 'Oh, dear, I've got it wrong!']

Client: Uh...OK. But what's to say? I've told you how I feel, haven't I?

Therapist: I guess the bit that really seemed important to me was the bit about thinking that you were just a textbook case to me ... that you didn't really matter to me, is that what you've been feeling?

Client: Well, yeah ... not quite as bad as that, I suppose, but, yeah, I keep thinking that you must see all these people all the time, with all these different problems, and to you I'm just another one in the line, you know. How could I matter to you?

Therapist: Well, it's not unreasonable for you to think that way. This therapy thing is pretty unusual really, isn't it? You come here and pay me money, and I listen to you and do my best to be helpful to you. But then you walk away from here, and that's the only contact we ever have, and you know full well that after you leave, there's the next patient in the waiting room, right? Perhaps that feels as though you don't count, you're just one in a crowd?

Client: That's about it. But it's partly how you talk to me, as well. Like you never tell me anything about yourself. Like you're keeping me out or something, you don't want me to know you.

Therapist: I can understand that it could feel that way to you. This is so different from any other relationship. OK, suppose I did tell you more about myself, or what I thought or felt… how do you think that would affect you?

[While not rushing to self-disclose in response to the client's challenge, the therapist finds a way to explore what the client's wish to know more about her actually means to the client.]

Client: I think I'd feel a lot more at ease, and I wouldn't feel so exposed… like, you know all this stuff about me, and I have to trust you, but it doesn't go the other way. It seems so unequal.

Therapist: Well, you're right … it *is* unequal. Like a parent and maybe a sixteen-year-old … the sixteen-year-old is sure that she can make her own decisions, and doesn't want to have to be told or warned or whatever. And that's natural. But the parent knows that she can't just assume that the girl knows it all, and just sit back and let her do things that are risky and may have serious consequences. So the parent steps in and gives a warning, or advice, and of course the girl resents it, but in a way, she'd feel unsafe if the parent didn't do that…she'd feel abandoned, I think.

Client: See, there you go again. You've turned it into something about me as a kid, not something about me now. I'm not a sixteen-year-old, I'm an adult. I don't know how old you are, but you don't look all that much older than me. I know how to run my life, you know?

Therapist: It feels like I'm ducking out of responsibility? Hiding behind the theory a bit?

Client: It certainly does. I can do without your judgements, and I wish you gave me a bit of praise sometimes for the things I'm doing right, instead of just commenting on the things I don't get right. I feel bad enough about those as it is!

Therapist: You'd like me to be a bit less like a critical parent, and recognise that you're doing pretty well in many ways. Is that it? [client nods agreement] Well, let me have a think about that [pause]. Listening to you talk, I wonder if I've failed to realise how much you need to feel accepted, and by not actually praising you, I've played into that feeling that you never get noticed for good reasons, you only get noticed when you do something wrong. Maybe I've missed something important there, something that's very important to you?

Client: That's right. That's how it feels. And it feels better to hear you say that maybe you've missed something. Like you're really listening to me. Like I do matter to you.

Now of course, in the dialogue we've just presented, it would have been perfectly possible for the therapist to simply continue to interpret everything the client said in terms of 'transference'—her longing to be praised, her feeling of being judged, her lifelong pattern of thinking that she only gets attention for being 'bad'. The therapist could have gone on batting it all back to the client, and refusing to accept any responsibility for the client's painful feeling that she isn't cared about. But this therapist is alert to the genuineness of the client's complaint, and, reflecting on her own behaviour, recognises that perhaps she has been partly responsible for the client's distress. She knows 'her own stuff' may be playing a part in what has happened. So she pulls back, and accepts some responsibility, sharing her 'shift' with the client. By modifying her own behaviour, and offering more praise and recognition, the therapist helps the client to gain a here-and-now experience of being attended to, taken seriously. The client's faith that things can change in her relationships is strengthened. This is the 'corrective emotional experience', a term first used by Franz Alexander.[4] When we, as therapists, are able to act in a way that is more flexible, more accepting, and more self-aware than the way the client's parents acted, then we are doing a small bit of 're-parenting'. And that, as we hinted in Chapter 5, lies at the core of the 'relational' approach to change. If clients realise that *we* can 'be different', can change our behaviour in relation to a challenge or plea from them, then they begin to develop trust that they can change too. That is how human beings are: we grow through relationship, and what we learn about a significant other person is also what we learn about ourselves.

In conclusion

If you are drawn to the notion that change occurs within a relational context, and believe that the most powerful changes occur in direct interaction between therapist and client, then hopefully, this chapter will have made sense to you. Even if you think the 'relationship model' a good fit for you personally, however, this does not mean that you will necessarily find it easy to develop the capacity to intervene in some of the ways we have been describing. Nor, as beginners, should you expect yourself to. Few beginners can consistently handle difficult confrontations and offer sensitive feedback to clients until they have had considerable experience of many different clients in medium and long term work, and processed their experiences in regular supervision. We hope that you, as students early in your training, will see this chapter as a useful map of what may lie ahead for you, further down the track. The most important thing we want you to grasp at this stage is that powerful 'here and now' encounters which confront clients with surprising truths about themselves cannot be staged in a vacuum. Rather, they come about only after much careful exploration, and preparation, often over many sessions. As we've repeatedly said in this book, the capacity to intervene in the ways described in this chapter depends heavily on your having experienced some or all of these interventions as a client in your own therapy. You need to know how it feels to have a theme brought to your attention, how it feels to connect past and present in a new way, how it feels to be told how you come across to your therapist. Without this crucial experience, you will be far less sure of yourself in handling similar encounters with your clients.

Some of you, on the other hand, may have read this chapter thinking, 'Yes, that's all very well—but it's not me. I know I couldn't interact with clients that way. And I'm not even sure that it's going to help them'. For those readers, Chapter 7 will provide a model that is more clearly focussed on the problems clients bring, and how we can assist them to change their behaviour in order to resolve their own problems, or influence the behaviour of others.

Chapter Summary

- The skills of encounter constitute the heart of the relational model of helping. They assist clients to change by deeper self-insight and self-confrontation, in which the therapist plays a more active role than he/she does in holding or exploring

- These skills come into play when the therapeutic relationship is solidly established.

Premature moves into challenge or offering feedback may cause clients to withdraw from therapy

- Skills of encounter require that the therapist demonstrate courage, sensitivity to client vulnerabilities, and most of all, good timing. Encounters between client and therapist require judgement calls as to 'how much reality' a particular client is likely to tolerate at any given time. Without the capacity for courage, good judgement and good timing, these skills can be risky.

- Skills of encounter attempt to move clients beyond their current level of self-awareness, by drawing their attention to connections, themes, 'blind spots', contradictions and denied inner conflicts. In this way, the skills of encounter shade over into what psychoanalytic therapy traditionally called 'interpretation'

- Confrontations with painful truths should never be offered 'cold'. They should form the final stage in a (sometimes slow) process in which clients learn to feel safe in approaching material or insights which they have defended themselves against lifelong

- 'Encounter' in its fullest sense directly involves the relationship between therapist and client. Naming openly what has been unspoken between the two, talking honestly about impasses in the relationship, and responding to client challenges of unhelpfulness can result in deeper self disclosure by the client, and shifts of attitude and behaviour

- The offering of here-and-now feedback requires 'gentle honesty'—a delicate balance between directness and diplomacy. It exposes the therapist's vulnerability as well as the client's. When well done, however, it often 'shifts' the client like nothing else, and constitutes part of that 'corrective emotional experience' which can be such a key to successful therapy.

Chapter 7

'Giving Wise Advice': The Skills Of Coaching

Meeting as equals

Throughout this book, we have used analogies drawn from parenting to help you understand what clients need from you, and how you may feel towards them. Perhaps some of you saw this, at first, as a bit patronising—'infantilising' clients or 'encouraging dependency', and putting the counsellor, by implication, in the position of power. We hope that any such misunderstandings will have been well and truly dispelled by now. Comparisons between counselling and parenting (some of them long established in the literature of professional helping) are not putdowns. Of course we do not see clients as helpless, wordless 'babies' or as impulsive, hormone-dominated 'teenagers'. Our developmental analogies are intended to remind you that at any given stage in the counselling process, you are going to be dealing not only with the rational adult who sits opposite you, but with that adult's younger selves who may be, in varying degrees, at different times, helpless, needy, distressed, rebellious, confused, and in search of a truth that is their own. It is these younger selves that counselling and therapy must address if the work is to be lasting and effective.

However, in this chapter, we will be describing something different. Conscious change work with motivated clients speaks to the rational, choosing adult within clients, rather than the confused, frightened or angry child. This is why we have used the term *coaching* to describe the skills described in this chapter. A coach works with an athlete's conscious motivation to improve, to reach her 'personal best'. A coach sets physical tasks and mental exercises that he or she knows will lift an athlete's level of performance, and generally speaking, coaches can depend on their athletes undertaking those tasks and exercises. Encouragement and praise for achievement are part of the equipment of most coaches (admittedly, some also use scorn, anger, and disappointment to motivate under-performers, which a counsellor would rarely, if ever, do).

However, just like counsellors, coaches also have to deal with 'resistance', which may well be partly or wholly unconscious in nature. Athletes and team members, like our clients, are perfectly capable of sabotaging their own potential, and can act in ways that contradict their consciously chosen goals. If that happens, the coach needs more than just lectures, homework tasks, encouragement and praise. In our profession, even with highly motivated clients, we must always be prepared to drop down to the child level, when the client needs this from us. In the counsellor–client dialogues later in this chapter, you will see many examples of counsellors moving flexibly between dealing with the client's adult (as transactional analysis would call it) and the client's younger selves, because the wish to change oneself is not a straightforward process. If it were straightforward, our profession would have no function, because everyone who desired to change would already have accomplished it without needing professional help!

Some of you may be wondering whether reading this chapter will make you a 'life coach'? No. What exactly life coaching is, and how it differs from counselling, is not within the scope of this book. The term *life coach* is one of those re-brandings that counselling/therapy seems to go through at intervals. Telling others that you're 'seeing a life coach' may make the pursuit of personal change look less embarrassing than telling them that you're 'seeing a counsellor'. Remember, too, that psychoanalysis was once trendy and cool (not the words they would have used in the 1920s, of course) at least to some people. In our view, change coaching is part of the territory of counselling: part, but not the most important part, or the part that should necessarily be addressed straightway.

'GIVING WISE ADVICE'

Traditionally, counsellors and therapists are not supposed to give advice. As we saw in Chapter 5, Carl Rogers insisted upon that, and his view has remained influential in the subsequent history of relationship-focused helping. In place of an orthodox psychoanalyst's blank-screen silence or transference interpretation, Rogers' paraphrase (reflection) conveyed understanding and empathy, but still refused to answer clients' questions, implying that clients themselves were the ones with the answer:

Client: So, what do you think? Do you think I'm normal? Are these problems sort of ordinary ones, or do they mean I'm crazy? I really want to know what you think.

Counsellor: You're concerned that there might be something really wrong with you, and you'd really feel reassured if I told you that you were just experiencing normal problems, like anybody else.

As we saw in Chapter 4, providing opinions and advice in the early stages of a therapeutic relationship is often unwise: counsellors are unlikely to be clear enough about the client's personality and issues for opinions to be soundly based, and the therapeutic relationship is not yet mature enough for clients to make real use of advice if it is offered. Yet in practice, the rule that forbids us from giving advice or making expert judgments is broken all the time. Like most rules, it is not absolute, but depends heavily on the particular client, the particular situation, and the timing of the intervention. For example:

- In the first few sessions, it can be helpful to many clients to be told that their problems are not uncommon and that many others have felt the same way (this is called *normalising*). This can be particularly true for clients who have never been brave enough to voice some of their concerns because they believed, 'Nobody but me has ever felt this way'.

- Providing limited information (of a factual nature) to clients in early sessions can be appropriate if the clients actually *lack* key information, and provided it does not change the whole tenor of the session into 'Ask the expert'.

- When a client is in serious crisis, and the client himself, or someone else, is at risk, the counsellor may need to respond directly to a client's plea for direction (*It sounds like you're really in danger. Your first priority should be your own safety. Then you can sort out how you feel about your partner*).

In a long-term therapeutic relationship, where the professional has come to know the client well, and they have faced similar situations together many times, offering direct advice may assist the client. In these instances, the counsellor's advice or warning may serve to scaffold clients' developing ability to anticipate the likely consequences of their own actions, and to make thoughtful decisions. Eventually, many clients internalise their therapist, and at key moments they can access 'what my counsellor would say' and use it to help them act wisely. Realising that we can have such influence should be humbling for us, and make us use our power wisely, in our clients' interests.

Listing these contingencies does not mean that it's always fine for you to go ahead and offer direct advice to your clients in the first few sessions, or even later, when you know them better. Whether or not it's appropriate to offer direct advice will depend on your ability to sense accurately who your client is, what she needs, and how she is likely to respond to your advice. You will get better at this as you gain experience. Pay attention to where your own urgent need to say something is actually coming from. Is it a real response to your client's situation, or is it more to do with your own feeling that if you don't answer the client immediately, you have let her down, or failed to offer the help that only you can provide? If the latter lies behind your strong need to offer advice, then resist your impulse. Wait; dig deeper into yourself for a reflection that acknowledges the client's situation more fully, and afterwards, discuss with your supervisor your need to rescue or to sound like an authority.

NORMALISING AND PROVIDING INFORMATION

Assuming that you are well informed about the matter in question, providing some limited information in early sessions is often positively received by clients. Helping parents with pertinent information about the typical behaviour of children at various ages might be useful where clients are unsure of whether or not their child is heading for serious trouble. Informing couples about which kinds of couple interactions are productive, and which are destructive, as found in John Gottman's self-help book *Why Marriages Succeed and Fail* (Bloomsbury, 1997), may provide an insight that a particular couple presently lacks. Information about automatic, involuntary responses in young children can remove blame and encourage supportive behaviour from parents. Information about the way that depression is typically experienced might assist a person who thinks he might be depressed or 'have OCD', or whatever. But this kind of general information giving needs to be carefully tailored to individual needs and readiness. It is hardly ever sufficient in itself. By contrast, when we provide information within the context of an ongoing counselling relationship, we give it the chance to be lastingly effective. The fact that some self-help books sell in hundreds of thousands while the majority of their readers do not change in any lasting way makes it clear that information and change strategies are not enough in themselves.

However, an attempt to change oneself in the presence of an informed, objective, and compassionate 'coach' is very different from reading a book or viewing a program on screen. Our clients are not left on their own with the information: they can talk with us about their fears of change, their reluctance to get started, their alarm when they do something different and it works (yes 'alarm'—think of the person who loses weight but reacts with anxiety to this 'new me that I don't recognise and don't feel comfortable with'). Clients can look to us for encouragement when those around them are scornful or sceptical. If they are unrealistic in their goals, we can advise caution. If they start to lose sight of how their changes may have an impact on those they care about, we can invite them to consider others' needs as well as their own. None of these things can be done effectively by a self-help book or You Tube video, however charismatic the presenter.

Research indicates that most readers of self-help books take away highly oversimplified messages, and that such messages are often summed up in the book's title;[1] for example, Susan Jeffers' *Feel the Fear and Do It Anyway* (Harcourt Brace Jovanovic, 1987), Eckhart Tolle's *The Power of Now* (New World Library, 1999) or Mark Manson's *The Subtle Art of Not Giving a F*ck* (Harper Collins, 2016). Readers tend not to remember the details of the individual examples described in self-help books—unless the cases are very similar to their own—and many of the authors' subtleties are blurred by readers into bland generalisations. All reading (and viewing) is governed by the laws of memory, which we mentioned earlier in this book (Chapter 4): details of new experiences that are too different from our previous experiences get forgotten. However, even though self-help books are of limited usefulness, it is well worth your while to be interested in them when clients themselves tell you about something they have read. You can explore what they got out of the book, how it was helpful to them (or if it proved not to be helpful, why they think it wasn't). When clients speak highly of a particular text, and can refer in detail to its approach or its teachings, then you may want to read the book yourself. (You may also want to listen to a particular song that clients say they 'love' and play again and again.) Whether or not you agree with the author's approach, you will have learned something about the kind of approach that your client is comfortable with, and you will have received some hints as to the client's theory of change. It will also give you clues as to the level at which your client reads, and takes in information (some clients need a book—or the on-screen equivalent—that is short and extremely simple in its language).

It is often much more useful to follow up a book or program of the client's choice than to recommend a self-help book of *your* choice. Some clients simply hand back the book you have lent them with 'It didn't grab me' or 'Yeah, I read a bit here and there'. A few may be affronted if you offer them a book about a particular person or situation, because they assume that, in doing so, you are telling them who you think they really are or what they need to do. Which brings us back to the fundamental principle we mentioned earlier: any information you provide should be tailored to the individual needs and priorities of this particular client. In this respect, offering a piece of information (or suggesting a self-help book to read) is no different from providing a reflection of what the client has been talking about. If your response doesn't engage with what is important to the client, then it will almost certainly fail, and your client may feel that you have not understood him or her: your holding will have been inadequate.

ARE CLIENTS READY TO CHANGE?

When clients ask you 'What do you think I should do?', your first question would normally be 'What do *you* think you should do?', and when they supply an answer, your second question might be 'What other alternatives have you considered? What made them less appealing?' *Generally, you would not start coaching clients into behaviour change without first having helped them to explore their own goals and ideas about being different.* The vital next question will then be, 'So what do you think has stopped you from achieving this change already?' Remember those self-help books? If clients knows what they want to do differently, yet have consistently failed to do anything about it, it is of little use to simply agree with them that yes, their ideas are sound and they should put them into practice. Psychoanalytic theory might see this question ('What's stopped you from …?') as helping clients achieve insight into their 'resistance', whereas narrative therapy might frame it as 'deconstructing the client's dominant story', but the process itself amounts to a compassionate but open-minded endeavour to understand why it is so hard for clients to alter longstanding patterns of feeling, thinking, and acting in the world. Most models of counselling/therapy pay attention to such patterns, albeit in somewhat different ways.

Notice how your clients respond to your questions. Do they engage actively in the exploration? Or do they wait passively (or impatiently) for you to take over and offer them the right answer? If the latter is the case, then going the next step and offering an answer of your own is unlikely to work because it will not come from their experiencing and their thinking. Nor is there much point in suggesting strategies or purposeful changes to clients who insist that the responsibility for their problems lies with someone else. They will not be able to use your advice in any meaningful way, and probably will not attempt to follow it, even though they may say they will. Before change is possible, clients must first embrace the understanding that if they desire change, it is up to them to instigate it. (Many couples in counselling insist that their partner must change first, and only then will they consider reciprocating. Since each of them holds firmly to this position, no change is possible. In fact, they are unconsciously co-operating to prevent any shift from occurring, although of course couples rarely acknowledge this.)

Paul Watzlawik and his colleagues at the Mental Research Institute in California famously divided clients into 'window shoppers', 'customers', and 'complainants'. Window shoppers ('visitors' in solution-focused therapy) are really coming to counselling to satisfy someone else. They are only playing with the idea of 'buying' anything. Customers are ready to 'purchase', provided only that their 'salesperson' (professional helper) seems responsive and capable enough to assist them. The third category, complainants, refers to clients who may be quite prepared to keep coming for session after session, but who only want to sound off about the impossible behaviour of someone else. They use the counsellor as a sympathetic audience, but not as a change coach, because in their eyes, the person who needs to change is not them, but the third party who causes them so much distress (see Brian Cade and Bill O'Hanlon, *A Brief Guide to Brief Therapy*, Norton, 1993).

It isn't always easy to know whether a client is a complainant or a customer, because many clients *start* by presenting the impossible behaviour of a third party as their reason for seeking help. What makes the difference is how they respond when you invite them to explore how they themselves—however inadvertently—might be contributing to the problem. While many clients find it difficult, at first, to shift from blaming someone else, they will, over time, be able to acknowledge their own part in the situation, especially as they gain confidence that the counsellor is genuinely sensitive to their needs, and prepared to be patient with them.

True complainants, by contrast, will simply dismiss any suggestion that they might bear responsibility for the problem. No matter how tactfully and slowly the counsellor proceeds, they will continue to insist that the problem has nothing to do with them. If the counsellor ups the ante, and confronts the client with his or her evasion of responsibility in the manner we described in Chapter 6, then true complainants will almost always drop out. They are not ready to change; they want only to voice their own belief that nothing goes right for them, and that they are the unfortunate victims of malicious, nasty, or irresponsible others. Even then, you should not be too ready to dismiss them as 'personality disordered' (which for many counsellors becomes synonymous with 'incapable of change'). It is possible that a client, having grown up in a highly critical or rejecting family, has never previously received empathy or understanding. He knows how to complain and blame, but being understood feels alien and even unsafe. These clients can be very difficult to sit with, because they will often push away attempts at empathy, and tax even the most patient of counsellors.

For example

One of us [Penny] had a client who seemed like a classic complainer. He talked about how unhappy he was, and how badly everybody treated him. No matter how empathically she reflected his concerns, he seemed to reject her attempts. Eventually she asked him, *'If I really understood you properly, what would I be saying right now?'* As the client started to answer the question, he burst into tears. The action of saying the words that were true for him—his own words, which he had probably never uttered before in his life—had enabled him to drop down into deep feeling that had previously seemed unreachable. Here is yet another example of where a counsellor's ability to calmly acknowledge that she does not know the answer, that she is not the expert, is the key to unlocking an impasse.

When clients have been traumatised, they may need to tell their stories again and again and again before anything else can happen. Whether or not someone has suffered trauma usually becomes evident as the work continues. But there are always those cases where you cannot be sure of what is happening. Here good supervision can help you to proceed cautiously and compassionately until you can. It is not always feasible to expect clients to accept full responsibility straightway. A mother with a school-refusing child cannot be advised that her child's problems are a result of 'attachment failure' in her own childhood, and that a lengthy period of intensive psychotherapy may eventually enable her to handle her daughter differently. The latter may well be true, and may lead to a more satisfactory and lasting solution to the problem, but it cannot solve the immediate crisis. The client needs to do something differently to avoid her child being excluded. Unless you are prepared to offer her that kind of immediate assistance, you won't have her as a client for more than a couple of sessions at best. She will either give up, and things will get worse, or she will go elsewhere for the kind of help she can accept at this time in her life, at her current level of self-awareness. In such cases, you have to work out how you need to be with particular clients in order to assist them to achieve their goals, in a way that they find acceptable.

Read more

Brief therapist Steve de Shazer was fond of observing that if a key doesn't fit a lock, then we don't blame the lock, we change the key.[2] In other words, if we offer a client a particular approach and they don't find it helpful, then there is little point in accusing her or him of 'resistance' or being 'incapable of change'. Instead, we need to find a new approach that will prove a better fit for the client's expectations and experiences. De Shazer's set of skeleton keys that fit many different kinds of client locks is described in his very readable *Keys to Solutions in Brief Therapy* (Norton, 1985). Barry Duncan and Scott Miller have discussed the 'client's theory of change' at some length in various publications, most notably in Duncan, Hubble and Miller's *The Heart and Soul of Change* (2nd edn, American Psychological Association, 2009).

Different individuals take different lengths of time to reach a point where they are prepared to act differently. Hugh's work with clients in small group therapy has reinforced for him how long some individuals may 'resist' before reaching the point at which they feel safe enough with the group to take the risk of talking openly about some traumatic, defining event in their earlier lives—five years, in one case—and thus begin a process of facing up to their own pain and anger. It would have been easy to dismiss these individuals as 'complainants' or 'personality disordered'. But they were not—they just needed longer in a highly supportive environment before they felt ready to make their move.

ASSISTING THE CHANGE PROCESS

When clients are truly committed to solving their problems, and are prepared to change their own behaviour in order to do so, how do you help them? Do you adopt the approach recommended in some manual of problem management, and simply take your clients through those steps, one by one? By now, you will immediately guess that our answer to that is going to be 'No'! Even straightforward coaching of clients towards behavioural change is often not nearly as straightforward as it looks. Here are some of the main principles involved in successful change coaching. Some of them are self-evident and straightforward; others will need elaboration, which we'll provide later in the chapter.

Each client is an individual. Each 'change plan' needs to be individual too. As we've already seen, self-help books fall short because their advice is necessarily generalised. Manualised programs for managing oppositional kids, mastering one's anger, or resolving conflicts successfully, may fail for the same reason. They cannot adjust to the sensitivities and needs of individual clients.

- *How much change, how rapid it is, and how wide ranging, is something that cannot be stipulated at the beginning of the counselling.* It is often discovered by trial and error, as the change process gets underway. Sometimes, of course, your client's stated goals and aspirations may be unrealistic, or unfair to someone else (as when one partner in a relationship has a goal that would look after him, but not look after the relationship) but they must always be listened to and fully understood before you begin to question or challenge them.

- Motivation is not a static thing, of which clients possess a fixed amount. *Relatively slight motivation can increase if the client experiences an early success.* Some clients' motivation may increase depending on the amount of encouragement you offer, *but others may be deterred by too much encouragement.* (Famously, the parents of Vincent van Gogh praised him extravagantly when as an eight-year-old he produced a wonderfully skilful clay elephant. Vincent reacted by smashing the elephant!) Motivation may decline once the immediate intensity of the problem has decreased; many clients are satisfied with some improvement.

- Framing change strategies as *experiments* rather than as homework lessens clients' fear of failure, and invites an attitude of curiosity rather than an anticipation of judgment. An experiment will yield valuable information, regardless of whether it succeeds or not. For example, the original experiment might prove to have required too ambitious a change from the client. Accordingly, the next experiment might be designed to require a much smaller amount of change, and more built-in cautions.

- *Never do for your client what that client is capable of doing for him- or herself.* That is 'rescuing' in the true sense of the word. *But be prepared to do for certain clients particular steps that may be necessary in order for them to be able to perform the next steps unaided.* Something as simple as making a phone call—which your client perceives as impossible—can be made do-able if you are prepared to find out what your client might need from you to support her in making the call (e.g. 'Could you be in the room with me when I pick up the phone?'). Parents repeatedly tackle this kind of challenge when teaching their children how to handle the world effectively.

- *Positive change—change for the better—can be stressful.* The changes that one individual may earnestly desire in him- or herself can come as a shock (especially at first) to that individual's significant others. Sometimes you will need to explore with your clients what the adverse effects of change might be, especially change that comes rapidly and profoundly. (See 'Why change is difficult' below.)

- *Change is rarely a smooth, continuous upward climb towards a desired goal.* You will often need to shift from change coach back to therapist: exploring the client's reluctance to do something different, gently drawing attention to blind spots, helping the client to realise that he or she may be repeating a dysfunctional pattern from the distant past. Skills from earlier in this book will be relevant here. An extended example is given below under 'Taking the long way round'.

- *The counselling relationship does not become unimportant simply because you are working actively to assist clients to change.* If clients try something new and fail to accomplish their goals, you need to consider the possibility that their failure may actually represent a hidden 'resistance' to being controlled by someone else: *you!* Or they may be so scared of letting you down that they don't feel they can try, in which case, you may need to explore their fears of disappointing or angering you. They may even need something more from you in order to act, only what that 'something' is hasn't been identified yet. Back to the skills of immediacy, and relational dialogue!

- *It is not necessary to address separately all the things that your client may want to change.* The left hemisphere of our brain breaks things down into logically related bits that it sees as distinct and separate, leading clients to construct mental lists of desirable changes, lists that can appear overwhelming. But to the right hemisphere, which perceives the world holistically, things can come right quite rapidly once a positive change has been sustained in just one bit of the problem.

TIMING AND MOTIVATION

Despite the current popularity of suggesting change homework in the first session of short-term counselling, we wonder how appropriate it is to move clients into action so early. As we saw in Chapter 4, clients often reveal only the tip of the iceberg at their initial meeting with you. They are still making up their minds whether you can be trusted with their deeper and more worrying concerns—in other words they are testing out the strength of the relationship. In the second session, fuller dimensions of the presenting problem may start to emerge, but many clients will still keep a lot back; there will be things that, at this early stage, are still partly or wholly unconscious. What sounds like an uncomplicated request for help with making changes may not be as simple as it appears. If you take the client's presenting problem too seriously, and move straight into suggestions that address it (*Could you try walking away instead of arguing?*) you may short-circuit a process that could (if you relax and let it happen) lead you in a very different direction.

If you are required by your agency to work within a very brief counselling model, some of the principles we have set out earlier in this book may need to be modified. If clients know from the start that they have only six sessions, then (in our experience) the third-session challenge will tend to occur earlier, perhaps at the end of the first session, or midway through the second. If the elephant in the room shows up as early as this, and is handled capably by the counsellor, then it may be possible to move into experimenting with change as early as the end of the second session. Appropriate handling of the challenge will also establish a firmer base from which any discussion of possible changes can proceed. Clients will typically feel more confident to say 'No, that's not what I mean' or 'No, I don't think I could do that'. By the same token, what you say to them will be more likely to be heard and digested than in the opening session.

However, if you are working within a medium-to-long-term model (several months to a year or more), you will notice that later requests for change coaching are different from those made in the first couple of sessions. By then you will have a clearer sense of who your clients are, and how capable they are of taking responsibility for change. One key way that you can assess motivation is by exploring where they would like to be (compared with where they believe they are now), and what attempts they have previously made to get there. Here is an example, taken from the fifth session of 12, where serious exploration of the wish to change begins:

Counsellor: So, Kate, you've told me that you hate being so secretive and not telling people what's happening for you ... even when you trust them. You've said how destructive this can be, and you've told me how you've lost partners in the past because of it. You're really clear that you don't want to lose this relationship that you're in now. And you want things to be different. Is that right?

[Counsellor summarises, checking the accuracy of her own understanding, and allowing the client the opportunity to correct her emphasis, or to back away from anything that she may have changed her mind about.]

Client: Yes, that's right. I feel like I've got to start doing something right now, or it'll be too late. I can't just hope that things might improve. I know it's up to me to make it happen.

[Client makes a strong, clear statement of intention to change, and indicates she is prepared to take responsibility for the change.]

Counsellor: OK, so. You've told me what you *don't* like about the way you act now. Could you tell me how you'd *like* to be around this?

[It's typical for clients to describe desired changes in terms of what they don't want, rather than in terms of what they do. To many people, change means the absence of something frustrating, annoying, or disappointing, rather than the acquisition of a new capacity or a new understanding. Here the counsellor challenges the client to rephrase her desired change in positive terms.]

Client: Well, I'd like to be trusting. You know, not always worrying about what he's doing or who he's with. He's never done anything behind my back, and I know he wouldn't. After all, we've been together for seven years now, and he's never cheated on me. But I just can't stop thinking about it all the time ... what he could do, you know, how he could betray me... And that's not fair to him. In fact it worries him, and I know he wishes I could just relax and trust him. I wish I could too!

[Notice how the client begins by attempting to adopt the positive frame that the counsellor has suggested, but soon reverts to the negative: what is lacking. The counsellor finds different words to help her towards a more solid or concrete statement of the desired change. Asking clients how they might behave after a desired change has taken place is a good way of doing that. This is a variant of the widely used 'miracle question', most often identified with Steve de Shazer, but in fact devised originally by Milton Erickson.][3]

Counsellor: You really, really want to be able to just relax and trust him. If you did feel trusting and secure, what would you be doing that would be different from now?

[The counsellor deliberately asks what the client would be *doing*, not what she would be *feeling*, in the hope of assisting her to state the change in behavioural terms.]

Client: Well, I suppose I'd, um [pause, because she needs to search for an answer] I'd be able to get on with other things that I wanted to do, like go to the computer and get a head start on tomorrow's work, or ... I don't know ... maybe figure out something new and interesting to make for dinner ... anyway, just be able to get involved in something else, instead of wasting so much time worrying and imagining what might go wrong, or ringing him to check that he's where he says he is, or ... Yes, that's it! [sitting up straighter and smiling] I'd be able to not ring him! I'd feel fine about not checking! I wouldn't feel the need to ring and check [breathing out fully]. [It's still difficult for the client to imagine how she might feel or behave in the absence of her persistent anxiety. But she has started to make mental pictures of it: to create a mental space for a future different from her present reality.

In *The Brain that Changes Itself* (Scribe, 2008) Norman Doidge describes how mental rehearsal—imagining yourself performing some action step by step, in detail—will activate the same parts of the brain that would be used if you were performing the real-world action. This is in fact the same phenomenon as occurs when you read about a dramatic event in a novel, and your brain activates neuronal patterns identical with those that would fire in response to a real event to which you were a witness.]

EXPLORING PAST ATTEMPTS TO CHANGE

It is vital to ask clients how they have, in the past, tried to bring about the state that they desire. Their responses to that question will give you an indication of how seriously they want things to be different, and also will inform you about the change strategies that make sense to them (as opposed to the ones that make sense to you!) Their responses will also remind your clients of successes they may have experienced in the past, a powerful counterforce to any current belief that there is nothing they can do to bring about change. (This insight is perhaps the most significant contribution of solution-focussed brief therapy, as described in Chapter 5.) Some clients will have a sense that if they just got going, they might be able to make things different for themselves. Others, by contrast, will tend to believe that there is nothing they can do. Psychologists would describe the latter clients as having an *external locus of control*; that is, their experience is that things 'just happen to them'. Psychoanalytic theory would describe them as operating at the same level as a helpless infant, who depends almost wholly on the actions of adult caregivers in order to survive. Clients who do not believe that their own actions can bring about positive change are also those who believe that their only hope is for a powerful, magical partner (adult attachment figure) to come into their life and make everything right. Such clients will also forget that they may have, in the past, actually succeeded in bringing about changes for periods of time. Being asked about past successes—however small, however temporary—can be a seed that later flowers into the realisation that future success is, after all, possible. But whether you are working psychodynamically or cognitively, these clients will need slow, patient work from you if they are to gradually form more of an *internal locus of control*.

Exploring past attempts to change behaviour necessarily involves asking *what led the client to give up*. Often, an attempt was abandoned because someone important objected to what the client was doing. Often, it will be because the attempt was actually succeeding, and the change was gathering momentum. This may seem counterintuitive, but here you need to remember that human beings, and human social systems, automatically react so as to protect themselves from change: the 'comfortable discomfort' they are so accustomed to. Only the naïve counsellor assumes that clients can desire change without also fearing it. (See below, 'Why change is difficult'.) A sympathetic discussion of clients' fears about change can make all the difference between a change plan that succeeds, and one that founders:

Counsellor: So, Julie, when you tried standing up for yourself with your sister, it seemed to be going OK for a while; is that right?

Client: Yeah, it did … I felt so good in myself that I wasn't just being a doormat and letting her walk all over me. But then I just sort of ran out of steam, somehow … [drifting off].

Counsellor: So, at first you felt stronger, that you were standing up for yourself. But then something happened, and you lost energy for it … What do you think might have got in the way there?

Client: Hmm. I suppose I started to think, 'What if I drive her away by being more assertive? What if she actually wipes me out of her life? [Pauses then speaks so she can hardly be heard] I might lose her forever … [a bit louder again] and that's such a scary thought, because in a way I've always depended on her, even though she was so critical and controlling.

[It is very common for clients to fear such catastrophic consequences. Rather than thinking, 'Wow, how irrational!', we need to realise that when clients become terrified that they might lose a relationship completely as a result of a small change in their own behaviour, this fear is coming from a very young part of themselves. We need to react understandingly and gently to it, not just challenge it at a rational level as advocated by some cognitive therapists.]

Counsellor: OK, so this real fear came up ... that she might abandon you completely if you kept on standing up to her. That's so scary, isn't it ... to think that you might lose someone who's so important to you? Maybe it feels like you couldn't survive without her?

Client: Yes, exactly. Um, I know I *can* live without her, it's just that ... actually, I don't think she would dump me. But it's really scary, even though I really don't think she would.

[As often happens, the counsellor's empathic reflection of the depth of the client's fear actually prompts the client to access her own rationality, where arguing with her might entrench her fear more deeply. Giving the client's right hemisphere what it needs has enabled her left hemisphere to come online and contribute. Now that the client has given an indication of accessing a more adult part of her, the counsellor engages at this level.]

Counsellor: Did you see any indications that she might be going to dump you? I mean, were you aware of her starting to pull away, or getting angry with you?

[Cognitive therapists would see this as challenging the client to find evidence that might support an irrational belief. Such challenges are much more likely to be accepted by clients if you haven't first told them that their belief is 'irrational' or 'dysfunctional!]

Client: Well, no, not really ... [thinking]... I suppose she did go quiet a couple of times when I told her what I thought, and that I didn't agree with her advice. She didn't do anything, though. Like, she still rang me the next week to ask how I was going. I guess that when she went quiet, I got really scared. I'd never seen her like that before. I felt like I might have really, really hurt her, and then this feeling came up, that I'd lose her, that she couldn't cope with that amount of hurt.

Counsellor: Sounds like you started feeling overwhelmed with anxiety, because something really new and different was happening ... you'd acted differently, and you could see the impact of that on your sister, and it scared you. It triggered a fear that you could, maybe, destroy her, or push her away. What do you reckon about that fear, thinking about it now?

Client: Well I don't really think it would've happened. I don't think she'd fall apart like that. When I think about everything she's coped with in her life: that's just not in her nature, to fall in a heap like that. It was more that I was scared of feeling so powerful. I'd never felt in control before ... it'd always been her that seemed in control. It seemed so different.

[The client now realises that she is scared of her own potential power in a relationship. Remember that preschool children, and even older children, often feel that when something bad happens in their family, they must have caused it in some way, the phenomenon that Piaget called *egocentricity*.]

Counsellor: So, in a way, if you started to stand up for yourself again, around her, you might feel that fear again? Even though you know now that it probably was more a fear than a real possibility?

Client: Well yes, I'd probably be a bit scared again. But I'd still like to try. I don't think I gave myself enough time then, to get used to feeling that way ... to get used to feeling grown up around her. It was really good to feel more equal. I wish I could feel that again.

[Now the client has managed to access a positive feeling from the past that she can draw upon to help her imagine being different in the future.]

Counsellor: So if you were feeling grown up with her now, what might you be able to do, or say?

[The counsellor has utilised the information the client has just provided, to help her fill out her picture of her own possible future relationship with her sister.]

WHY CHANGE IS DIFFICULT

Freud developed the idea of *resistance*, where disowned ('unconscious', 'repressed', 'split-off') feelings within people get in the way of their conscious desire for change. Behaviourists countered that anything someone has learned can, at a later point, be unlearned, or supplanted by a different behaviour. If particular behaviours were simply *habits*, then they could be altered. Some half a century later, a different explanation for human unwillingness to change was offered. Systems theory argued that social systems (notably families, but by extension all sorts of groups and communities) embodied *status quo-maintaining mechanisms* in exactly the same way that a thermostat turns off a heater once the temperature reaches the desired point, and turns it on again as soon as the temperature drops below it. Early family therapists, informed by this analogy from engineering, noticed that when a family member who had previously occupied the position of the problem child began to function better, a different child (previously healthy or normal) often began to develop physical, emotional, or behavioural problems, as if to create a new problem child in place of the first. It seemed that the system (the family considered as a whole entity) would (without anyone making a conscious decision, or even wanting this) tend to revert to the status quo: the way it had previously functioned.

Similarly, systemic therapists noticed that couples tended to evolve fixed roles in relation to one another: the nag and the procrastinator, for example; the over-responsible one and the under-responsible one. But a sudden change to the relationship might reverse these roles. The previously irresponsible partner could suddenly develop a strong sense of responsibility, and the previously high-functioning or care-taking partner might need to be taken care of by the other. If this could happen, then clearly, these roles were not set in stone. An individual's personality might, in fact, develop certain potentials at the expense of others, depending on his or her interpersonal context. 'Acting weak' might develop in relation to being with someone acting strong, and if one partner started functioning less well, the other might automatically be drawn into over-functioning, as if there were a vacant space in the relationship that required filling. Once begun, such roles rapidly became entrenched, and harder to change. Over time, partners might come to believe that this was the way they were, and that change was impossible.

This new way of looking at 'resistance' opened up new possibilities for change. If a therapist could encourage one family member into behaving differently, then others might automatically find themselves behaving differently, without any conscious decision to do so. *Altering the interpersonal context of a behaviour—even something as seemingly individual and intrapsychic as depression, or addiction—might alter the behaviour itself, by removing some of the things that reinforced or maintained it.* If one spouse ceased to nag and criticise, then the other might start to resent his own dysfunction instead of resenting his partner. Behaviourists such as B. F. Skinner had argued that if we altered the environment so that it ceased to reinforce a problematic behaviour, then the behaviour itself would start to diminish. Similarly, systemic family therapists argued that altering the interpersonal environment so that it ceased to reward one family member's dysfunction would lead to a diminution of that behaviour, even though it appeared to be 'inside' one particular family member.

Family systems theory could even be seen as an application of Skinner's *operant conditioning* to the arena of interpersonal relationships. But a psychoanalytic theorist looking at family therapy could equally well see systems principles as a development of Freud's idea of unconscious resistance and internal conflicts. The shifting, unconscious forces within a family (or any other social system) were the equivalent of the unconscious dynamics within the mind of an individual. A family, or a work group within an organisation, would find itself acting in ways that tended to maintain dysfunction. Thus a firm would get rid of a dysfunctional employee, but nine times out of 10, would then end up replacing him or her with an equally dysfunctional new employee, although nobody would have consciously intended to do so. It is as if there is a slot for such a person within the system, and the system then acts unconsciously to fill it. If no new staff member is employed, an existing staff member will start to be drawn into the vacant role, just as a functional child will be drawn into the space vacated by the previous problem child in a family. (Think about most work teams that you have been a part of, and you will soon find examples of this!)[4]

Regardless of the theoretical explanations offered, it is clear that human systems, like human individuals, do resist change, albeit unconsciously. Significant others in a client's life can either assist the client's change, or subtly undercut it. The fact that we can see unconscious resistance to change on a collective level (the level of the whole system) does not mean that there is no unconscious resistance within the mind of the individual. An example would be the very common problem of someone attempting to give up smoking (or any other addiction), where very often, both internal and external resistance are involved. Lasting changes to entrenched behaviours rarely come about quickly. The typical change graph is one of progress followed by regression, and of slow shifts over time. It's hardly surprising that so many people give up after trying to change, and then finding that they slip back (or somebody else in the system reacts badly to the change). Lasting change often requires that people persist in their new behaviour and many are unwilling to persist. Their original change strategy might well have worked, had they only hung in there long enough.

Signs of change-for-the-better are often difficult for clients to perceive, and the counsellor needs to function as a witness to change and a memory aid for the client. In the extended example that follows, notice how the counsellor is just as interested in learning about the resistance as she is getting a cure or a positive outcome. Often, successful change coaching can be about 'taking the long way around' (the Dixie Chicks' song written after the crisis induced by Natalie Maines' impulsive statement about then-President George Bush in March 2003). The following section presents an extended example of 'taking the long way around'.

Taking the long way: change coaching in action

Counsellor: Liz, we've spent quite a bit of time looking at your feelings about your weight. You've told me the story, and we've talked about why you feel comfortable being the shape you are, and yet in some ways you actually don't feel that comfortable, and you'd like to lose some kilos. And we've discussed what happened when you've tried to lose weight before. Can I just check with you? ... What would you say were the key things that made it difficult for you, when you've tried to lose weight before? How did the various programs help you, or hinder you?

[Counsellor first summarises, as a platform for asking questions designed to help the client spell out what got in the way of previous attempts to lose weight.]

Client: Well, I'm pretty clear on that now. Every time, I've started off doing really well, and whatever program I was involved with at the time really seemed to be working. I'd feel pretty happy with myself, you know. And then after a while … I think we talked about three months, didn't we? … I'd somehow start to slip. And what happened then was that the counsellor, or whoever it was, would be really nice about it, and encouraging, and tell me that I'd be fine, it was normal to have a setback on the way to permanent weight loss, and so on. And then I'd feel worse and worse. I'd feel I was disappointing her and I didn't want to tell her what was worrying me. I felt I just should be trying harder … and that felt so bad that I'd just go to the ice cream to make me feel better.

[In her own summary, Liz reminds her counsellor of a key thing that went wrong for her in previous attempts to change: the fact that the then-counsellor was stuck in a position of encouragement. Her previous counsellors were of course intending to be helpful. But Liz did not respond as the counsellors expected. Instead, their comments made it harder for her to talk honestly to them about what was getting in the way of her progressing further. These counsellors may well have been focussing entirely on the goal of behaviour change and not factoring in the possibility that the client's relationship with them might be part of the problem. They would fail to 'see' this because the client appeared to trust and like them. They wouldn't consider that maybe the client might be scared of disappointing them, and consequently would not be fully honest with them.]

Counsellor: Liz, I think you've just reminded me of something I might have missed when we talked about this before. When things started to get difficult, and you began to slip, it sounds like it wasn't that helpful for your counsellor to just encourage you to keep trying. In fact, in a way it made it harder for you.

[The counsellor doesn't immediately ask Liz if her own 'encouraging' behaviour might be creating a similar problem. Her sense is that the client needs a gentle lead-up to an honest encounter with her.]

Client: That's right. I felt I was letting her down. She …well, most of them actually … was so sincere, she really wanted me to lose those kilos. I could tell how much she wanted it. And I felt like I was just a failure. I didn't dare to tell her about the funny comments that Steve [the client's husband] made, or Mum having a go at me for even trying to lose weight. I think she would've thought I was making excuses.

Counsellor: This sounds important. Could you tell me a bit more? What sort of things did Steve say? And your Mum?

[The counsellor wants to help Liz explore the ways in which significant others in the client's life resisted her attempts to change.]

Client: Oh, he'd make these funny little comments like, 'Well I won't know you soon, will I!' or 'I'll be wondering who this woman is that gets into bed with me every night.' He said it sort of jokingly. It sounded a bit sarcastic. … I felt like he was having a go at me, poking fun at me. I felt sort of confused [rubbing her forehead]. What was he saying? Does he want me to stay fat? Is he saying he can't cope with a new me? … I mean, it's just the same me, only a few kilos lighter … Can't he see that? [She holds both hands out as if to show the counsellor what she means.]

Counsellor: It sounds really confusing. But it sounds like you were a bit angry with him, too, that he didn't really seem to want something that you wanted so badly?

[The counsellor reflects back the anger which is hinted at in Liz's choice of words, 'Can't he see that …?' Liz also hints at anger in the word she chooses to describe her husband's comment: 'sarcastic'.]

Client: I guess I *was* angry. I don't think I realised that at the time. I get worried that other people are going to reject me for trying to be who I want to be. And then I feel torn about letting myself have what I want. I start to feel it's not OK to be me.

Counsellor: You've got a really strong feeling of needing to be how other people want you to be, and maybe that gets in the way of you being able to stick to something that's really important to you.

[The counsellor articulates more openly a conflict within the client, so that the next time she sets out to lose weight, she will be more likely to be aware of it, and value her own goals more.]

Client: It's true. I've always felt as if it's up to me to keep them happy. Like with Mum and Dad, how I used to think I had to be really, really good, because if I was, they mightn't fight so much. I suppose it wasn't anything to do with me ... I realise that now, but at the time, I really thought I had to be more what they wanted, so they could be happier, and then I'd have the family I needed. [tearfully] It makes me feel really sad to say this.

[The client reflects from an adult space on her beliefs and actions as a child, connecting her present behaviour with how she felt in the past, but putting this into words for the first time touches her deeply on an emotional level.]

Counsellor: You used to try so hard to keep them happy, and touching on this makes you realise how impossible it was for that little girl. So very sad that you tried and tried ... and your parents still kept fighting and you couldn't make it better.

A little later in the session:

Counsellor: And your Mum? You said that when you've tried to lose weight before, she's made it hard for you too, somehow?

Client: Well, you know how I've told you she sort of disapproves of me; it's like she thinks of me as a failure or something. Every time I'd make the mistake of telling her that I was on a new diet, with a program and a counsellor and everything, she'd be saying, 'Oh, I know you; it won't last; you've done this before and it never works.' I'd feel so flat after she said that [sagging in her chair, as if to show how it made her feel]. Like I couldn't be bothered telling her about how I was going, because she wouldn't really want to know ... She'd already made up her mind.

Counsellor: You'd think 'she's not interested', that what you wanted wasn't important to her ... a bit like with your husband, in a way. So you didn't feel like telling her what was really going on? Sort of like—she didn't believe in you, and that seemed to take away your own belief in yourself?

[Here the counsellor is tentative so the client can feel free to correct her.]

Client: I hadn't thought of it that way ... Um ... Yes, I guess. I hadn't thought that Mum and Steve were the same, in that way. That neither of them cared about what was important to me. They weren't listening to me, or supporting me, so I just lost confidence in myself.

Counsellor: OK, so when you try this next experiment with losing some weight ... like we've been talking about ... it sounds like there are a few things for us [the use of 'us' makes the client a partner in the enterprise] to watch out for. One would be how other people start to react ... Would it be Steve and your Mum that would still be the ones that you'd be watching out for?

Client: Yeah, it would. I'm really reactive around Mum. Anything she might say could trigger me. With Steve it's not like that, so … well, I'm not sure. In a way, I guess I want his approval just like I want Mum's. Only I've kind of given up on getting Mum's, and so that just leaves Steve, and when he makes those funny little comments, like he's having a go at me, I feel kind of flattened again, and then I start to question whether this weight thing is so important after all.

Counsellor: OK … so it's both of them … but in a way, Steve is the one you're more vulnerable with, because with your Mum, you kind of expect her to be negative anyway, whereas with Steve, it sounds like you're still half hoping that he might support you … You've told me that generally, he does support you on other things, is that right?

Client: Yeah, he does. I don't understand why he's so negative about me losing weight. It's not like him at all.

Counsellor: It feels a bit weird when your partner behaves in a way that you don't expect? Like you kind of don't know him any more? [client nods agreement.] What's that like for you?

Client: Um, well, it's a shock. Like you can't rely … like, um, you start questioning yourself, because you're questioning him, and he's normally someone you rely on, you know.

[Here the client has started to use 'you' instead of 'I', suggesting that this idea maybe too painful for her to encounter up close at this stage.]

Counsellor: You're used to relying on him because he seems kind of solid and dependable, but then he changes when he talks like that, and that kind of pulls the rug out from under you, is that right? And then you start wondering whether you should go ahead with losing this weight, because you need to be how he needs you to be, and you can't afford to rock the boat?

Client: [pause] I guess, um … maybe he doesn't want me to be different, because, um … maybe because he's used to me the way I am?

Counsellor: You might have hit on something really important there. I'm wondering now whether maybe Steve might actually feel a bit, I don't know, even a bit anxious at the thought of you looking so different. From what you say, he's used to you looking the way you do now, and he's sort of worried about having to get used to you looking different. And maybe you're feeling different about yourself, too.

[Counsellor offers an empathic insight into how her partner might be experiencing her changes, to reframe the client's original perception of him as sarcastic or critical. This allows connection to remain between the client and her husband, rather than the counsellor giving energy to the client's perception of his behaviour as an attack on her. The dialogue continues with the client beginning to feel more confident that she can go ahead with her planned program of weight loss, without having to fear that her partner might permanently withdraw from her, and no longer be a reliable source of support.]

Let's now jump ahead several sessions, and return to Liz and her counsellor after Liz has successfully kept to her weight loss goals for more than a month, and has reported with surprise and pleasure that Steve's attitude seems to have become less critical. Now, however, Liz is confronting resistance from a different part of her family system: her Mum. Remember that resistance to change can 'shift around' within a family, so that one person no longer resists but another one starts to get anxious and oppositional instead.

Client: I'm feeling really down this week. I was going so well, and now it feels like someone's put the brakes on. I'm starting to lose confidence again. And it's Mum … just like we talked about a few weeks back. I thought I could manage her reaction this time, after talking about it here. But you know what, I'm just as hopeless as ever. Talking to you about it hasn't made any difference. As soon as I hear her voice at the end of the phone, you know, I start to feel really beaten [her shoulders sag]. She just can't say anything nice or encouraging, so I start thinking, 'Maybe she's right. Maybe I am hopeless, and can't do this.'

Counsellor: I think when we talked about it a few weeks back, you said you'd given up hoping that she would be supportive, and so her comments probably wouldn't worry you. But now we've discovered that maybe you didn't realise how easily you feel squashed and defeated by what she says.

Client: Yep. I didn't. And to be perfectly honest, I did expect that it would be different this time. I thought that we'd dealt with all of that, in sessions, and that I ought to be different now, more able to cope … She wouldn't have that control over my emotions any more. But I was wrong. It didn't make any difference. Maybe talking isn't the answer.

[The client hints that more than just talking is required, that she needs strategies to defuse her Mum's resistance to her changes. But she also hints that the counsellor has let her down. The counsellor decides that her first priority is to explore the in-the-room feelings between the client and herself—which she deliberately avoided doing several sessions earlier.]

Counsellor: So it's really disappointing, and it kind of makes you mad, too. You were feeling really hopeful, because we'd talked about it in advance, and you thought you should be able to do it differently this time. And now you feel almost back to square one, with your Mum still able to pull those critical strings, and your confidence seems to collapse. And I suppose I'm thinking, I've been working with you on this, and so far we've gone pretty well, but here we've hit a spot where maybe it seems like I've let you down, or … I don't know, where I've done something that hasn't been helpful. What do you think?

Client: No, not really.

[Very often, when clients say 'Not really' they are hinting to us that they are censoring something, something they don't feel able to say out loud. If you 'listen' carefully you can 'hear' the unsaid 'but…..']

Counsellor: Not really?

Client: It's not that you've let me down. You've been really helpful. I've enjoyed coming here and talking about all this with you.

[Clients often feel the need to save face for the counsellor, by denying anger or disappointment.]

Client: But I feel, um, well I suppose I feel a bit frustrated, because you were so encouraging, I mean with Steve, and that worked, and then I started to feel like if I didn't manage to get through the Mum bit, I'd be failing. I felt this, I don't know, this sort of pressure to do it right. And then, talking to Mum, I just fell in a heap. She was so critical and so sure I was going to fail, I started to feel the same way. And that was the last thing I needed to feel at that moment!

Counsellor: Hmm. So in a way, I was acting like your earlier counsellors had? Remember, you told me that they'd sort of been too encouraging. And maybe I was too encouraging, is that it?

Client: Um. Not really. Well I guess that was part of it. I suppose you'd been there for me with the Steve thing, and I'd got through that, and I was kind of depending on you to get me through it with Mum as well. And this is going to sound really stupid, because you didn't do anything different, but I felt scared that maybe you were going to give up on me. Because I'd failed. I should have been able to handle Mum, not overreact to her. And I just couldn't.

Counsellor: [softly] All these things you were *supposed* to do. Get it right. Do everything that everyone else expects. Including me ... do everything that you thought I expected. And if you can't, you're worried that I'll give up on you in some way. Is that right?

Client: Yeah. I suppose you didn't really say anything about expecting me to do well with Mum. But when you were so encouraging with me and Steve, I just started to think that you were there cheering me on, and ... and that was a scary feeling. I started to feel I was sure to get it wrong, then.

[This is the same thing that happened with the client's earlier weight loss counsellors. The client experienced their cheerful support as a kind of conditional love, in which she was obliged to keep 'winning', and that if she didn't, expected that they would become critical and negative, like her Mum. What is new this time is that the counsellor is actively engaging the client in a discussion of what has been going on, and assisting her to explore her disappointment and anger, without judgment.]

Counsellor: So I think you're letting me know that when I was encouraging to you over the situation with Steve, that actually got in the way? Was it like I was caring too much about you succeeding with this weight loss thing?

Client: Well, no, I mean, I liked you being on my side and cheering me on, sort of, but I suppose then I started to feel like I'd disappoint you if I didn't manage Mum as well as I'd managed Steve, you know?

Counsellor: Maybe when I was supportive and encouraging, you started to get worried because your experience of your Mum is that she doesn't stay supportive for long. She gets critical as soon as you start to slip ... or even before you do. And maybe you started to expect that I'd behave the same way.

[Psychodynamic therapists would call this an example of transference interpretation.]

Client: You're not at all like my Mum. You're ... I think you do believe in me, and I'm not sure she does. But yeah, I probably did feel that you were going to turn cold and critical. I wasn't aware of it at the time, I just started to lose confidence in myself all over again, you know?

Counsellor: What has it been like, letting me know all this? Actually telling me to my face?

[Counsellor invites more immediacy from the client.]

Client: It's been a bit weird, but a relief. Like I've just done something I didn't really think I could do. I mean, I'm always so worried that if I say what I feel, I'll get into trouble. And I didn't. At least, I don't think so [giggles]. I wish I could talk to my Mum like this.

Counsellor: So it'd be really nice to be able to talk to your Mum like you did with me. Well, we could work on that sometime, if you want. But around how I am with you, how could I help you with this stuff about cheering you on? Like, is there some way I could behave that'd be more useful?

Client: [pause] I don't think so, actually. I think what you're doing is fine for me. It's like the feeling [her feeling that the counsellor might turn critical], like it's gone away now. When I was able to tell you what I felt, suddenly it wasn't there so much any more. So the problem with my Mum is that I'm so sure Mum's going to push me away that I just react badly to it.

Counsellor: Like you find that you always have to be on guard when you're talking to her? Is this something you've ever talked about with your Mum? [client shakes head] You haven't talked about it with her? What's stopped you, do you think?

Client: We don't have those sorts of conversations, I suppose. I wish I could! I don't think she realises how she affects me. I think she's just trying to be helpful, in her own way, it's

A Safe Place for Change

just that it doesn't work for me.

Counsellor: So you can see that she's trying to help ... I'm wondering what ideas you might have about why she seems so negative when you try to lose weight? Why might she be so negative towards that?

[Now that the client has experienced a shift in how she perceives the counsellor in the here and now, the counsellor can safely ask her to explore new aspects of the 'there and then': what might lie behind her mother's reactions.]

Client: I don't know. Maybe she's scared that I'll change, I mean, change towards her ... Like with Steve, how we worked out he was worried that I might be a different person, and not feel the same towards me. Or maybe she doesn't want me to succeed because she's never managed her own weight that well. I mean, she's big. And I think she feels bad about it, but she never says.

Counsellor: You've got some interesting ideas there. I hadn't realised that she struggles with her weight too. And look, in my experience, when one person starts to change, it is a bit confronting for other people in their family, even for their friends. It kind of challenges them, and initially they tend to react quite negatively. I don't think they always mean to be negative; it just happens automatically. What clients have told me in the past is that if they can hold onto their changes while the other people adjust, after a few months things start to improve. The other people settle down, and even seem a bit pleased about the changes.

[Here the counsellor becomes a teacher for a short time, explaining to the client how the change process tends to work in social systems. The counsellor is building upon an awareness that the client is already starting to develop for herself. Framing the advice as 'something clients have told me in the past' makes it less patronising than an 'expert' pronouncement coming from the counsellor herself.]

At this point, there are several ways that the dialogue could go. The counsellor could assist the client to explore the history of her relationship with her mother; or she could rehearse a conversation she might have with her Mum (assuming that the client is willing to undertake this). Or the counsellor might return to the therapeutic relationship—how the client feels towards her—because it is possible that more dynamics between Liz and her mother may also play out in the counselling room. Or the counsellor might invite the client to talk more about her own fears of losing weight, apart from the anxieties that others might have. These are not mutually exclusive alternatives. Nor do they all need to be explored in order for change to occur. If counsellor and client are well attuned, then the counsellor will soon grasp which direction is the most productive, and the client's feedback will confirm it.

Although this is only an extract from a longer, ongoing dialogue focused on change, we hope that we've presented enough for you to see what 'taking the long way round' might be like in practice. We hope also that you've been able to see how the counsellor needs to move backwards and forwards between the therapeutic relationship in the room, and the client's external relationships with others out there in the world. And how what happens in one of these domains often parallels what happens in the other—which is the whole point of drawing attention to transference. What emerges is that the relational and the problem-focused approaches that we discussed in Chapter 5 may not be as diametrically opposed as they seemed. Rather, they may both be necessary and appropriate at different times, and as you gain experience and confidence, as well as deeper self-knowledge, you will develop the capacity to move flexibly between the two in response to your client's needs at that particular point in the counselling process.

Bearing witness to change:

Increasing motivation by operant conditioning

We've seen that encouragement can be a double-edged thing. Some clients respond straightforwardly to encouragement; it increases their motivation. But others seem almost instinctively to be put off by too much encouragement. They may fear to disappoint the counsellor (as we've seen in the extended example above). Or they may start to feel that if their counsellor seems so invested in their success, then the counsellor might 'own' the changes that they are making. They may be so scared of changing that they prefer to slide into change without thinking about things too much. Or they may actually fail to recognise changes that they have already instigated.

In some of these cases, where straightforward encouragement does not work, it can be useful to adopt a different stance. We might celebrate change only after it has already happened, or we might explore the potential risks of change that has started to happen. These approaches originated in strategic family therapy, and have been developed further by the solution-focused and narrative schools. Celebrating change and bearing witness to change can be powerful interventions when employed with clients whose past history has been marked by failure, disempowerment, and conditional love. An example would be where parents or other attachment figures have relentlessly focused on what the child failed to do or failed to achieve, as in, *'So you got 98 per cent for your exam. But what about the other 2 per cent?'* These are the clients who, as we mentioned earlier, fail to realise when they have succeeded in something, and who almost cannot believe that they can have agency in their own lives (internal locus of control). As we saw earlier, exploring a partial success in the past can be one way of beginning a process that may lead to clients having, for the first time, a mental space within which it is possible for them to contemplate the possibility of change in a desired direction. Such a space can be expanded, sometimes, if the counsellor pays a great deal of attention to *a success in the present* (a success that occurs during the counselling process) in such a way that it is harder for the client to forget this success later, or to dismiss it cynically as 'just luck' or 'a flash in the pan'. Here is a brief example of this kind of intervention, which early family therapists, following Gregory Bateson, saw as *conveying news of difference*:[5]

Counsellor: Rob, just wait a minute here. I'm sorry to have to interrupt you ... you know I try to avoid that, because this is your time ... but I just want us to have a chance to talk about what you've just told me. I wonder if you maybe don't realise how significant it is. You've told me that you stood up to your Dad for the first time that you can ever remember. You told him where to get off, and he actually respected you, and backed off. Is that right?

Client: Yeah, that's right. It felt good. But you know, I don't trust him. After all, he's treated me like shit most of my life. What's the point in standing up to him if he just goes back to being the way he's always been?

Counsellor: Yeah, well, you might be right about that. But we don't know yet. And I guess that when you focus on what your *Dad* might do or not do, you're kind of failing to realise what a significant step *you've* taken. You did it, and you felt good. That sounds huge!

Client: Ahh ... I dunno. How do you mean, a significant step? I thought I just did it; I didn't even really intend to do it, the words just came out, and he kinda took it on board. I didn't expect that, but I still don't trust him further than I can throw him.

Counsellor: Yeah, let's just leave your Dad out of it for a minute.

[This is quite directive, but deliberately so. The counsellor knows that the client will revert to his 'comfortable discomfort' as soon as he focuses attention back on his father.]

I want to stay with talking about you for a moment, even though that might feel a bit uncomfortable. You're saying that you didn't intend to say the words ... they 'just came out'—what that means to me is that something inside of you had decided to do something different. You didn't need to make a big, conscious effort ... you already sort of knew what to do, and when the right time arrived, you did it ... it just came out. To me, that's big.

Client: I hadn't thought of it that way ... I suppose now you put it like that, yeah, maybe I was ready. But I dunno whether I'll ever be able to do it again, though. What if he gets worse?

Counsellor: Let's talk about what might happen to him in a minute. I still want to stay with *you* for a sec.

[Again the counsellor resists the client's 'pull' to return to negative possibilities.]

You're saying that maybe you were ready to act differently, with your Dad. And I need to let you know something. I know it's going to sound kind of hard to believe, so I wouldn't be surprised if you thought I was being too optimistic, or something. Do you want to hear what I think?

Client: Go on, shoot.

Counsellor: Well, what I was going to say was ... but I'm not sure this is really the right moment to say it, I don't know if maybe you'd prefer to talk about how your Dad might get worse ...

Client: Nup. You're right. I think too much about him. Just say it. I can take it.

Counsellor: What I was going to say was that now you've done it once, you're going to be able to do it again. Not necessarily straight away, but sometime soon. And how I know it is that once you've taken a step like this one, that you've just taken, you can't go backwards. It's not possible, because now you've got a memory of what you did, and you've got a memory of what you felt about it, and you've got a memory of how your Dad backed off. And that's going to make a big difference to how you act in the future. Not just with him, but with other people too.

[This isn't just glib 'positive thinking', because it is firmly based in a knowledge of how our brains work. Having done something once makes it that much easier to contemplate doing it again. Even *imagining* ourselves doing something different will make it easier for us to translate the 'rehearsal' into real-life action.]

We could continue this dialogue for pages, but by now you should have a clear idea of what 'celebrating change' and 'bearing witness to change' might involve. Many more examples can be found if you watch recordings of strategic and solution-focused therapists such as Insoo Kim Berg and Bill O'Hanlon, or narrative therapists such as David Epston and Michael White. Narrative therapy has in fact pioneered a whole new approach to celebrating change, which it calls *definitional ceremonies* or *outsider witness practices* (see Michael White's *Maps of Narrative Therapy*, Norton, 2007: 165–218). In this approach, the therapist asks clients to nominate particular people in their lives who they think might be interested in attending a session to listen to them talking with the therapist about the changes they have been able to make. These people (there might be just a couple, or there might be quite a few) are invited to observe in silence while client and therapist discuss the changes that the client has successfully implemented. They are then invited to comment on the changes, and on how the client's story has affected them. They are not permitted to ego trip, or to turn the conversation in a negative direction, or to bring in outside issues that don't relate directly to the clients' changes. As the clients listen to these 'outsider witnesses' talk about them, they become aware, often for the first time, of their potential to influence others, and to move and impress them with what they have achieved. This, as you can imagine, is a dramatic experience, particularly for clients who have always seen themselves as insignificant, powerless, and little valued by others around them.

As you continue with this work, you will notice how difficult it often is for clients to accept compliments. It can be very useful to ask, *What was it like to hear me give you that compliment? It sounds as though it was hard to hear—maybe even uncomfortable for you?* This can help the client to become more self-aware, and to reflect on what his or her behaviour might mean. When clients develop the capacity to be aware of what they are experiencing in the moment, they can exercise more choice over their reactions, instead of reacting automatically in patterns learned long before, which may no longer fit their current situation.

All of the examples we've given might well be described by a behaviourist such as Skinner as examples of operant conditioning. Instead of encouraging change before it occurs (which can sometimes lead clients to fear failure), these approaches reward change *after* it occurs; and not only do they reward it, they do so in a particular way, altering the interpersonal environment around clients, so that they do not get the kind of response they have received in the past, but instead, are required to take on board the fact that their own behaviour has changed in a positive and significant way.

HIGHLIGHTING SUCCESS BY OFFERING WARNINGS

When clients indicate, early in the change process, that they feel anxious at the prospect of change, and then react to a success that they've achieved by downplaying or dismissing it (or even failing to report it in the sessions), it can also be useful to take a different path to achieving news of difference in the client's life. In this alternative, the counsellor avoids celebrating the success in the obvious ways. Instead, the counsellor explores the client's *fears* in relation to what has happened.

While this line of counselling may seem a bit odd, it can assist the kind of client who finds great difficulty in accepting the counsellor's praise or encouragement. Questioning of this type is specifically designed for clients who have earlier indicated a deep ambivalence about change. We are not recommending it as a 'one size fits all' solution, to be used with the whole range of clients, although in a milder form, it is always useful to remind clients of the possible adverse consequences of their changes, and to check with them whether, having made a change, they may now experience greater anxiety about its consequences. Such questioning is ultimately informed by the important learnings about change that our profession has evolved over the past century, and to which we've already referred. For the final time in this chapter, we remind you that *if change were easy and natural, our profession would not exist.*

CHAPTER SUMMARY

- While clients may appear to request change coaching in early sessions, it is unwise to rush into taking these requests too seriously. Clients need space and time for deeper, underlying concerns to emerge, and these may need to be thoroughly explored before change strategies are set in place.

- Generally speaking, change coaching should only commence when the counselling relationship has survived the third session challenge. It may take many more sessions until it is evident that clients really want to change, are clear about *what* they want to change, and are willing to take responsibility for change, instead of insisting that others must change first.

- Change coaching is often a three steps forward, two steps back progression, in which the counsellor must be prepared to move from straightforward coaching back into therapeutic exploration of the client's struggles (*What gets in the way of you doing this? Is it possible you're scared to disappoint me if you fail?*).

- Significant others in the client's life are often key to the client's difficulty in persisting long enough for changes to become established. The counsellor can easily become one of these 'significant others'.

- When clients experience real difficulty in hanging onto a memory of their own successes, or seem dismissive of what they have achieved, a different kind of stance may be required of the counsellor. This involves a celebration of success that makes it much harder for the client to dismiss the achievement, or else the taking of a risk-focused attitude to changes that the client has begun to make.

Chapter 8

'But How Do You Know When They're Finished?':
Supervised Work With Clients

In this chapter we look ahead to some of the issues you will grapple with as you continue your training into the stage of supervised practice with clients. We have tried to focus on the kinds of questions that beginning counsellors wonder about and worry about, and have provided our personal answers—some of which we hope will reassure you—and to forewarn you of some problems and dilemmas you may not yet have anticipated.

WHAT WILL THE NEXT YEAR BE LIKE?

There is a clear pattern in two-year counselling training programs, a pattern that, in a modified form, can also be detected in longer (three- or four-year) programs.[1] First-year trainees typically experience a high. They discover lots of things about themselves, they make new friends with whom they often find they can communicate on a more meaningful and intimate level than with their existing friends—or even their partners. It's exciting, and maybe a bit alarming. First-year students can idealise their trainers and to see them as larger than life: embodiments of all wisdom, patience, and empathy. They have found new role models. In the second year of their program, however, much of this changes, at least for many trainees. By the second year, some are starting to feel overwhelmed by what they have been learning (especially disturbing topics such as domestic violence, sexual abuse, depression, and psychosis). They begin to realise that they themselves have experienced some of these things, if not personally, then through their interaction with a close family member or partner. It is as if the pain that unconsciously drove them into a helper role (see Chapter 1) has now risen to the surface. Previously acknowledged at a safely cognitive level, its reality at the emotional level cannot be denied any longer.

And then there is the placement or internship, which in many programs (not all) happens in the second year of study. As students move from working with 'tame clients' (fellow trainees) to real clients who present at community agencies and organisations, they must confront painful feelings of incompetence, and the serious consequences that may result if they are, indeed, incompetent. Most students worry about failing their clients: about the risk that a client may suicide on their watch, about maybe having to report 'danger to self or others'. Staff in the agency where they are placed may reinforce these worries, as many agencies are understandably preoccupied with risk, and the procedures that they hope will protect them from such risks. In high-burnout settings like domestic violence and child protection, many staff may feel (deep down) incompetent and despairing and focussing on 'the rules', on 'risk' and 'danger' can be a way of coping with their own understandable sense of failure and helplessness. Even experienced therapists are tested by situations where clients continue to be at risk and they have nothing to offer other than 'being there' (connection with the client) and a consistent listening ear. If even experienced counsellors can start to doubt the value of 'just holding', it is far easier for beginning counsellors to do so, because they have not yet had the experience of sitting with clients over months or longer, and seeing how the connection in itself can be healing. Earlier in this book we quoted the client who testified to the fact that her therapist had 'held the hope for her' at a time when she herself had none. Penny tells the story of a student on placement who was confused about why her client continued to see her after moving away. The client now had an hour and a half journey on public transport to come to sessions! Penny encouraged the student to ask the client 'How come?' and the client replied, 'Are you kidding?! It's because you care!'

Trainees will inevitably lose some of their initial clients, who will cease to attend sessions because of things that the student has unwittingly done, or failed to do (see below: 'What if they don't come back?'). This leads some second-year trainees to doubt that they can ever help anyone. Often, trainees at this stage experience a lack of fit between the model in which they have been trained, and the urgent anxieties of their clients. When trainees become involved with a client who is intensely anxious, deeply depressed, or hopelessly self-defeating in relationships, some trainees forget the principles they have learned, and begin to feel they must somehow 'produce a change' in the client: *doing to, not being with*. Their natural helping styles—compulsive problem solving, advice giving, or judgmental lecturing—bob up again, and get in the way of their ability to sit with the client while waiting for the time when the client may feel safe enough to risk change.

Some second-year trainees will experience a different kind of lack of fit: a lack of fit between the model in which they have been trained, and the model used by the agency in which they are placed. This will set up tensions within them, as they struggle to do what they have learned to do ('hold' their clients non-anxiously and 'follow the client') in the face of a very different set of expectations from their agency ('Start handing out worksheets at the end of the first session'). Many trainees feel that they have to jettison much of the learning they acquired the previous year, and adapt to a structured model of assessment, a prescriptive map of what to cover in each of the few sessions the agency allows, or a toolbox of miracle questions, cognitive homework, and relaxation training.

Whatever happens to you as you progress through your second year of training, the very best advice we can offer is this: *accept your situation, and allow it to teach you something*. Every client you fail to help is a potential source of learning, if you are prepared to consider not only the client's 'resistance' to change, but also how you may have inadvertently passed on your anxiety to him, by hurrying him into changes he was not ready to make. Every time you have to compromise between the principles of intervention that you have been taught in your training, and the requirements of the agency in which you are working, you have the opportunity to learn something about the strengths and weaknesses of the agency's model—and the strengths and weaknesses of the model your own trainers have taught you. If you treat such conflicts as a laboratory for your own learning—an experiment rather than a homework task (see Chapter 7)—you will minimise the frustration and anxiety you would otherwise feel in the clash between what appears to be an irresistible force and an immovable object. If you are prepared to take your dilemmas to supervision, you will often find that both models can be incorporated (remember that the right hemisphere embraces 'both-and' where the left insists on 'either/or'). Occasionally the two models may be mutually exclusive, but even if you have a 12 page assessment form to fill in, you can ask the questions they require you to cover, but in a more 'natural' order, and you can still use the skill of reflecting before going on to the next question.

Personal awareness and working on your own issues is not something that only happens in the first year of your training, and then abruptly gives way to the 'real work' of helping clients. Personal development should continue through your second year, and beyond; ideally, through your entire professional career. Watching yourself calmly and curiously as you become caught up in your clients' hopelessness or helplessness will show you parts of yourself that you may need to work on, certainly in supervision, possibly in your personal therapy as well (see below: 'You can't take your clients where you haven't been yourself').

In what we have said so far, we may have given you the impression that the second year of training is all struggle, conflict, and painful self-realisation. These things are certainly real enough for many advanced trainees. But there is another side to it. As the second year progresses, some of you will begin to break through to a new level of confidence. Often, this occurs when, with a particular client, you feel safe to rely on your own instincts instead of mechanically following a set of rules and prescriptions. You start to trust that this is the right way to be with this client, even if it is not exactly what you are supposed to be doing, and you find that it works: that it produces a positive shift in the client's attitude and behaviour.

Second-year trainees who have experienced this shift talk of 'spreading their wings' or 'taking the training wheels off'. Now, at last, they are operating autonomously, relying on their own resources. Now they have begun to integrate what they learned as students with what they have learned lifelong as individuals. Personal knowledge and professional knowledge have begun to meld into a single entity: *a new therapist is being born*. Like falling in love, or having a spiritual experience, you will know when this happens to you, but earnestly searching for it will not produce it. It is just like the changes that clients desire, changes that will come when they are ready, but which cannot be ordered on demand. Exhilarated, the trainee realises, '*I can do this! I can help people! And I can do it by being me!* (more realistically, 'me, with significant modifications.') Helping just one client in an effective way is a powerful boost to confidence, and an aid in diminishing anxiety and self-doubt. And, as we have emphasised throughout this book, the lower your level of anxiety, the more you are fully 'present' to your client, the better you will be as a helper.

Not all second-year trainees experience such 'Wow!' moments. Some may take longer to start spreading their wings. For others, the experience of actually working with clients helps them acknowledge that counselling is not for them. As one of our past students said, 'I've realised that I'm not a counsellor. I'm a nurse. I like finding out where the pain is, and then treating it. I like telling people what they need to do. I can't do those things as a counsellor—they get in the way and I can see that they often don't help the client. But as a nurse, they're part of my job. I love doing that job, and I'm going to stick with it.' A couple of years into his first job as a student counsellor at a local college, another new graduate explained, 'I just get this awful knot in my stomach every time I have to see a client. It's not that I do anything bad, and I know some of my clients think I've helped them—but I don't feel good about what I'm doing. It's stressing me out, it's affecting my health, and it's not right for me.' He resigned from his job, took out a loan, and enrolled for a PhD in agriculture (remember, that's what Carl Rogers originally saw as his career). He has continued his journey of personal and spiritual growth, but not as a counsellor. As we said in the first chapter of this book, there is no shame in realising that you are not cut out to be a counsellor. It is far better that you realise it early, and make a different choice, before your doubts and anxieties create problems for your clients as well as for you.

THERE'S ALWAYS MORE TO LEARN

Students may feel disappointed or angry when they find that the end of their training is really only the beginning of their professional education. Some institutions train their students in a broad-based model that cuts across specific theoretical approaches, similar to the model we have presented in this book. Graduates of such programs sometimes decide that this isn't enough, and embark on another training, this time in a particular therapeutic modality. They wonder which of the many approaches they should invest time and money to learn and generally search out one that seems a more comfortable 'fit' for their personality. Other students, already trained in some depth in a single approach—solution focussed brief therapy, for example, or cognitive behavioural therapy—realise after a while that there were gaps in their original training, and that they need more skills than they presently possess, or a more flexible model for understanding clients and the change process. They, too, may feel let down and ripped off. As one psychologist memorably observed, 'When I'd finished my clinical Master's degree, I knew most everything there was to know—about rats.' MClinPsych programs have improved since she said this, but her wry comment is still echoed by young psychologists today.

At the other end of the spectrum, graduates of personally intense, highly demanding training programs in psychoanalytic psychotherapy—sometimes stretching over seven years— can find themselves with a model that is well suited to private practice, where some clients are prepared to stay for the long haul and to pay large amounts of money to engage in often-painful self-examination. But, they realise, that model is a poor fit for the average client in most agencies, whose pressing needs are often for brief intervention and crisis management. So, whether your original training program has been generic and broad-based, or specific to a particular therapeutic model, at the end of it new skills may still need to be acquired, and the assumptions of your original model may need to be modified.

It is common for newly qualified counsellors to attend lots of conferences and other training events. Their professional organisations will require them to do so, but many would do it anyway. They are hoping for *answers*: techniques or models that might make sense of the confusion or stuckness they feel. Often, they will feel inspired by a workshop or presentation, go away, and try out some of the approaches they have learned. If there is a good fit between their own helping style and the model in question, then this can work quite well, at least for a while. But newly qualified counsellors often attempt to graft a new model (or more typically, individual interventions drawn from that model) onto their existing approach, which they themselves have not yet fully mastered. That may leave them more confused, and it may well confuse their clients too. Rapid adoption and discarding of new interventions is common among professionals who have failed to master the core skills (the ones presented in this book) or whose training has not offered them the self-knowledge to sense whether a particular model fits their personality or not. They do not persist long enough to learn the core of any one approach before mixing and matching it with another. Nor do they form a clear notion of what types of clients are best suited to that approach, because they have not stayed with it for long enough to try it with the full range of clients.

Read more

Hybrid approaches can work very well indeed, if those who formulated them have sufficient grasp of the essence of the various models they have combined. A good recent example is psychologist Marsha Linehan's *Dialectical Behaviour Therapy* (DBT): its coherence comes from the fact that it was devised, and continually tested against, the particular needs of a single, challenging client group: those with borderline personality disorder. The seemingly disparate understandings and techniques involved in DBT seem to work for this population, which has notoriously failed to respond well to pure psychodynamic, cognitive, or mindfulness-based approaches. (You can read more about Linehan's approach in her *DBT Skills Training Manual*, 2nd Edn, NY, Guilford, 2014) A successful eclectic model (one that combines elements of several models) works because its elements are selected according to a central organising principle. In the same way, many of you will eventually become eclectic in a meaningful way, by intuitively organising your approach around the needs of a particular client, drawing upon what you know has worked with similar clients in the past. 'Integrative' is now the term that is being used instead of 'eclectic', as it better suggests this need for an organising principle in what is 'borrowed' from other models. Edward Teyber and Faith Holmes Teyber's *Interpersonal Process in Therapy* (7th Edn, Brooks/Cole, Cengage Learning, 2016) is another example of an 'integrative' approach. This excellent book takes elements from the psychodynamic, person-centred and systemic models—but they are elements that belong together and 'map onto' one another in a meaningful way.

There's a lot to be said for completing a thorough training in a single model (in large part because it takes two years to develop the competencies effectively, much like building the muscles of a performance athlete) and applying it consistently in practice for several years, before branching out in new directions. That will give you a real understanding of the model's strengths and weaknesses, and at the same time, a grasp of what it is in you that may make the model frustrating or limiting in certain respects. Having mastered that model, you will be in a far better position to embark on learning a different one.

An alternative way of furthering your ongoing training is to work for a couple of years with a single client group; for example, alcoholics, or eating disordered clients, or individuals with depression, or couples with anger issues. Seeing dozens, and eventually hundreds, of clients with similar presenting issues constitutes a training program in itself. You will learn the advantages and limitations of your existing model as applied to this group; and you will (no doubt) be trained in the model that your agency or organisation favours for dealing with that client population. Of course every client is a different person, but there are similarities in personality structure and attitude that you'll be able to observe in those who present with the same diagnosis or set of issues. Nearly all addicts (even if their drug of choice is not an actual 'drug' but compulsive gambling, compulsive work or compulsive sex) share strong common features (trauma expert Bessel van der Kolk would say they all lack the chemicals that are generated within the body by rewarding human interactions). Depressives exhibit predictable patterns of thinking and behaviour. So do those struggling with anger that keeps getting out of control. Keeping some of the client variables constant may well assist you to refine your understanding of the approaches you are using with these clients. Then, when you have learned enough to feel confident in dealing with that particular client group, you might apply for a position working with a very different set of clients, and notice which of your key principles and assumptions still work, and which ones need to be modified. One of the reasons the gurus of the therapy world seem to go straight to the heart of the matter with clients in the very first session is simply that they have served such apprenticeships, over many years. Those who don't possess years of focused experience with a particular client group cannot expect themselves to do the same.

WHERE DO YOU STAND?

Most of you will have firmly held views on certain controversial issues. For example, if a relationship is in trouble, you may believe that the partners should stay together and work hard to see whether they can improve things, or alternatively, you may believe that there is no point in the couple staying together once 'the feelings are gone'. You may believe that if one partner is unfaithful, such a betrayal should automatically end the relationship, or you may believe that affairs may be a wake-up call to both partners, signalling that something is wrong, and that this something may not necessarily mean the end of the relationship. If a couple have children, and are in serious conflict, is it better for them to stay together, at least for the next few years, for the sake of the children's emotional security, or are the children actually better off if their parents separate? Where do you stand on abortion? On adoption? On breast feeding? On euthanasia? Should kids be made to complete their high school education even though they hate it and want to leave, or is it better to let them quit school, on the grounds that they will be able to take up further studies later if they need to? How appropriate is it to cut off from a 'toxic' family member—have no contact with him or her at all? (Many people, including many counsellors, have families full of such cut-offs.) What about forgiveness? Clients often say, *'Everyone says I have to forgive him, but I just can't, and then they tell me that I'll never be able to move forward until I do.'* Are there any circumstances, do you think, in which such a rule should be modified?

These issues often embody ethical dilemmas to which there is no simple right or wrong answer. They are also things that many people feel very strongly about, and the strength of their feelings will be compounded by cultural prescriptions and unwritten family rules. Sooner or later, you will find yourself working with clients for whom one of these issues is very real, and you may well find that your client's position is diametrically opposed to your own. Of course it will rarely be appropriate for you, as a counsellor or therapist, to debate such issues with your clients, let alone attempt to influence clients to abandon their own position in favour of yours. However, you still need to be aware of your own bias. Having the opposite position to theirs may make it difficult for you to empathise, and to be objective about the choices that they seem to be making. Yet holding the same views as they do can also get in the way of your being objective. Even if your biases remain unchanged, just identifying them, and discussing them with other trainees, will enhance your ability to remain neutral with clients when such issues come up. Counselling and therapy are, above all, professions which involve dealing with complex, ambiguous issues, and those of us who do this work must be capable of tolerating considerable uncertainty and ambiguity without a rapid resort to rules, prescriptions, and dogmas. (This is a view elaborated upon in Garrett McAuliffe and Karen Eriksen (eds), *Handbook of Counselor Preparation: Constructivist, Developmental and Experiential Approaches*, Sage, 2011.)

Individual clients, relationship issues

Many new counsellors expect that they will only be seeing individual clients. They have trained for 'one-on-one' counselling, and though they may have been introduced to couple or family counselling, they don't feel that comfortable with the idea of having more than one other person in the counselling room. Individual counselling can be gratifying: you can give your whole attention to one person, and in response, your client may become devoted to you and rely on you. Having to 'split yourself' between two (or more) clients, having to be equally interested in each of them, and having to avoid 'siding' with one against another— many counsellors find such things pretty challenging and prefer to avoid seeing couples, parent-child combinations, or whole families. Yet although you can choose not to be a couple or family therapist, you cannot really escape from the fact that most human beings live in relationships with others.

One thing that you will encounter over and over again is individual clients who spend much of their time worrying about, complaining about, or even obsessing about another person in their lives. Most often, this will be an intimate partner: lover, wife, husband, former partner. At other times, it will be a relationship with a parent, a sibling, or a child. Clients who present relationship issues pose two problems. First, how much should you allow them to focus on the other person (who is not present in the room); and second, what might be the potential problems of listening to one party describe a relationship, in the complete absence of the other? On the first count, most counselling texts will tell you that your job as an individual counsellor or therapist is to focus the client back on him- or herself. They will tell you that to allow too much time to be spent talking about anyone else is inappropriate, because the client is, after all, there to work on him- or herself. Above all, you will be told, you should not enter too much into a detailed analysis of any other person's behaviour, because that is to collude with clients in their avoidance of their own issues.

This approach makes good sense, up to a point. Clients do avoid self-knowledge by focusing on the behaviour of others. It is important for you, as a counsellor, to ask questions such as 'So when he does that, what happens for you?' or 'How might you be playing some part in what's happening between you and your girlfriend?' or 'You've spoken a lot about how angry he is. Do you ever find yourself getting very angry? What does "angry" feel like, for you? How do you handle it?' All of these questions invite clients to *take back projections* (to realise that something they object strongly to in another person may sometimes be a denied or disowned part of themselves).

However, to our way of thinking, there will also be times when it is appropriate to help the client to explore and understand the attitude of someone else, especially when this other person seems to be acting in extreme ways, ways that appear odd or wildly out of proportion to the situation in question. For example, what if your client, who has clearly tried hard over many years with a difficult Mum, describes sending Christmas presents to her Mum, with messages from her children (her mother's grandchildren), only to find that her Mum sends them back with a curt note: 'We've got too much junk cluttering up our house already'? Of course there is always the possibility that the daughter—your client—has acted in extremely hurtful ways towards her Mum in the past, which might explain such an extreme reaction. But what if this is not the case? What if it turns out to be the daughter who has, lifelong, put up with abusive and dismissive remarks and actions, feeling deeply hurt, but convinced that she must continue to behave towards her Mum in a loving and generous way, in spite of everything?

As you explore such situations carefully with clients, and discuss them with your supervisor, it can become apparent that your client is not distorting the picture to any great extent. You may eventually surmise that your client is dealing with a person (in this case, a parent) whose attitudes and actions are genuinely destructive and whose capacity for empathy, remorse and responsibility taking are either very limited, or completely absent. These are the individuals that professionals sometimes describe as 'personality disordered'. In these cases, *you cannot simply assume that the real problem lies with your client*. Often, all your client can really do is to find better ways of coping with the other person's hurtful or destructive behaviour. This may even involve an acceptance that the other person may never change, and that there is nothing the client can do to produce such a change. This can be difficult if the counsellor believes that their client should take a strong position and let the other person know that their behaviour is not OK. Many clients are not ready to take such stands, and the counsellor may compromise the therapeutic alliance unless she is prepared to work within the limits of what feels possible to the client at this time.

Conversely, adults often describe a parent (or both parents) as 'toxic' and if their counsellor is already of the opinion that there are 'toxic parents' who are better 'cut out of your life', then that counsellor may easily accept a client's exaggerated and unfair description of the other parties at face value, and urge them to have no contact at all. This is why it is so important not to leap into premature opinions about your client's situation, until you get to know your client well enough to have a sense of how reliable a 'witness' he or she is when talking about significant others.

Complicating the whole issue of clients who focus on relationship difficulties is the problem of talking about a relationship with one participant when the other is not present. The strict understanding of therapeutic boundaries originally evolved within the context of psychoanalysis and precluded the therapist from having any contact—even phone contact—with a client's significant others. It certainly precluded the therapist's seeing the client *in the presence of the other person*: the partner, parent, or child. Once individual work had begun, there was no possibility of including even a single session with the client's significant others, let alone modifying the boundaries to include ongoing conjoint work. Of course, there were good reasons for this rule, and there can be real pitfalls in starting with one partner, and then inviting the other in, especially if counselling is well under way and you don't think through how you could mitigate potential difficulties. But it is not always 'wrong' and on many occasions, it can be more helpful than simply continuing to see only one half of the relational problem.

What is lost forever in the purist approach to boundaries is the possibility of a therapist developing a more objective view of a client's relationship through direct observation of both parties interacting. As anyone who has done couple work knows, a relationship that a client has previously described to you in an individual session can appear dramatically different as soon as both partners attend the next session. Immediately, you have a chance to see for yourself not just the reality of the other person, but the reality of how your original client relates to him or her. And access to that perspective can dramatically alter your entire view of what the problem is, and how it might need to be addressed if the client's stated goals are to be achieved. That is why it is invaluable to have done some training in conjoint (relationship or family) work, even if you still intend to specialise in seeing individuals. After repeated experiences of seeing how partners, children, and parents of your clients can be very different from the way your clients have depicted them, you develop a more accurate relational radar!

One thing we can assure you about couples is this: however much it may appear that one partner is emotionally healthier than the other, this is hardly ever the case. People rarely get into a committed relationship unless there is significant matching at a deep emotional level, even though surface differences will initially obscure it. This was the insight of Murray Bowen, who insisted that people partner with others whose level of *differentiation of self* (solid selfhood) is very close to their own.[2] It is not an easy understanding to tolerate; it is much simpler to see one partner as right and the other as wrong, or one as emotionally immature and the other as self-aware and responsible. Think about yourself and your own adult partner—how many of you are already pretty sure that you are the one who is more 'emotionally mature', more 'honest' or more 'grown up'? It's not easy to consider the possibility that you yourself may have some of the same deficits as your partner—although probably they will be displayed in different ways, or in different spheres of life (some people can be emotionally mature at work but lapse into childlike tantrums at home for example).

WHAT IF MY CLIENT DOESN'T COME BACK?

As a beginner, you will almost certainly run into this one early in your period of agency placement. If your client attends only a single session and then drops out, it can be quite difficult to know what the dropout means. Responsible beginners tend to assume that it must have been their fault; they must have done something wrong. Those with more confidence (or stronger defences) tend to assume that it was simply that the 'client wasn't ready to do any work', or 'the client lacked motivation'. Both possible explanations need to be entertained, because either or both may be true; quite often, a beginning counsellor's errors (such as moving too rapidly into an area that is very sensitive for a client, or offering homework too quickly) can compound and reinforce the client's existing ambivalence. If a client has doubts about whether he or she wants to be seeing a counsellor at all, then he or she will seize on anything the counsellor does that might jar a bit, and make that a justification for giving up. This client, needless to say, is probably one of Steve de Shazer's 'window-shoppers'.

It helps to know that statistically, a substantial proportion of clients do attend only one session (see Chapter 4). It also helps to know about the three-session phenomenon, as discussed in the same chapter. You can see dropouts as an opportunity to learn something worthwhile. What do you notice about those clients who only come once? Is there anything that seems similar in their behaviour, or in what they say? What sort of personalities are involved? Or is this more a matter of socio-economic status and education level, as some have suggested? Researchers have investigated such things, of course, but it is still useful for you to make your own observations. You will also need to navigate your agency's responses to 'no shows'. Some agencies require you to send an email warning clients they may lose their time if they don't make contact. Others let you ring the client, showing that you noticed their absence, and were concerned that something had prevented their keeping the appointment. Whether you ring to 'chase' a client who doesn't arrive, or don't, would ideally be a decision you would make after careful thought. Some clients hope you will care enough about them to make contact. Others may be very differently motivated.

Unless you are working in a rehab or other unit where clients are expected to attend sessions as part of their contract, you are bound to lose some of your early clients and that doesn't feel good, no matter how much you tell yourself 'it isn't personal' Some of the time, it will be at least partly a result of miscalculation or mistiming on your part. Learning to sit with a distressed individual without rushing into offering solutions is something that takes time to develop. Some beginners find it difficult to avoid such anxious rescuing. But as we saw in Chapter 7, some clients in crisis do need you to do more than 'just be with' them. Some intervention, practical or emotional, may be required, or they will lose hope and drop out. The experienced worker is better able to sense what a client most needs than a beginner. In two or three years' time—even in one year's time—you will be probably be able to retain many more of your clients than you do now.

While losing clients is frustrating and disappointing, you need to get used to it. We all have to learn, again and again, that sometimes people don't really want to be helped, at least, not right now, or at least not by us. Dropouts may be as much a matter of counsellor–client fit or chaotic life circumstances, as of counsellor error. In other words, if your client instinctively likes you and feels comfortable with you, she or he is far more likely to come back for another session. If a client does not like you, or senses your dislike of him or her, then dropout is a far more likely outcome. There is little you can do about this in the short term.

Even if your client does like you and feel comfortable with you, things can still go wrong. Some clients (as mentioned earlier) disclose too much, too early, and then feel that they cannot go back for a second session and face what they imagine will be their counsellor's judgement, or their own shame. Some clients have a distinct tendency to leave some significant disclosure until late in the session, blurt it out when they realise that there is hardly any time left, and then crawl away feeling dreadful. Then the counsellor (who has another client waiting) is left with no chance to explore what has been said so suddenly, no chance to hold the client's feelings—and so the client feels 'dumped' by the counsellor and the counsellor feels 'dumped on' by the client! Human beings are complicated and difficult in many ways and hopefully you will realise and begin to accommodate this reality as your training progresses.

IS IT WRONG FOR CLIENTS TO DEPEND ON YOU?

Clients who drop out very early pose one challenge, but another may come from those who seem to stay and stay. When you are a beginner, clients who return are generally seen as a sign of your competence. 'She keeps her clients', agencies say approvingly. Yet when the weeks and months turn into years, things change—unless of course you are working in private practice. If clients keep coming, some people will assume it means that you are failing to confront them, or not 'moving them into action' rapidly enough. The current popularity of short-term models of counselling supports this view—ignoring the fact that there are many clients who are simply not ready to make the changes that professionals see as important for them.

There exists a widely held opinion that it is a bad thing for clients to become 'dependent' upon their counsellor or therapist. Sometimes dependency is seen as taking away clients' sense of empowerment—they don't 'learn to stand on their own feet'. Sometimes it is claimed that therapists encourage dependency to gratify their own wish to be needed by their clients.

Many agencies actively discourage dependency by setting rules (for example, no phone contact outside of sessions). These rules offer sensible protection for inexperienced counsellors. It's not generally a good idea to give your mobile number to a client you barely know—although an experienced counsellor might sometimes choose to do so, on the basis of an accurate appraisal of the risks involved. Policies on funding may limit the number of sessions that an agency is officially able to provide and pressure is applied to staff to terminate clients who have attended for 'too long'. Too often, this pressure results in the premature termination of isolated older people (and some younger people too) for whom their counsellor may be the only person they really trust. Of course it is our job to encourage such people to widen their circle of friends and other supportive people, so that they are not so dependent upon us. But that is easier said than done.

While your placement agency will (rightly) expect you to observe its own rules, it is important in the longer term to consider your personal response to the idea of clients being dependent upon you. When your client rings you twice in the week between sessions, does this mean that she is going to start wanting more and more contact, and end up ringing you at home at 2 a.m.? Do you feel 'gratified' by a client who tells you, 'I really look forward to these sessions'? Or do you feel anxious and burdened by the thought that this person has invested so much in his relationship with you?

Dependency is not necessarily bad, and in fact it may be necessary, especially in the earlier stages of a counselling relationship, just as many new counsellors need the weekly or fortnightly support of their clinical supervisor as they begin their professional journey. Some clients may initially appear extremely needy, and require lots of contact and support from you. Yet we have noticed that when the helper is prepared to offer what the client seems to need (within the limits of the helper's own ability to do so), this can often result in the client settling, becoming more capable of getting through the time that remains until the next session. As time passes, the client seems content with less frequent contact, only wanting to touch base around a renewed crisis or some unexpected development. Of course if clients cannot take in the extra support you are offering them, then none of the above is true. This minority of clients may indeed 'cling on' to the relationship with you, without being able to internalise your presence as a resource for themselves between sessions. They seem to need your physical presence to feel safe and grounded. By contrast, clients who appear totally self-contained and *independent* can be problematic in the opposite way. They may refuse to allow themselves to be vulnerable, or to be helped at all.

Traditionally, psychoanalysis explicitly encouraged dependency, because it was believed that unless patients allowed themselves to regress to childhood feelings of helplessness and neediness, they would not be able to do the real work of analysis. The aim was that the patient would eventually outgrow this dependency, but this might take years. The re-parenting model of counselling/therapy, as outlined in Chapter 6, broadly shares this assumption. If the therapist or counsellor does not become part of the client's life—a consistent witness to the client's experience—then damage cannot be repaired, and no corrective emotional experience is possible. One client told her counsellor, 'I can't believe that you trusted me with your phone number!' For this particular client, the effect of this trust was profound. 'You were there when I really needed to talk to you,' is what other clients have said. This is a clear example of the principle that 'it's the relationship that heals' (as Irvin Yalom frequently says). When clients are asked what they remember from counselling they mention relational moments: 'When my counsellor had a tear in her eye'; 'When she let me stay in her waiting room even though our session was over'. They rarely talk about our clever insights, or the clever strategies we taught them.

Many of you may not wish to make yourself as available as some counsellors do, because you know that it would stress you unduly, and that is perfectly acceptable. But if you are comfortable making yourself available out of hours to clients who seem to need it, you may be offering them far more than you realise. As always, you should check with your supervisor, but also pay close attention to how your client responds to what you have offered. If your willingness to be available simply encourages more and more demanding and inappropriate conduct from your client, then there is your answer. You have indeed 'encouraged dependency' of an unhelpful kind. If it doesn't, then you are probably on the right track for this particular client.

FEES AND GIFTS

Many new counsellors—and many experienced ones—have considerable difficulty asking clients for payment. If you work for a free service, or if your agency handles fees at a reception desk, you may not have to worry about this. But anyone who has to remind clients that they owe money, or who has to negotiate a fee with a client whose income is low, will have encountered the issue. Even writing a receipt and giving change can cause awkwardness to some of us. Probably this is because counselling and therapy involve trust and intimacy. What we do seems too close to 'friendship' to be paid for. One of Penny's clients said, 'It's hard to handle. I have to pay the one person who I feel is there for me.' For her, the financial transaction seemed to cheapen the whole enterprise.[3] Perhaps there are other reasons why we do not feel quite right about charging for our services. Could it be because we doubt that we have really done enough, because we fear that just listening and empathising is inadequate? (Feelings like these are sometimes described as the 'impostor syndrome'.)

But suppose you think of it this way: how often do most human beings get another person's undivided attention for an hour at a time? Most conversation, even between close friends or family members, does not approach the level of care and intensity a good counsellor can offer. Rightly understood, the fees we charge compensate us for being prepared to offer this service, not to a lover or a friend (from whom we expect to receive the like in return) but to someone we have never previously met, someone we may very well not have sought out in a social setting. The fees are there to ensure that we do strive to be objective, to act in our clients' best interests, that we do not resent their drain upon us; that we do not feel burdened by them. (When they pay $50 to have their nails done, but say they can only afford to pay you $20 for a session, you might wonder about their priorities, or question your own belief in the value of what you are providing.) As you gain experience, you will notice that sometimes the clients who complain the loudest about the fees they pay are relatively well off. And some of the poorest insist on paying more than they can really afford. Face it: if you choose this way to earn your living, then you have a responsibility to charge appropriately for what you do, and so does your agency.

Sometimes clients want to give you extra things—presents, flowers, invitations—over and above the fees they have already paid. Often counsellors are uneasy about that too. The longstanding rule of psychoanalysis was that analysts should never accept gifts. Rather, analysts are advised to analyse the patient's motives for offering the gift (is the patient attempting to buy love, forestall the analyst's anger, or assuage guilt?) This makes a lot of sense in a very long-term, intensive therapeutic relationship, where the analyst can become a very important person in the patient's life, and where the ultimate goal is to understand every aspect of the patient's behaviour. But there can be long term relationships with clients where gifts have meaningful but less neurotic motives. In less intense relationships, over much shorter periods of time, where the work is problem-focused rather than relationship focused, the acceptance of a gift may be less problematic.

Clients often feel very grateful to us. They try to show their appreciation in ways that in any other social context would be considered perfectly appropriate. It is hard for them when we respond with, 'I'm sorry, but I can't allow you to give me a present. Let's talk about your reasons for wanting to give me something', especially during the final minutes of the final session!

Is a wish for more than a formal handshake at closing always something you must refuse? If a client wishes to hug us as a goodbye, is that the same as a client wanting to be hugged at a much earlier stage, where it might well complicate the relationship, or blur the boundary between therapy and a different kind of intimacy? If clients have gone to a very scary place during the session, or faced something that they have previously denied, or kept out of their awareness, they may want to express their relief or gratitude with an embrace. It seems to be their way of thanking the counsellor for being able to 'go there with them', face their fears, or say out loud whatever it was that badly needed to be expressed. They may feel so good about what they have achieved that they want to give something back.

With some clients you might feel reluctant to respond to the client's request for a hug, and for good reason, even at a final session. With others, it may feel comfortable to accept a hug at the end of the counselling. You are supposed to be dealing sensitively and caringly with your clients' feelings. If you awkwardly reject a gift that means a great deal to them, have you been consistent with your professional values about holding and attunement? One thing that remains clear however is that *it should not be you who asks a client for a hug!* Such an action on your part risks serious misunderstanding. The client might well assume that you are making a romantic or sexual overture, or that you are 'falling apart' and need the client's support and friendship.

WHAT IF ONE OF MY CLIENTS COMMITS SUICIDE?

Having a client commit suicide is the average trainee's greatest fear. Yet it rarely happens, even when you are working with high-risk clients. Logically, trainees ought not to be so anxious about suicide. But they are. Trainers may inadvertently enhance this fear, by talking about how great a responsibility counsellors and therapists carry, and how dreadful it would be if your client took his or her own life while under your care, or shortly after leaving your care (something that apparently happens to one of Paul's clients in the first series of *In Treatment*).

The blunt truth, which many counsellor educators do not tell their trainees (perhaps because it is socially unacceptable to admit), is that if someone is absolutely determined to take his or her own life, then nobody can stop that happening. Asking about suicide plans, checking on whether or not clients possess the medications, firearms, or other means of doing the deed, making a no-suicide contract: all of these things are important, but their relevance and usefulness is for clients who are still to some degree ambivalent about whether or not to commit suicide, and who are not fully resolved to end it all. These clients (sometimes consciously, sometimes unconsciously) want to issue a dramatic wakeup call to those around them, to get others to take over and help them (perhaps via hospitalisation or medication) in ways they have not been able to do, or to prove to themselves that others really do care. Clients who are motivated by such factors may miscalculate, and hence *risk* ending their lives, but that is not the same as a premeditated decision to die. Taking seriously clients' talk of suicide ('I wish I were dead'; 'There's no point in going on'; 'Nobody gives a shit about me anyway') is a first step towards helping them to find more mature ways of drawing attention to their pain and sense of isolation.

But completing suicide prevention checklists and asking about suicide plans, important though these measures are, will never stop those who really want to end their lives: they will simply go away and kill themselves anyway, and in most cases, they will not announce their intention of doing it to their counsellor, or to anyone else. Nobody, however experienced, however high his or her level of skill and compassion, can persuade another human being to stay alive once the person has made that final decision. To believe that we can, or that we ought to be able to, is a 'self-assigned impossible task'.[4]

There is another, even more confronting, truth. For some people, the mere act of living can be so painful that suicide seems preferable to continuing to force themselves through day after day of abject misery and hopelessness. By what right do we insist that such individuals stay alive? To make *ourselves* feel better? Might not the analogy be with hospitalised patients who are clearly dying, but whose lives are prolonged artificially by heroic surgical procedures that keep them alive for another few weeks or months, without in any way restoring a higher level of functioning, or giving new hope of improvement?

While we are speaking about confronting truths, what about adult clients whose own mother or father has committed suicide? Knowing that a close relative has committed suicide, particularly during one's growing-up years, is something that often makes it easier for a person to feel that this is an option, albeit a dreadful one. For this reason it is important to find out (if you have not previously asked) whether there might have been other suicides in the family, how old your client was at the time, and what impact the suicide had on her/him. Such explorations—especially if the client has hardly ever spoken of them before—can make a real difference for some clients, in understanding the reasons for their own conviction that suicide is the only 'way out'.

How many depressed or despairing clients might still be alive had they not experienced this terrible permission in the form of a parental suicide? It is impossible to say, and of course parental suicide is only ever one of several factors predisposing clients to take their own lives. By the same token, the wish not to inflict such a legacy on one's own children can be a powerful incentive to clients (especially mothers, but fathers too sometimes) to stay alive, despite their hopelessness and desperation. If clients have become too deeply sunk in their own misery to have considered it, counsellors are surely entitled to ask, 'What effect to you imagine your decision may have on your kids?' To do so may well sound like a judgment or a threat to the client, yet can a counsellor afford not to invite the client to explore the issue? Here, as so often, there is no easy answer, no pat formula.

Occasionally, talk of suicide can enter the realm of emotional blackmail. For example, at the end of a 90-minute couple interview, in which the man had wept for much of the session (while maintaining that his wife must terminate her pregnancy because he was 'not ready for children and could not cope with a baby'), the husband waited for the counsellor to end the interview, and then, as his wife was paying and discussing whether or not they would come back, turned to the counsellor and said suddenly, 'Never a day goes past that I don't think about killing myself'. The counsellor sent him off to see a psychiatrist and to be medicated for depression, which was an appropriate response to his individual pathology, but at the level of couple interaction, his dramatic disclosure looks very like a way of reclaiming the counsellor's attention and sabotaging the couple work that had just begun. Yet it is also possible to argue that nobody asks for attention in this way without having a real need for it. What would you have done? A career as a counsellor or therapist is going to confront you with difficult moral dilemmas questions like this, and you need to ask yourself whether you are up for that.

With a potentially suicidal client, ensure that you have sufficient support for yourself. Here the rulebook says, 'Never be the only one to know', and that rule must be followed. If your client is at real risk of suicide, you are not bound by confidentiality, nor should you be, since to be the single person that knows of such an intention is too great a burden of responsibility for anyone. If the worst-case scenario does eventuate, and you learn that your client has taken his or her own life, access your support network immediately. If your workplace provides support only in a limited, inadequate form (like a single session of debriefing with a manager), find a viable alternative. A good supervisor is the obvious choice if you have one, but you may need a deeper level of support and exploration than your supervision can provide. However well you think you may be coping, however rational you may appear, it is likely that you will still experience shock and deep disquiet. You may 'know' that your client's death is not in any way your responsibility, but you will find that your unconscious probably keeps disputing that. In fact, a client tragedy, and what it provokes in you, can be a valuable exercise in learning about yourself.

Read more

If you read one book on suicide, it should be Kay Redfield Jamison's *Night Falls Fast*. Kay Jamison is a world expert on bipolar disorder, which she herself knows intimately. She writes about suicide as an academic expert, with a sure grasp of the research literature, but also, commandingly, as a person who knows from personal experience what it is like to feel suicidal, and to attempt suicide. So her book takes you right inside the world of the suicidal individual, as well as providing you with insights and tools with which to approach a suicidal client. You'll find details of Kay Jamison's works in 'Must-read books'.

WHAT SUPERVISION CAN DO, AND WHAT IT CAN'T

Good supervision is crucial to the development of your ability to help clients in a compassionate and competent way, without ending up drained, dispirited, or burnt out. You will already have experienced some supervision from your lecturers or trainers as they commented on your practice sessions with fellow students and volunteer clients. You will also have experienced a range of comments, questions, and suggestions from your fellow students as they listen to you talk about your sessions. You will know, already, what sorts of comment you find helpful, and which are more likely to get in the way. Some of you will welcome challenges: 'Why are you so invested in this client, Jen? Is there something about her issue that reminds you of your own life?' Others will feel invaded by such invitations to look inwards, and will retort that supervision shouldn't be personal therapy. Some of you will earnestly seek practical suggestions: 'The first thing to do with a depressed client is to ....' Others again will listen politely to such advice, but it won't hit the spot for them. When seeking a supervisor, you will need to take your preferences into account, while recognising that your preferences might also indicate your blind spots.

Your fellow trainees' reactions to different types of supervision run roughly parallel to clients' reactions to different approaches to counselling, as described earlier in this book (see Chapter 5). Some want the problem solved, via practical suggestions for what to do. Others want a more open-ended exploration of self, and operate on the assumption that if they can unblock themselves, their clients will automatically do the same (and it is amazing how often this does happen!). The latter is a form of parallel process.[5] At its most basic, good supervision should hold you in the same way as a counsellor holds a client: it should hold your anxieties, your wishes and professional aspirations, your conflicts and self-doubts. It should offer an environment in which your own ideas and insights can grow and develop. It should not be a stage on which your supervisor demonstrates to you his or her dazzling clinical skills or superior insight, or sits in judgment on you for dealing with your clients in the 'wrong' way.

You should feel safe with your supervisor in the same way as your client needs to feel safe with you. You should not anticipate a supervision session with dread, as it seems many trainee psychologists do.[6]

Especially in the early stages of a supervisory relationship with a beginning counsellor or therapist, most supervisors will (quite reasonably) offer a higher level of support and encouragement and a lower level of challenge than might be appropriate when the supervisee is more experienced, and the supervisory relationship better established. When they provide practice wisdom and suggest particular ways to handle particular clients, supervisors of beginning counsellors may act more like problem-focused counsellors than like relationally orientated psychotherapists. While it is entirely reasonable to expect a lot of support and encouragement from your supervisor while you are still in the early stages of learning your craft, you should also have the sense that your supervisor is prepared to challenge you. If you cannot tolerate a supervisor politely and sensitively pointing out something you may have missed, or indicating an area where she thinks you may have more personal work to do, then you probably should not be pursuing this profession. One of the reasons supervision exists is to help you see the bits of you that are out of your awareness, and to identify your own countertransference. Even the most experienced of us cannot always do those things, although we can get better at it over time.

You can't take your client where you haven't been yourself

Throughout this book, we have insisted that having your own therapy is one of the keys to acquiring fully developed capacities for helping others. Why exactly is this so? First, if you have experienced successful therapy as a client, you know how it feels to be on the receiving end of a professional's interventions. You know how vulnerable you can feel, how sensitive you can be when certain things are said, how important it is that your therapist 'get you'—understand you correctly—and how devastating it can be when your therapist appears to judge you, or fails to take you seriously. All of these experiences will help you to sense what your clients need from you. Second, you will know what to say in many circumstances, because you have internalised what your therapist has said to you. The right words come from your mouth when you need them, without your having to frame them in a conscious way. Not that this is an infallible guide to every client and every situation, but it certainly helps.

Finally, you will have had a personal experience of the process of change over time. You will know what you felt like at the beginning of your therapy (your doubts, your worries, your wariness, the high expectations you may have had). You will know what you felt like when firm trust was established, and when you were being challenged and confronted on difficult areas. You will know how it felt to be changing, and maybe even losing parts of yourself, yet unsure of where you were going, or who you were going to be when you arrived there. Such experiences should assist you to sense the point your client has reached on his or her therapeutic journey. No client will be identical with you, and many will be quite different from you. But at least you will have a personal map of what the change process felt like.

Counsellors often say, 'You can't take your clients where you haven't been yourself.' In other words, you can learn techniques and forms of words, you can study the theory of interacting with clients, but if you haven't experienced these things in your own therapeutic journey, your attempts to help will often be compromised, and your capacity for deep empathy, and effortless 'Yeah, I know' responses (spoken and unspoken) will be far less. In fact, clients usually sense—perhaps not consciously—whether or not you have the capacity to go with them where they need to go. Mystical and unscientific though it may sound, clients will not normally access painful and vulnerable places unless they feel that you can handle it. This is one of the many forms taken by 'right hemisphere to right hemisphere connection'.

Ideally, your therapist and your supervisor should complement one another. Supervision will usually deal with counsellors' response to their clients (and, by agreement, to their work situation generally). Often, though, your response to both your clients and the dynamics of your agency will be affected by attitudes, values, and ways of relating that have deep roots in your personal history. When you get blocked or 'stuck' with a client, it may be because that client reminds you of someone in your past (transference), or indeed, reminds you of a part of yourself that you feel uncomfortable about and may even pretend you don't have (projection). Even if your supervisor is comfortable engaging with you about these more personal dimensions of your work, supervision will probably not allow you the luxury of fully exploring them. For this, you need the personal space provided by therapy, and your therapist's close knowledge of you over time. Many students don't realise initially that they can talk about conflicts or difficulties with clients in their own therapy sessions, and that exploring these impasses may well lead to significant personal discoveries and new awareness.

One experience of personal therapy is not always sufficient. That does not mean that the first experience was a failure, or inadequate. Human beings are constantly changing, whether they like to acknowledge it or not. Many people find that they need to re-enter therapy ten or more years after their first experience, when perhaps their situations are different and they are encountering new challenges in living and relating. The process of ageing potentially brings new wisdom, but it can also bring back old issues that seemed to be 'dealt with' at the end of an earlier therapy. Clients who have had previous therapy often exclaim 'Oh, I've worked through all that before—I don't need to rake it all up again' but this is sometimes a self-comforting statement that helps them avoid a painful awareness. If clients say this, it is always worth exploring with them what made talking about whatever-it-was in their previous therapy so uncomfortable or painful. And similarly it can be very useful for you as a therapist to ask yourself 'when I say I've 'dealt with' that, what do I really mean?

WHEN FOLLOWING THE CLIENT ISN'T ENOUGH

In this book, we have taught you a relatively nondirective model of how to conduct a counselling session. Until you have learned to follow your clients' agendas, to respect their needs and their sensitivities, you will not be in a position to intervene in a more directive or challenging manner. But clearly, there are going to be times when following the client patiently and sensitively is not sufficient. We have already looked at some of these occasions, in Chapters 4 and 6. But quite aside from the kinds of interventions considered there, you will find as you gain experience that you will sometimes need to cut across clients' agendas, in the interests of helping them to pursue their own stated goals. Some clients will have a 'pitch' to which they return repetitively. For these clients, repeating the same message over and over becomes a way of reassuring themselves, and avoiding the hard work of change. Telling long stories of how much pain or hardship they have endured would be an example, and so would protesting over and over how much they love and care about someone else. Of course we don't mean that you shouldn't listen closely to such stories, or respond to them empathically. But as they are repeated, session after session, it gets more and more apparent that these clients are simply spinning their wheels.

In this sort of situation, what you may need to do is to *redirect* the session. Nearly always, there will be a core of something real—real pain, real fear, real anger—lurking underneath clients' endlessly repeated stories, and that is what you can help them to feel able to access. Once again, the more experience you have, the more easily you will recognise when you need to cut across the client's flow (hardly ever, of course, within the first few sessions!) and take charge of where the session goes, so that it can go *somewhere*. That 'somewhere' should be determined by what the client has already stated as important to him or her, or what you have increasingly realised matters to him or her. Often, clients who talk and talk but remain stuck are clearly in a lot of distress and pain, yet they seem unconnected with themselves, and more than likely, not connected with anyone else either. Typically these clients don't seem to notice when you, as the counsellor, speak. This is where process-focussed interventions are so useful. Interventions like *'What's it like to have me listen to your story when there's so much hurt there for you?'* or *'I'm not sure what that was like for you to hear me say that ...'* bring you, the therapist, into the dialogue. 'What is it like to hear yourself talk about this?' or 'What do you notice as you tell me about living on your own agasin?' are questions that start to *bring clients into relationship with themselves.*

The need to be directive in this way becomes far more obvious as soon as you are working with a couple, a parent–child combination, or a whole family. There is no way you can sit back and try to be solely client-centred when there are several clients, often with strongly differing needs, feelings, and goals. Your session will go nowhere, and your clients will rapidly lose faith in you. This is a big subject, and a complex one. But even with an individual client, therapy 'gurus' seem effortlessly to take control from the very first session, appear to know where to go, and to take the client along with them. What they do is impressive, but you cannot expect to follow in their footsteps until you have gained knowledge and sensitivity equivalent to theirs. Check with your supervisor, and rely on your own instincts. If you do take control, and find that your client responds negatively, then you will have learned something. If you take control and your client responds almost with relief, then your instinct may well have been correct.

How do I know when they're finished?

If you adopt a problem-focused approach to the project of helping, then you will have a clear benchmark by which to assess when your clients have achieved their goals: they will report that the problem has been solved, or improved sufficiently that they don't need to come any more. If you adopt a relational approach, then the indicators of completion will not be as clear. Having undertaken your own personal therapy will provide you with a gut sense of whether your clients have reached a point at which it is appropriate for them to 'spread their wings' and fly alone. You may remember times that you yourself terminated a counselling relationship prematurely; you may recall own ambivalence about whether or not you felt confident to walk ahead without your therapist's support.

However, deciding whether or not clients are ready to terminate is not simply a matter of your own judgment and your own experience. Nor is it simply a matter of what your clients say. Some clients believe that they have finished when, as far as you are concerned, that is far from the case. Some flee after only a few sessions, telling you that they 'feel much better' and 'can manage on their own now' (This is Freud's flight into health, also noted in a family therapy context by Murray Bowen.[7] Others (especially within the relational model) may insist that they need to keep coming, when you can see that they have reached a plateau, and are only marking time, perhaps enjoying the luxury of enjoying your uninterrupted attention. This need not be wrong, but it does need to be talked about in a session. The great thing about psychotherapy is that everything that happens can be talked through. If it is happening, but isn't being talked about openly, then therapy is not doing its job.

Many clients end their work because of external circumstances: relocation to a different city, state or country, getting a new job, or entering a new relationship. We particularly draw your attention to the last named of these, which often complicates the issue of whether or not clients have finished. Falling in love normally makes people feel good. In this respect, it is little different from a shot of heroin, except that the euphoria lasts a lot longer, and it does not damage your body or endanger your life. In the early phases of being in love, clients typically feel more confident, more optimistic, and this flows over into the way they talk in counselling as well, and convinces them that they are 'OK now', and that their earlier problems are a thing of the past. You may know that this is unlikely to be the case—when the glow wears off, their problems will still be there—but this is not something most clients want to hear, and neither, most probably, would you, if you were in their position. Sometimes it is clear that the new lover has actually replaced you, the counsellor. Yes, you listened and understood, but you did not offer the delights of romance and sexual intimacy as well. Can you really compete with such a beguiling relationship? All you can do is point out, soberly, that perhaps they are being led astray by the power of their own feelings, and that to continue in therapy might be a very good insurance policy for the new relationship. A few will heed these words, many will not, and there is little you can do about it, except wish them well.

Leaving aside such circumstances, how can you tell when your clients really are coming to the end of their work with you? There are some reasonably reliable indicators. When a client tells you that she or he 'feels different' or 'is thinking differently', that is something that you may, or may not, consider good evidence for change. But when (spontaneously) clients start reporting that *other people in their world are telling them that they are 'different'*, that is of greater significance. Take this seriously, and explore it, just as you would have done at a much earlier stage in the counselling process, when clients were telling you about their presenting difficulties. Getting the details of who, when, and how will help you to know ascertain how real, and how lasting, these reported changes are likely to be. Vague assertions of being different that are not backed up by specific details are not likely to be worth much.

If you know your clients well (as, in longer term work, you should), you will have your own 'change indicators' that will assist you to assess their statements. For example, if your client has always struggled to consider the consequences of his actions, then you will notice when he starts giving you evidence of greater ability to think ahead, and more reliance upon cognitive functions. More 'change indicators' are discussed in Chapter 9.

Clients often indicate (unconsciously) that they are ready to finish by referring someone else to you, perhaps a friend or a work colleague. In this way, perhaps, they replace themselves in your caseload, or present you with a gift, to convey how much they have felt helped by you. Others inform you that they are considering training to be counsellors themselves: they want to 'become you', by occupying the role that you now play for them. Some of these clients may indeed go on to become successful counsellors; probably many will not, perhaps because they have formed an idealised image of you, and an idealised image of what the profession would mean for them (see Chapter 1). Either way, it is often an indication that they are nearing the end of their work with you, or at any rate, believe that they are.

The other way in which you can know if the work is finished is by a diminution in the level of energy that your clients bring to their sessions. If there seems little to talk about, if they seem to be casting around for topics, or just filling in the hour, then you can legitimately use the skill of immediacy to involve them in a discussion of what you have observed, and what their lack of energy might mean for them. It could mean that the work has bogged down, and that the two of you have been skirting around an elephant. But at other times, such discussions will lead clients to remark, 'I'm used to coming here, and I like it. But for a few weeks now, I've had this sense that we've done what needed to be done, and that maybe it's time for me to see how I go on my own.'

How can I be there for clients if I'm falling apart?

This is a crucial question if you intend a continuing career in counselling and therapy. The more experienced you get, the easier (other things being equal) you should find it to sit with clients, and to be there for them in a non-anxious way. But even the most experienced of us are going to feel seriously burdened by a crisis in our own lives. It is very hard to concentrate all your attention and empathy on your clients when you yourself are crying inside, or full of anger at something that has happened to you. If your state of emotional turmoil or overload continues, then (for some of you, at least) it may prejudice your ability to offer your clients what they need. It will be more difficult for you to keep your own distress from flowing over into the responses you offer your clients, especially if their situation is similar to your own. If, for example, you are going through a relationship breakup, with strong feelings of bitterness towards the partner who has left you, or strong feelings of guilt because it is you that is doing the leaving, then it may be quite hard to listen to a client speak of similar feelings and remain reasonably objective. Bias or judgment may creep in without your being fully aware of it. Alternatively, you may find that your clients' words may affect you so strongly that you can no longer concentrate on what they are saying, so vivid are the thoughts and feelings you are experiencing—feelings and thoughts about yourself, not about them.

What are you supposed to do in this situation? As when a client speaks of suicide, you need to involve your supervisor and your therapist. You may need help to work out what is best for you—to take a period of time away from your clients, or to soldier on (as one therapist said, 'Even when everything else in my life was falling apart, my ability to be involved with my clients was the last thing to go'). For some, there may even be a decision to quit the profession for good. It can be helpful to read how other professionals have coped, and to talk to those who have struggled with similar issues. Just as with suicide, the one thing you must avoid at all costs is to be alone with this situation.

If your life has always been a series of crises, and this simply seems to continue after you become a counsellor or therapist, then perhaps you need to reconsider your choice of profession. That is not meant to be a cruel judgment. Rather, it is realistic and (in the long term) kind both to you and to your clients. Those of you who would like eventually to work in private practice with long-term clients should be aware that it is very difficult to build up and maintain a practice unless you enjoy a fair measure of stability in your personal life. Suddenly having to relocate, going through a messy relationship breakdown, or becoming embroiled in your children's problems with drugs, crime, and/or abusive relationships can all erode your ability to offer your clients the consistency of care and the level of attention that they need. Most clients (other than those who are themselves in crisis) can tolerate you having the occasional off day, when you seem more scattered and less able to focus on what is most important to them. They know you're human, and they make allowances. But no client should be expected to tolerate continuing lack of focus, lack of empathy, and obvious distraction. Think of what your clients need, as well as what you yourself need. Balancing the two is not easy, and you'll probably need the help of your therapist to work it through adequately.

What being a counsellor or therapist will mean

If you follow through on your training and go on to take up counselling–therapy as a career, you will find many rewards, but there are some drawbacks too. Being a professional helper of others does not necessarily make for an easy life, and for some of you, the price may be too high. Best to be alert to this from early on.

First, don't expect that you will earn a lot of money. In Australia, where counselling and psychotherapy do not command the public credibility of psychiatry, social work and psychology, many of the better-paid positions are presently tied to membership of one or other of those established professions. Most of the jobs available to beginning professionals whose training is specifically in counselling or therapy are relatively low-paid, low-status ones, without good prospects for promotion to higher levels of status, salary, and responsibility. Professional bodies are working hard to change this, but convincing the government that we offer a genuine alternative to psychology and social work, with comparable standards, ethics, and expectations of our members, has not proved easy.

Many students don't worry too much about this, because they expect that after a few years they will establish private practices, where they will be free to see the kinds of clients they find rewarding to work with, and convinced they will make a good living. Some intend to move into their own practices straight after graduating. In fact, very few new graduates (however confident they may feel) are ready for full-time private practice without five to 10 years of supervised agency experience first. Most newly qualified counsellors are insufficiently experienced to retain a high proportion of the clients who come to them, and not well enough networked to receive a good flow of new referrals. A viable practice takes several years to establish, and ongoing work to maintain. And, as the stability of your practice will depend on a core of long-term clients who will continue to see you for years, you must be prepared to stay in the one area to avoid having to start all over again. In your early years as a counsellor or therapist, it may be a good morale booster to have a few private clients as an adjunct to a salaried job with an agency—if your employers allow such an arrangement—but you should see a private practice as a medium- to long-term goal, and certainly not as an immediate source of a secure income.

As we have already seen, working in this profession can well be pleasant enough when things are going well for you personally, but once you hit a rough patch in your life or your relationship, you can find seeing four to five clients a day (which agencies generally consider an appropriate load) a real strain. Being a counsellor or therapist brings additional stresses to your private life, however. Your clients will expect you to be a perfect human being with no problems, and this expectation is part of the reason for the professional code that therapists and counsellors disclose little or nothing about their private lives. At one level, everyone knows that people in our profession have as many problems as anyone else (hence all those jokes about 'shrinks' who are more crazy than their clients), but clearly, if we reveal our own struggles, some clients (at least) are going to lose faith in our ability to help them: 'If he can't solve his own problems, how on earth can he help me with mine?' *In Treatment* depicts the stresses and strains of Paul's private life as well as the challenges provided by his patients, and (confrontingly) shows the difficulty he experiences in facing his problems in his own therapy.

For the same reason, we can't afford to enter into debates with our clients on issues of religion, politics, morals or environmental issues, even if we strongly disagree with our clients' stance, or think their values are poorly based. It makes sense not to reveal our position on these things, because some clients' trust will immediately be eroded if they find that we are 'on the other side' from them—and, of course, entering into debates of this nature changes the whole character of our interactions with clients, bringing it back into the arena of conventional social relationships, and removing a key part of the non-reciprocal nature of the healing relationship (see Chapter 5).

If you live in a tightly knit rural community, or a suburb where lots of residents know each other, there will be other restrictions on your freedom to do and say what you like. Letting your hair down in public can't easily take place. Allowing clients to see you dancing on the table, enthusiastically participating in karaoke, or having a few too many drinks, is unlikely to be good for your professional image. If you are essentially a private person who is happy with a small circle of trusted friends or professional associates, and who does not see the need to make public statements at political rallies, enter reality TV competitions, or to perform on stage, then none of this will matter very much. But if you are extroverted, sociable, opinionated, and enjoy going out, you may find it quite restrictive, and may even feel that you cannot be yourself as much as you would like.

In a rural community, you will also encounter your clients in all sorts of places and at multiple levels: in the street, while shopping, at your children's schools, even in the change room at the local swimming pool. As well as being your client, someone may also be your professional colleague, a fellow member of a committee, or a fellow coach of your children's sporting team. In a large, anonymous city you may find that this rarely happens, but in a small place you will need to find ways of handling such contacts that feel comfortable both for you and for your client. It is a good idea to talk about this eventuality with your clients before it happens, rather than allowing an unscheduled and unexpected encounter to occur. What is it going to be like for you to run into a client whom you have failed to help, and who, perhaps, has left you feeling dissatisfied? What is it going to be like for a client who knows that you know 'all of this stuff' about him or her, especially when you run into one another in the street, where others are listening? You need to be clear about how you want to handle such encounters, and you need to have negotiated a mutually agreeable way of doing so.

Focusing on these restrictions may seem like a negative note on which to end this chapter. But most professions have their down side. Some involve lengthy periods away from home, others the strain of frequent overseas travel, some involve physical risk, emotional drain or responsibility for large numbers of others. But if you have been strongly drawn to counselling or therapy in the first place, then you are more likely to be able to sustain the lifestyle that practising our profession entails. And the rewards will be great, not in financial terms, but in terms of life satisfaction. The privilege of having someone trust you enough to share their unspoken dreams, deepest fears and shadow selves is richly humbling and rewarding. Many clients teach you and touch you, and remain with you in unexpected ways so your sense of what it means to be human is constantly expanded. And finally, to know that you have truly helped another person to turn their life around, to assist others to break a generational cycle of bitterness, disappointment, or abuse, to see clients make contact with their own denied talents and creative energies, to realise that children will grow up feeling more secure because you have assisted their parents: these sort of things make it all worthwhile.

Chapter 9

Further Along The Road Less Travelled: What Counselling And Therapy Can Accomplish

At one time (and not so very long ago, either) many postgraduate students of counselling were taught how to conduct the first two or three sessions (essentially, how to conduct 'assessment interviews', as in clinical psychology). After that, the lecturer's guidance ceased. Students were left in the dark about how the counselling process would unfold in subsequent sessions, and with little idea of what to expect as a therapeutic relationship of a few weeks turned into one that might last years. Lecturers assumed that trainees would learn about the unfolding counselling relationship in the same way they had—by trial and error, with the assistance of a supervisor when things got badly stuck. One ex-student, who'd graduated a year before Hugh did, told him, 'You don't really understand the process of therapy until you've seen a client for at least a year'. She was right. Though a new therapist herself, she had started to relax into her work, confident that her client would stay with her for long enough for changes to occur. With experience, anxiety diminishes and we listen better. Glib formulas and rules drop away, and we slowly feel more confident to 'be ourselves' with our clients. As they come to trust us, we trust that things will improve for them. We develop hope for them—the hope that, as yet, they may not be capable of developing. As one client said after her therapy had ended 'At times when I had no hope any more, she held the hope.'[1]

Of course it is very difficult to generalise about the way longer-term work unfolds, because every client is different, and each counsellor or therapist works in his or her own way. Those readers who have already had an experience of longer-term therapy will know how it felt for them and what happened for them, but another client's experience might be very different. Nevertheless we believe it is possible to provide at least some kind of 'map' of what happens, a map that should be useful as you and your client embark on a journey down what F. Scott Peck, borrowing from Frost's famous poem, called 'the road less travelled'. If you are a reader, then you should definitely supplement our account by reading some of the small but growing number of accounts of personal experiences with therapy, written by those with the capacity to articulate what the vast majority of clients have left undocumented (Sarah Ferguson's *A Guard Within;* Marie Cardinal's *The Words to Say It;* Irvin Yalom and Ginny Elkin's *Every Day Gets a Little Closer;* Jewel Jones' forthcoming *Now You See Me*.[2] Reading narratives like these will help you to see how very differently therapy can be experienced by clients, depending on their personalities, the approach taken by their therapists, and the nature of the issues they struggle with. But at the same time, there are some generalisations that can be made. In this final chapter, we'll look at how trust develops over time, how clients' initial goals may become almost irrelevant, how long term therapy 'goes in cycles'; in what ways clients typically change and how we know that a therapy has been successful. Finally, we return to 'the person of the therapist'—how our capacity to be *our* 'authentic selves' helps our clients to contact *their* authentic selves. As we have said all the way through, it's not about 'doing things to' our clients, it's about being with them in a certain way.

CYCLES, NOT STAGES

Some writers on long-term therapy talk about an 'opening stage', a 'middle stage' and a 'termination stage'. In the opening stage therapist and client get to know each other, clients establish trust, the therapist sets ground rules and the client sets goals. In the middle phase clients work towards their goals (according to psychologists) or (for more psychoanalytically inclined writers) work through transference issues. In the termination phase client and therapist prepare the ground for therapy to finish and for the client to feel comfortable with moving ahead on her/his own. The client no longer needs the therapist's physical presence, because the client has internalised the therapist, can hear her voice, can recreate her calming presence, or, for many psychologists, has learned the strategies taught and practiced in therapy. This three part 'summary of therapy' is true enough as far as it goes, but a little too neat, in the manner of the left hemisphere. It misrepresents the intrinsically spiral nature of long-term therapy. Once a solid therapeutic alliance is achieved, the ongoing work of therapy proceeds less in defined 'stages' than in a series of cycles. The main issues may be established early, but they come back again and again as clients cycle back and back over different manifestations of the same issue. Whatever the issues are, they come back as often as they need to, until some form of shift or resolution occurs. Experienced therapists can sense their clients' progress when they tackle the same issue yet again, but each time at a slightly deeper level, coming closer to painful or shut-off feelings, and showing more self-awareness in the process (see further later in this chapter).

TRUST—SHORT TERM AND LONG-TERM

As we've seen in earlier chapters, some clients will establish 'basic trust', which, for one client might mean 'you get what I'm saying' or, for another, 'I can rely on you', in their counsellor within a session or two. Generally, such clients are those who were securely attached as young children. Other clients may take months, or even years. One client sat in almost total silence for ten sessions. Her counsellor wisely sat with her, making only minimal attempts to maintain contact with her seemingly unresponsive client. Finally, the client began to talk. For this client, establishing trust was an enormous step and she required extraordinary levels of skill and sensitivity from the counsellor in order to do so. Fortunately, her counsellor was able to give her what she needed to reach the point at which many other clients would have started. In longer-term work, we often need to remind ourselves that *if our clients keep coming, then they must be getting something*, even though to us it appears that they are 'not getting anywhere'. That doesn't mean that we can simply sit back and ignore what is blocking them. It needs to be acknowledged, but delicately—so that they are less likely to take it as criticism or rejection. After all, they may not know themselves what is going on.

Therapist: I've noticed that you come along every week, and yet you're still feeling a lot of distress and nothing I'm saying seems to be making a difference. What is it that keeps you coming? Is there something that happens here that you appreciate, even though you're not getting anywhere with the things you wanted to improve in your life?

In asking these kinds of questions, we need to be careful not to give the impression that we are asking out of our own need for reassurance. So we listen carefully to their answers, and if need be, we rephrase the question so that they can start exploring what is happening for them instead of just trying to help us.

With some clients (often these were ambivalently attached as children), trust seems easily established initially, but sooner or later, there comes a 'rupture'—the therapist says or does something that triggers the client into feeling abandoned, shamed or judged. The therapeutic connection has temporarily been broken. We discussed this in Chapter 4 but with some clients there are many ruptures and repairs in the course of a long term therapeutic relationship. Good therapists generally lay 'groundwork' in advance for how such ruptures can be dealt with in a constructive and non-blaming way:

Therapist: Remember what you told me about that other counsellor you saw one time? How it all broke down when he said that judgemental thing to you? And you just left the room and never came back? [client nods] Well I'm wondering whether maybe at some stage I might say something that triggers you in the same way—so that you feel you just have to get away?

[Client first disputes that this would happen (saving face for the therapist) then admits that 'yes, it might happen although it's not likely'.]

Could we talk about how we might deal with that if it does happen? For example, could we have an agreement that whatever I do and however bad it seems at the time, you'll agree to stay and talk about it—or if you do walk out, that you'll come back and talk about it next time?

Sometimes (particularly in the earlier stages of therapy) it is important for the therapist to ask, *How would I know that you were starting to distance yourself from me? What would you do that would show me that you were 'cutting off'?* Often clients know precisely what they do— other clients have no idea and will need assistance from the therapist, who can remember their typical behaviours preceding earlier ruptures: *I noticed that last time that happened, you said at the end of the session, 'I'll have to get back to you about the next one'—my daughter's coming up and I'm not sure when I'm going to be available'. I'm wondering if that was your way of telling me that you were feeling unsure about whether or not you could still trust me and not sure that you wanted to come back at all?*

Of course, there will be times when clients tell you they're uncertain about when they can return—but it does not mean that they have cut off from you. Their statement is 'reality based'. So how does an experienced therapist tell the difference between the two situations? Partly this is a matter of knowing your client better and better as time goes on, learning to pick up the subtle signs that he or she is 'moving away' from you, beginning to 'cut off'. Experienced therapists usually know when they can take a client's excuses at face value, and when they would be unwise to do so. But even experienced therapists can be wrong! It is important always to hold in your mind the possibility that a rupture may have occurred, which your client is unwilling or unable to tell you about in words. And it's always a good idea to check: *When you said that, I found myself wondering whether perhaps you were feeling a bit uncertain about whether you wanted to keep coming here. Is that right?*

All of this is just one facet of learning to put into words what would once have been felt but concealed, or even not felt at all but simply 'enacted' (demonstrated in behaviour but not acknowledged in words). In long-term therapy, clients learn to take right-hemisphere feelings (even 'unacceptable' feelings) and express them verbally (thus bringing the right hemisphere's instinctive feeling into the conscious awareness of the left, and making it available to the therapist). The client is 'coming into relationship with self' and simultaneously, enriching the relationship with another person (this person will be the therapist, in the first instance, but in time the client will be able to do the same with significant others in her/his life).

While these ruptures are shocking for the client, they can also be alarming for the therapist, who has felt secure in her relationship with the client and suddenly finds that the same client has lost trust in her and simply wants to run away. When long-term clients do this, therapists may question their own skills and wonder what is wrong with them. Responsible therapists, who have spent time in therapy themselves, will often be able to spot their counter-transference reactions and admit that they may have (for example) projected something of their own onto the client—something that might have contributed to the temporary breakdown in the therapeutic alliance. They will discuss the rupture with their supervisor—and their therapist—and these actions will assist them to help their client through the initially painful process of examining what went wrong. Ideally, it will lead to a corrective emotional experience in which the client will discover that it is possible to handle painful feelings in a close relationship without simply cutting off from that relationship temporarily or permanently. Connections that feel 'broken' can often be repaired and in many cases the patient process of restoration will strengthen rather than weaken the original connection. For most people this healing process is uncommon outside the therapy room. Many individuals react to a relationship rupture by attacking or walking away (the limbic lobe's fight or flight) instead of giving themselves space and time to observe their own feelings and actions, and then expressing them honestly to the other person.

With some clients trust is going to be constantly broken, because clients who have experienced disrupted attachment in early childhood are likely to act (as adults) in ways that unconsciously invite others to respond to them in the same unpredictable and unreliable way their own caregiver did. Such clients can take their therapists down a very bumpy road. As time passes, however, the client's 'on-again, off-again' pattern will become more familiar to the therapist, who will be more able to seize the chance to turn the client's experience of mistrust or betrayal into an opportunity for valuable learning. This kind of learning rarely occurs as the result of a single dramatic 'breakthrough'. More usually, it occurs slowly, with the client 'doing it again' (feeling the same as before and acting on those feelings) followed by a discussion with the therapist in which the client is invited to examine the feelings that prompted his action, and to consider how he might act differently next time those feelings come up. This sequence may be repeated many times over a long term therapy, but clients who stay the distance will gradually learn to respond differently to their own urgency—in part because the therapist has offered them the patient, reliable assistance that their childhood caregiver failed to offer, but in part too because of the quality of connection that has occurred during crucial interactions (more on this shortly).

Sometimes trust may need to build over several years before clients will feel safe enough to risk a highly significant but seemingly shameful disclosure—perhaps of childhood sexual abuse, or a wish to harm someone—that they have never previously admitted to anybody. Once the disclosure is made, and the client discovers to his shock that the therapist does not reject him or judge him (as he has been rejecting and judging himself for so many years), all kinds of things can fall into place. Rigid behaviour patterns begin to dissolve, offering the client the possibility of behaving in new and more constructive ways. Love begins to flow instead of bitterness and hate. The key thing in all of this is the therapist's consistent 'being there', her ability to wait for her client to get there, her capacity to pull back from confrontation when the client signals he is not ready. Many professionals can be patient for a while but there comes a point where they lose their patience (and, unfortunately, their tempers) and start telling clients 'I can't help you any more' or 'You're never going to change' or 'I think you like being miserable, in fact I think you're addicted to it'. As we saw earlier, Freud occasionally yelled at a 'resistant' patient, and no doubt he was not the only one! Of course there is a place for confrontation, but it must be caring and honest. It should not just be a knee-jerk reaction to the therapist's frustration, and it should not leave the client feeling that he has 'disappointed' the therapist or 'let her down'. *You cannot fail in my eyes.* That is the message that many clients need to receive, over and over again, from their therapist.

The wise therapist waits and waits, noticing subtle signs that the client is getting gradually closer to the core of his problem, until eventually the 'ah-ha!' moment comes (educational experts speak of 'the teachable moment'—the 'window of opportunity' for new learning to occur). British psychoanalyst Donald Winnicott (whose books on parenting we mentioned earlier in this book) famously advised that analysts should never push an interpretation on a patient but wait until the patient himself seemed to be trembling on the edge of saying the exact same words that the analyst was silently framing in his mind. When you find your client saying out loud the thought that you yourself have just been thinking, then *there* is your evidence that you are well 'attuned' to that client. Right brain-to right brain communication is what is happening in these cases: therapist and client are connected so deeply that the feelings and thoughts that one is having can 'flow across' into the other, even without being spoken out loud. You and your client are 'in the same place' or 'on the same wavelength' (spatial or auditory metaphors that convey the same thing). Fantasy literature (especially science fiction) has often featured some form of 'mind to mind' communication between individuals, across great distances, without the need for words—'mindspeaking' is what SF award-winner Ursula le Guin calls it. Surely this 'fantastic' idea has its roots in the real-world potential for two people to share awareness, often at a level below that of words, via the older parts of their brains?

GOALS—IN THE SHORT TERM AND IN THE LONGER TERM

Counsellors are generally advised to ask their clients to set goals very early in the process—sometimes even at the first session. There is some merit in this, especially for beginning counsellors. A goal provides a structure to the ongoing work so that both client and counsellor have something to measure progress by. However, the goals clients are likely to come up with in early sessions are probably going to be of two kinds. Some goals are big and vague *(I want to feel more self confident; I want to feel better about myself)*. These goals suggest that the client wants to be a completely different person. Other client's goals are highly specific *(I want to control my anger; I want to let go of my grief)* and often couched in negative terms, which strongly suggest that the client sees problems in terms of getting rid of the 'something' that is causing trouble for him or her.

Both types of goal are unrealistic. While people can change in many ways, it is virtually impossible to change one's temperament (the bundle of genetically-influenced traits we are born with). Shy people will always be shy; loud, expressive people will always be loud; thick-skinned people will always be less sensitive than 'highly strung' people. We can learn to conceal some of our temperamental traits—for example, unconfident people can learn to act confident even though they do not feel it—and this may improve things for us. However, adopting new behaviours will not transform us into different people. We have simply added new, learned behaviours to our repertoire.

Similarly, it is not possible to 'get over' feelings like grief within a time frame set by ourselves. Grief takes the time it needs to take—which is too long for some people, who simply don't like feeling the pain, and far too long for most of the people they know (who just want the grieving person to 'get over it' so that everyone else can feel comfortable with them again). Media reporters are prone to conclude their reports of public mourning (after mass-shootings and natural disasters) with the words, 'Now the healing can begin'. Ritual mourning does generally assist healing, but true healing takes far longer than the reporter's clichéd assurances would indicate.

Likewise we are going to feel anger in certain circumstances whether we want to or not—though we can certainly learn less destructive ways of expressing and dealing with that anger. Again this is generally a lengthy process. The trouble with anger is that it is often righteous, that is, the person feels entitled to his anger, because of the unfair way he has been treated (at least in his perception). This kind of 'righteous anger' is not going to be 'controlled' or 'managed' in simple steps: it is only when the angry person is able to focus not on his 'rightness', but on the damage he is doing to others whom he values that his anger will become more open to being 'managed'. 'Anger' is also used, misleadingly, to refer to rage—a primitive, animal-level surge of aggression directed outwards, in the grip of which the person feels that he is fighting for his own survival and that nothing short of extinguishing his 'opponent' is going to ensure it. This is the 'fight/flight' instinct recognised by neurobiologists, and understanding this can help clients: their rage is no longer 'blind'. If his perceived 'opponent' is actually his intimate partner, physically weaker than he is, then the situation is grave. Alan Jenkins, an Australian psychologist much influenced by narrative therapy, has evolved some innovative and effective ways of helping entitled, rageful men to face up to their own destructiveness—by using the same stereotypes of 'courage vs 'cowardice', and 'strength vs weakness' that men themselves typically employ.

The kinds of goals clients initially set reflect common misconceptions about therapy (and by extension, about human change processes in general). The first misconception might be termed 'detonate and replace'. The second might be thought of as 'surgical removal of a cancer'. Both share the idea that *something has to be taken away or got rid of* in order for things to improve. In the first, the client acts as if she believes that her 'old personality' can be sloughed off like a snake's old skin, leaving a new one in its place, all gleaming and handsome. In the second, the client acts as if impossible-to-control feelings like passionate anger or profound grief can be cut out (like a cancer) or medically controlled (like high blood pressure) leaving their existing personalities intact. The truth is that change is unlikely to happen in either way. More usually, we humans change by adding on new capacities and behaviour patterns rather than by subtracting or deleting patterns that are established within us. In the evolution of the brain, new structures and capacities have been added to those that already exist—as when the mammal brain (in humans the limbic lobe) replicates the functions of the existing survival-oriented reptile brain but also extends them with new capacities. In psychotherapy, old structures and capacities are not 'detonated', but they may be supplemented by newer behaviours and capacities which enable them to be circumvented and give us more control over the brain's more primitive impulses than we previously enjoyed.

So even if clients set goals at the start of a long-term therapy, it is likely that these goals will need to be revisited and redefined later—perhaps many times. In some cases the initial goals are simply forgotten, as clients explore their thoughts and feelings in greater depth and realise that what they thought was the problem is not the real problem at all. In other cases clients may realise, as therapy nears its end, that they have actually achieved some of their original goals even though they have not consciously 'worked on them' since those far-away early sessions. At all events, it is often useful to ask clients in the concluding sessions '*Looking back on yourself as you were when you began, what changes do you notice in yourself?*' or '*Can you remember what you said you wanted to achieve when you met with me for the first time? Do you think you've got there?*'

Some personalities are goal-oriented: it is part of their whole attitude to life. They will feel lost and dissatisfied if not asked to specify goals. Others will be perfectly happy to proceed without any goals being specified at all. In longer-term work, both may end up modifying their initial stances. The goal-directed personality might learn that happiness is possible without always having 'something to work towards', without a series of 'benchmarks' to achieve. The goal-less 'drifter' might learn that it actually helps sometimes to have a deadline that forces her to be more organised, and is surprised at how much she can achieve that way. In long term work, people often modify rigid attitudes ('I could never do that!') and develop more behavioural flexibility.

Our old behaviours stay in place, but it is a less prominent and influential place, unless in some unexpected crisis, old behaviours temporarily take over again. This used to be called *regression* ('going backwards')—corresponding to the common sense metaphor of 'three steps forward, two steps back'. Psychotherapy assists us to be aware of our regressions to old behaviour so that their effects are less long lasting and destructive. And while clients will probably feel some disappointment and even shame at a 'slip-back' or stumble, most will also learn to be 'less hard on themselves'. *Greater self-acceptance is a very common outcome of successful therapy.* We cease to try so hard to be 'better', and so, paradoxically, the less hard we strive and the less we condemn ourselves for our lack of progress, the more likely we are to progress—albeit slowly and often in 'spurts' followed by 'slip-backs'.

Therapists can play a key role in the change process—not so much by urging clients to change (the beginner's mistake) but rather, by being precise *observers* of their clients' changes and by being able to remember accurately what the client was like when she or he first came to therapy. In the process of trying to be different, human beings tend to lose sight of their starting point. Notoriously, they also tend to focus on negatives rather than on positives. If a client 'slips back' and becomes dispirited *(I feel like I'm right back at square one!)* then the therapist can remind him or her of the gains she or he has made, gains which have not been lost (though they may be temporarily obscured). A consistent focus on strengths rather than deficits and weaknesses is of considerable use to many clients who are 'experienced failures' (remember David Epston's words, 'Experienced failures fail to learn from their own success'). You do not have to subscribe to Solution-focussed Brief Therapy or Strengths-based Therapy in order to remind your client of what they have achieved in their lives (and earlier in their therapy). Thus as a therapist you preserve an 'external record' of your clients' successes and good qualities, at times when the clients themselves in the grip of temporary slip-back and depression are likely to forget or minimise them.

How do experienced long-term therapists recognise that their clients are making progress when the same issue returns again and again? What is it that tells therapists that their clients are actually getting somewhere, rather than simply spinning their wheels? First, the therapist may spot a change or a shift in the *way* that the client is talking about the issue. Little may have changed in the way the client is acting 'out there' in the real world, but *the client is perceiving it differently and in particular, perceiving his/her own behaviour more accurately.* This usually involves the client being more aware of his/her feelings, and more aware of what is happening in his/her own inner life than previously. We elaborate on both of these below. Second, *small shifts in the client's actual behaviour* may be noticed. If so, then the therapist may choose to comment on them and 'expand them' by asking questions, so that the changes have more chance of 'sticking'. A typical statement might be:

Therapist: You know, we've talked about this issue a lot over the past year or two, but what I'm noticing today is that you seem much more 'alive' to what is going on than you used to be. And I think you may be handling the situation a little differently too.

[Therapist elaborates on the shift she has noticed.]

Do you have any ideas about what might have made it possible for you to act differently this time? I remember you saying that you used to feel completely helpless and your own feelings just took over and made everything worse. What's altered that?

Asking clients to think about changes is (as we saw in Chapter 7) one way of keeping the changes alive—but it is also a way of assisting the client to be more introspective, more self-aware.

Another thing that sometimes happens when a familiar issue raises its head for more attention is that *clients may remember more*. The picture of their personal past becomes richer in detail, more emotionally alive. Discussion of an issue facing the client in the present prompts the client to recall an incident or a feeling experienced many years before. When such memories are explored, they can lead to new insights, which in turn catalyse changes in the client's present behaviour. Clients' initial stories are often impoverished—like sketchy black-and-white drawings, with little colour, texture or specificity. *As clients get further down the road of long-term therapy, the details are gradually filled in and the story 'comes alive' with memories of things said and felt.*

Narrative therapists have based their approach on the idea of helping clients to replace personal stories that limited or oppressed them *(I have failed at everything I do; I am worthless and I will never amount to anything)* with new 'stories of self' that remind them of what they have achieved, and empower them to 'stand up to' their fears, self-doubts, and destructive self-criticism. (This approach has much in common with Cognitive Behavioural Therapy's emphasis on replacing 'dysfunctional beliefs' and 'negative self-talk' with positive beliefs and encouraging self-talk.) However it is not so much a matter of replacing a 'bad' story with a 'good' story as adding details to the 'bad story' so that it expands and can embody what is positive and life-enhancing in a client's life-course as well as what has 'gone wrong' or failed. Narrative therapy assists clients by encouraging them to locate much of the 'bad influences' in their lives *outside* of them (for example, in destructive social beliefs like 'only thin people are attractive'). A somewhat similar process can occur in any long-term psychotherapy, however, as clients increasingly learn to separate out what is 'their own responsibility' from what is not their fault, and thus gradually free themselves from shame and self-doubt.

Awareness and honest expression of feelings

Most clients feel unsure, anxious and vulnerable in the early stages of counselling or therapy, though only some of them will openly express those feelings. Being open about 'embarrassing', 'weak' or 'confused' feelings is not possible for them at this stage. They do not feel safe enough. But learning to be open in expressing shame, fear and anger is something that does normally happen in the course of longer-term work. *At the end of a successful therapy, clients should be more comfortable in admitting 'weak' feelings like vulnerability or socially disapproved feelings like anger.* They should be able to name their feelings more accurately, and experience the corresponding emotions when using the words. Tears may well up while they are talking about sad experiences, they feel anger when admitting to feeling angry with the therapist, and they radiate joy when they feel joy.

Being able to 'feel your feelings' might seem a pretty insignificant goal for those who have never had any difficulty in doing so, but many clients really are cut off from their feelings (or at least some of their feelings). Sometimes this is the result of early social conditioning (avoidant attachment, for example). Often it is the result of trauma, where a child shuts down her feelings in response to overwhelming pain or terror. Within a conflicted relationship, one partner often assumes that if the other has difficulty voicing his feelings (or seems completely out of touch with his feelings), then this must be a diagnosable disorder like Asperger's (high-functioning autism) or Alexithymia (inability to name one's feelings). Their partners may or may not actually deserve those labels, but regardless, the 'disorder' is much more likely to be the result of early trauma than something embodied in the personality, something genetic that the partner cannot change, only learn to live with. Here is where the slow and careful exploration of early experiences, for which psychotherapy is known, can provide the possibility of answers that diagnosis and medication simply ignore or 'leap over'.

Full awareness of our feelings provides us with more information to guide our decisions and thus contributes to making better decisions because both sides of the cortex—the 'rational' left hemisphere and the 'emotional' right—can co-operate fully. Dialectical Behaviour Therapy calls this 'wise mind'—a third alternative to 'reasonable mind' and 'emotion mind'. If we can speak from that fuller awareness to our partners, children parents and siblings, it helps with our relationships too. Of course, being aware of our feelings does not mean the same as 'dumping' them on others in a self-indulgent way. But, contrary to what many clients fear, 'waking up to our feelings' does not necessarily mean being taken over by them. *The experience of being 'held' and 'contained' by a good therapist can assist many people to hold and contain their own feelings, even when the therapist is not present.* Again, this is something that generally happens over the longer term. Individuals often restrain themselves from crying (or feeling any emotion for more than a few seconds) because they are convinced that 'If I started crying, I'd never be able to stop'. It can be useful sometimes to assure them that they may, indeed, cry for a long time, but that this may not in itself be a bad thing. Maybe there is a great deal to cry about? Some humans need a therapist's assistance to feel their feelings properly (instead of 'choking them back' or 'squashing them down'). Others need the therapist to help them regulate their feelings instead of allowing them to gush forth inappropriately. What works for one is unlikely to work for the other! Sometimes the client fears her feelings, and so the feelings expand into panic and hide the original concern.

BECOMING AN OBSERVER OF ONESELF

Alongside gaining fuller awareness of their feelings, many long-term clients become better observers of themselves. It is the brain's left hemisphere that allows us to be 'detached observers' of ourselves, but without access to the emotional and sensory information provided by the right hemisphere, our ability to observe ourselves accurately is severely curtailed. Sensitive reflections by a therapist can help us to acknowledge more of our whole experience—feelings along with thoughts. By the end of therapy, clients are making statements indicating that they are not only 'noticing themselves' but also incorporating awareness of their own feeling states into their noticing. In turn, this enables some clients to begin separating 'me' from 'you'. How does that happen? When we notice and acknowledge our own feelings, we take ownership of them and are less likely to blame someone else for 'making me feel this way'. Awareness of our own feelings is also crucial in avoiding dissociative responses. Instead of automatically removing their minds from what is being said in the session and simply 'going away' somewhere inside their heads, a client who is well into therapy might say:

I just noticed that I drifted off somewhere then—like I didn't want to think about what you were saying.

Similarly, instead of saying indignantly to the therapist:

What the hell gives you the right to say that! You hardly know me! [a statement that blames the therapist and assumes that she has just 'caused' the client's angry feelings] the same client might say something like:

I had a reaction to that idea—I started to think, 'What right do you have to tell me that?' I guess I was feeling put down or shamed or something—probably my stuff—nothing to do with you! [recognising that his angry feelings tell him something about himself rather than something about the therapist. In this example, an external locus of control has shifted to an internal one].

Long-term therapeutic work helps clients understand their inner worlds, and encourages them to pay more attention to what is going on inside them. This may be disconcerting for partners or friends, particularly those who live on the surface of life and have little interest in delving more deeply into what motivates their actions. While most clients find that their relationships with others (particularly intimates) are enriched, some report the break-up of relationships that had previously seemed stable. Clients' journeys towards self-acceptance and self-knowledge will inevitably take them away to some degree from the mainstream of human life, where people are completely absorbed in the daily round and the pressures of work, rarely pausing to think about what it all means or whether they are achieving joy and satisfaction in what they do. Such people dread deeper knowledge and self-questioning and may only risk those things when in the grip of (or just after) a serious life crisis. Clients who have completed a successful therapy report losing some of their previous friends—but acquiring others with whom they can talk meaningfully about the things that now matter to them. As Joni Mitchell put it, 'something's lost and something's gained in living every day'.[3] Life itself will eventually teach us many of the things therapy helps us to see—but therapy can help us to learn these things earlier than that.

Think About It

In Chapter 2, we mentioned the way that to most people, recorded counselling sessions sound 'slow' and 'boring'. We noted that this is because therapeutic conversation does not display the 'anxious haste' that occurs in social conversation. Interestingly, clients who have had a successful experience in ongoing therapy often speak more slowly than they did at the start. Simultaneously, they begin to perceive ordinary social interactions as rapid, superficial and competitive—they have learned what 'good listening' really is, and now notice when it is absent!

PIVOTAL MOMENTS

In long-term therapy, it is reasonable to expect that some sessions are routine—the 'bread and butter' of therapy. In these sessions, clients recount 'the events of the week', familiar issues may be worked on, or clients talk about something new that has come up for them (which often turns out to be something old in an unfamiliar form). Coaching of clients to experiment with new behaviour, even the offering of advice (provided it is based in the therapist's intimate knowledge of, and sensitive attunement to, their client) can be part of what happens in such sessions. Advice-giving is often inappropriate in early sessions, but over the long term it can often be helpful. By then, therapists know their clients well enough to trust that the clients will not 'swallow whole' any advice they are given—or know them well enough to refrain from advice because the client *will* swallow it whole! This mix of therapeutic stances is sometimes referred to as 'supportive counselling' or (confusingly) 'supportive psychotherapy'. It helps maintain clients in difficult situations without putting undue pressure on them to explore their own contribution to the impasses and challenges with which they are faced.

But there will also be times when all this changes, when clients risk encountering the core of themselves in the presence of a therapist whose reliability has been tested again and again, and whose presence assures safety. In such sessions, clients will 'drop down' into profound feelings, sometimes silent, sometimes expressed in words, sometimes physically expressed.

Now the therapist is witness to these moments and needs *the capacity to respond in that moment* in a genuine, feelingful but non-intrusive way. The therapist's response will come directly from her or his right hemisphere—not from the calculated, rational thought processes of the left. In that 'pivotal moment', words will be comparatively unimportant. Right brain-to-right brain connection means that the client will know that the therapist is with her. If words are needed, the therapist will not need to 'think about' what to say—the right words will come. This may sound mysterious, even magical. Perhaps the best word for the feeling in the room at such 'pivotal moments' is *numinous*—there is an apprehension of the divine, the sacred. It is not a matter of either client or therapist being religious. In some cases client or therapist may possess a faith, in many cases, neither will. Deep connection, connection of one person's limbic lobe with another person's, *feels like a spiritual experience*. It is in these moments that clients feel 'deeply received' (as Carl Rogers expressed it) by another person—accepted, valued, understood. They can experience their own worth, their own goodness in the eyes of another person. It cannot happen if the therapist does not actually feel that acceptance, that belief in who the client actually is. But in long-term therapy, we come to care deeply about our clients. It is hard not to. We know their faults, and we appreciate their inherent value as people. This is the true meaning of intimacy—a knowing of the whole person, which necessarily involves a full knowing of ourselves. We have to be completely open to receiving and being moved by our clients, with no other agenda but to be with them.

Remember that it is not the right hemisphere that divides people into 'good parts' and 'bad parts' or tries to weigh up which 'side' predominates. It is the left hemisphere that insists on such distinctions, while the right hemisphere sees people as wholes. When we are operating out of our right brain, and connecting with the right brain of our clients, we can experience that total acceptance. 'Both-and…' replaces the left hemisphere's 'either/or'. *It is these moments of profound connection, acceptance and peace that catalyse change at the deepest possible level.* This is the sort of deep connection that should occur in infancy between a baby and its loving caregiver. For many of us, it does not occur then, or it does occur sometimes, but not reliably. As adults we need to experience this deep connection in relationship with an adult who cares enough about us, in a way that is free from selfish investment, to give us what we did not receive all those years ago, and who will stay with us long enough for us to make it part of ourselves. Our capacity to provide that presence for another individual is not something that can be learned mechanically or 'grafted on' to our personality. It is indistinguishable from our own individuality—from who we are as a person.

THE PERSON OF THE THERAPIST

And so in the final words of this final chapter, we return to the 'person of the therapist'. 'Who you are' is not an array of techniques to 'use on' your clients (*armamentarium*—literally, an 'array of weapons!'—is the word that you may still find in American clinical texts!) It is not a list of 'strategies' that you can teach them (or hand them on a worksheet). You are not these things. You are a person (like your client) who struggles with some aspects of your life and sometimes feels like a failure. But hopefully, you are also a person who knows that change is possible. You are a person who has learned to be in contact with your own feelings, rather than being closed off to them. You have learned to be a good observer of yourself. You are (at least some of the time) calmer and more at peace within yourself, more accepting of yourself, than you once were. You trust that your clients can change because you have experienced change in your own life—within a deep relationship with another person that was not tied to romantic or sexual investment on your part or theirs. You have risked being vulnerable and been accepted for who you are—connection!

All of these things enable you to 'be there' for your clients in a non-anxious way, to focus on who they are rather than focussing inward on your own anxious wish to 'help' them. At the heart of the alchemy that can occur in long term therapy, but occasionally also in short term therapy, is a meeting of two people, in which one feels deeply understood by the other, deeply accepted by the other, and deeply trusted by the other. It is as simple—and as complex—as that. We wish you—and your clients—well on your journey further down the 'road less travelled'. And we hope that this book will have helped you to continue that humbling and rewarding journey with optimism and a realistic sense of what may lie ahead.

Endnotes

Chapter 2

[1]'Our "babies" are not infants who cannot communicate with words, but adults, or children old enough to speak fluently.' When your client is a child, the ways that we hold may be somewhat different. Virginia Axline's classic account of play therapy with a lonely, emotionally distant little boy, *Dibs in Search of Self* (Ballantine Books, 1964) demonstrates the principle of being with someone in a way that is almost as applicable to adults as it is to young children.

[2] 'point 2s on the Enneagram, Pia Mellody's "codependents"': We use the Enneagram system, in preference to the other established systems of personality typing, because its nine types are easier to master than the larger number that make up the MBTI, and more fine-grained than systems that have only four types. The Enneagram acknowledges both the potential strengths and the potential weaknesses of each type, making it much less focused on pathology than the DSM. We recommend Helen Palmer's *The Enneagram: Understanding Yourself and the Others in Your Life* (HarperCollins, 1988) and Don Richard Riso's *Understanding the Enneagram: The Practical Guide to Personality Types* (Houghton Mifflin, 1990). Pia Mellody's books on codependency and the recovery movement may be overstated and simplistic, but many clients have read them and it is worth your while to familiarise yourself with the ideas (Pia Mellody, Andrea Wells Miller, and J. Keith Miller, *Facing Codependence*, HarperCollins, 1989).

Chapter 4

[1]'The rules of counselling and therapy in our society dictate that clients will, mostly, be people that you do not know.' Mainstream counselling and therapy have evolved in a predominantly urban context, and assume anonymity. The client and the counsellor do not have previous knowledge of each other, and their relationship will be limited to the one hour a week (or whatever) occupied by the professional consultation. It is also assumed that they will have no continuing relationship once the counselling is over. In a small community, particularly an isolated, rural community, these expectations are much less likely to hold true. There, you may already know your client, and in fact, the client may only feel safe to consult you because of that prior relationship (you seem a trustworthy person); moreover, you are going to encounter your client outside the therapy room, and quite possibly, you will be expected to maintain some level of relationship thereafter. Handling professional boundaries in such circumstances does pose problems that most urban practitioners do not face, and demands some adjustments. With a flexible and sensitive attitude on the counsellor's part, the situation can still be handled without anybody being compromised. See H. Crago, R. Sturmey, and J. Monson: 'Myth and Reality in Rural Counselling', *Australian and New Zealand Journal of Family Therapy*, 17, 2, 1996: 61–74; M. and H. Crago: 'The Connectedness within Me: An Interview with Rural Counsellor Jenny Monson', *Psychotherapy in Australia*, 3, 2, 1997: 36–41.

[2] 'If you allow your client to take the initiative in this way, what happens in the first three sessions will have a degree of predictability to it'. There has of course been a good deal of research into early dropouts from counselling–therapy, and a mean length of attendance for clients in the mental health system is variously quoted as 'six sessions', or 'five sessions, plus or minus two'. An entire therapeutic approach (single-session therapy) has been devised in response to the frequency with which clients attend only one session (Moshe Talmon: *Single Session Therapy*, Jossey-Bass, 1990). However, the three-session process described in this chapter has rarely been recognised in the same way (a broadly comparable account to ours can be found in Michael Jacobs' *The Presenting Past: The Core of Pyschodynamic Counselling and Therapy* (2nd edn, Open University Press, 1998). To provide just one example, an old study by Andrew Firestone and Bernadette O'Connell's 'Does the Therapeutic Relationship Matter? A Follow-Up Study of Adherence and Improvement in Family Therapy', *Australian Journal of Family Therapy*, 2, 1, 1980: 17–24, reported that of 72 client families studied, over half had dropped out before or directly after the third session. Comparable statistics could be cited from more recent studies of both individual and conjoint treatment.

[3] 'In Treatment': *In Treatment: The Complete First Series*, 9 DVDs, HBO, 2008. There are two subsequent series—all make riveting viewing.

[4] 'the main attachment strategies empirically identified by the attachment research of Mary Ainsworth and Mary Main': Although Karen Horney, a German-born psychoanalyst based in New York, wrote at a time when attachment theory was still in its infancy (*Our Inner Conflicts*, Norton, 1945) she observed in adult clients the same types of interpersonal 'style' that characterise what we would now call the three main attachment styles or attachment strategies. See M. D. S. Ainsworth, M. C. Blehar, E. Waters, and S. Wall: *Patterns of Attachment: A Psychological Study of the Strange Situation* (Erlbaum, 1978); M. Main and J. Solomon: 'Procedures for Identifying Infants as Disorganised/ Disoriented during the Ainsworth Strange Situation', in M. Greenberg, D. Cicchetti, and E. M. Cummings (eds): *Attachment in the Preschool Years: Theory, Research and Intevention* (Chicago University Press, 1990). Horney's mover towards may be either a type B (secure) or a mild type A (insecure– avoidant). Many 'avoidantly attached' individuals look very like securely attached ones, because they have learned to smile and seem confident and trusting as a way of avoiding getting into trouble. Inside, they actually do not trust the counsellor all that much, and reserve judgment. By contrast, those who are securely attached trust readily (which does not mean trust blindly or trust indiscriminately), and their trust will grow once they are assured of the other person's goodwill. The mover against is likely to be a Type C (insecure–ambivalent), who blames or attacks as a strategy for gaining the counsellor's attention and concern, or alternatively acts helpless and clingy when blaming does not appear to work. Horney's mover away (schizoid in traditional psychiatric terminology) is probably similar to a more extreme type A, where the avoidant features are not masked by superficial social poise.

[5] 'Humankind cannot bear very much reality': T. S. Eliot: 'Burnt Norton' (first published 1935) in *Collected Poems, 1909–1962* (London, Faber: 190).

Chapter 5

[1] 'It does not take long to see that these distinctions tend to break down in practice': See Hugh Crago: 'Counselling and Therapy: Is There a Difference? Does It Matter?', *Australian and New Zealand Journal of Family Therapy*, 21, 2, 2000: 73–80.

[2] '[Freud] did not actually "discover" the unconscious mind, because the concept was already in existence': For example, Charles Dickens' early novel *Barnaby Rudge*, published in 1841 (London, Folio Society, 1987), contains both the word 'unconscious' and the equally Freudian term 'repression', though neither is used in the technical sense that we identify with Freud. Dickens, who died in 1870, was an amateur hypnotherapist, and actually treated the wife of a friend for the same kind of 'hysterical' symptoms as Freud's early patients displayed!

[3] 'At its core, the ideology of psychoanalysis is not dissimilar from Buddhist teachings': Indeed, it may be that all therapeutic models eventually converge on core principles that are indistinguishable from those acknowledged within most major spiritual traditions. These principles are what transpersonal psychologist Ken Wilber calls the 'perennial philosophy'. See K. Wilber: *Eye to Eye: The Quest for the New Paradigm* (Anchor Books, 1983): 127–33.

[4] 'In some forms of counselling today ... that understanding is still accurate': For an example of this, see Eric Timewell: 'Counselling and Psychotherapy' in E. Timewell, V. Minichiello, and D. Plummer (eds), *AIDS in Australia* (Prentice-Hall, 1992): 325–6.

[5] 'For Rogers, confusingly, continued to use both terms': Carl Rogers' early book, *Counseling and Psychotherapy: Newer Concepts in Practice* (Boston: Houghton Mifflin, 1942) offered his original thinking about the two terms, as well as introducing the term client, which he had first employed in 1940. Rogers later replaced the term non-directive with client-centred (*Client-Centered Therapy*, Houghton Mifflin, 1951), and then person-centred (*On Personal Power*, Houghton Mifflin, 1980).

[6] 'Empathic paraphrase ... has been reinvented ... under the labels of vicarious introspection and empathic immersion': See Heinz Kohut: 'Introspection, Empathy and Psychoanalysis', *Journal of the American Psychoanalytic Association*, 7, 1959, 459–83. The topic is clearly introduced in Stephen A. Mitchell and Margaret J. Black: *Freud and Beyond: A History of Modern Psychoanalytic Thought* (Basic Books, 1995): 155–9.

[7] 'Psychoanalysts in the 1920s had set up free or low cost clinics…': See E. A. Danto: *Freud's Free Clinics* (Columbia University Press, 2005).

[8] 'Rogers taught that the professional's warmth, empathy, and personal honesty were crucial to creating an environment in which change was possible for the client': This change of emphasis from neutrality to warmth and honesty reflected personality differences between Sigmund Freud and Carl Ransom Rogers, as well as cultural and historical differences. Freud grew up in nineteenth-century Vienna, a rigidly stratified society, where polite middle-class behaviour meant reserve and respect, and overt warmth would not be expected between doctor and patient. Rogers, by contrast, grew up in twentieth-century America, a more egalitarian society, where the cultural style was cheerful, optimistic, and friendly.

[9] 'Many new models start off by claiming … a cure for schizophrenia': A cured schizophrenic patient of Jung's later became one of his closest associates. Rogers conducted a large research study that he hoped would demonstrate that people suffering schizophrenia would benefit substantially from his client-centred approach. Unfortunately, the evidence did not bear out his initial expectations (see C. Rogers, with E. Gendlin, D. Kiesler, and C. Truax: *The Therapeutic Relationship and Its Impact: A Study of Psychotherapy with Schizophrenics*, University of Wisconsin Press, 1967). Early family therapists argued that their novel approach could result in substantial improvements in the functioning of schizophrenic individuals, yet once again, the early successes were not replicated by later studies. In 1965, Murray Bowen made a more modest claim: 'Although family psychotherapy has not been successful in resolving the underlying problem in severe schizophrenia, it has been effective in helping families achieve symptomatic adjustments' (*Family Therapy in Clinical Practice*, New York: Aronson, 1978: 141).

[10] 'The problem-solving model of counselling and therapy seems to have been evolved by individuals whose own preference has been for problem solving over relationship, and it suits clients with a similar preference': See for example Skinner's autobiography, *Particulars of My Life* (New York: Knopf, 1976) and Daniel W. Bjork's *B. F. Skinner: A Life* (New York: Basic Books, 1993); contrast Rogers' autobiographical 'This is Me' in *On Becoming a Person* (Constable, 1967: 3–30) and Howard Kirschenbaum's biography *On Becoming Carl Rogers* (Delta Books, 1979).

Chapter 6

[1] 'Confrontation (often defined quite narrowly)': See for example Allen Ivey, Mary Ivey, and Carlos Zalaquett, *Intentional Interviewing and Counselling: Facilitating Client Development in a Multicultural Society*, 7th edn, Brooks-Cole, 2007: 245–7; Valerie Chang, Sheryn Scott, and Carol Decker, *Developing Helping Skills: A Step-by-Step Approach*, Books-Cole, 2009: 192–5.

[2] '"Feel the fear and do it anyway", as the well-known self-help book advises': Susan Jeffers: *Feel the Fear and Do it Anyway*, New York: Harcourt Brace Jovanovich, 1987; New York: Ballantine Books, 1988. Many reprints.

[3] 'Telling gap': This term appears to have been coined by German literary scholar Wolfgang Iser, who talked about how authors would often deliberately omit key pieces of information about characters or plots, 'telling gaps' that prompted readers to question and speculate in order to fill them, thus involving them more deeply and personally in the narrative. When clients tell their stories, they leave similar gaps, but unlike the gaps left by authors, these are rarely consciously planned (Chapter 3). See Wolfgang Iser, *The Act of Reading*, (Routledge & Kegan Paul, 1978).

[4] 'Corrective emotional experience, a term first used by Franz Alexander': Franz Alexander: 'Some Quantitative Aspects of Therapeutic Technique', *Journal of the American Psychoanalytic Association*, 2, 1954: 685–701).

Chapter 7

[1] 'Most readers of self-help books take away relatively simplistic message': See Paul Licherman: 'Self Help Reading as a Thin Culture', *Media, Culture and Society*, 8, 4, 1991: 404–20.

[2] 'We don't blame the lock, we change the key': See Steve de Shazer, *Keys to Solution in Brief Therapy*, New York: Norton, 1985: xv.

[3] 'The widely used miracle question most often identified with Steve de Shazer, but in fact devised by Milton Erickson': Milton Erickson (not to be confused with Erik Erikson, the psychoanalytic developmentalist) was a highly original American psychiatrist whose ideas about hypnotherapy, paradoxical messages, and metaphors lie behind much strategic family therapy and brief therapy, as well as informing NLP and Frank Farrelly's *Provocative Therapy*.

[4] 'Think about most work teams that you have been a part of': A fuller account of this phenomenon is described in Hugh Crago's article 'Programmed for Despair? The Dynamics of Low Morale/High Burnout Welfare Organisations', *Australian Social Work*, 41, 2, 1988: 31–5.

[5] 'Which early family therapists … called news of difference': See Gregory Bateson: *Mind and Nature: A Necessary Unity* (Dutton, 1979): 94–100. The idea became a shaping metaphor for first-generation family therapists. See Lynn Hoffman, *Foundations of Family Therapy* (Basic Books, 1981): 176–218.

Chapter 8

[1] 'A clear pattern': First noted, to our knowledge, by Robert R. Clark in 'The Socialisation of Clinical Psychologists', *Professional Psychology: Research and Practice*, 4, 2, 1973: 329–40. This pattern resembles the three-session phenomenon. There is the same initial euphoria, accompanied by unrealistic or grandiose expectations, followed by a loss of hope, as the realistic challenges must be faced. Some trainees, like some clients, give up at this stage, it is all too hard. Those who survive the first half of the second year (in two-year programs) or the end of the second year (in three- and four-year programs) are likely to continue to the end, having settled into the more mature 'depressive position' required of those who intend to do this work.

[2] 'Whose level of differentiation … is very close to their own': Murray Bowen, *Family Therapy in Clinical Practice* (Aronson, 1978): 264–5.

[3] 'A self-assigned impossible task': See Vega Zagier Roberts: 'The Self-assigned Impossible Task' in A. Obholzer and V. Z. Roberts (eds): *The Unconscious At Work: Individual and Organisational Stress in the Human Services* (Routledge, 1994): 110–20.

[4] 'The financial transaction seems to cheapen the whole enterprise': See William Schofield: *Psychotherapy: The Purchase of Friendship*, Englewood Cliffs, NJ: Prentice-Hall, 1964.

[5] 'This is a form of parallel process': Parallel process is one of those therapeutic concepts that tends to be orally transmitted by trainers and supervisors, rather than written about to any great extent. See Bill Kell and William Mueller: *Impact and Change: A Study of Counseling Relationships*, Englewood Cliffs, NJ: Prentice-Hall, 1966. Belgian systemic therapist Mony Elkaim uses the term resonance, but he means the same thing. See *If You Love Me, Don't Love Me: Constructions of Reality and Change in Family Therapy*, New York, Basic Books, 1990: 130–1; 138–42.

[6] See Analise O'Donovan, Leanne Casey, Marchienne van der Veen, and Mark Boschen, *Psychotherapy: An Australian Perspective*, IP Communications, 2013: 337.

[7] 'This is Freud's flight into health': See J. Oremland: 'Transference Cure and Flight into Health', *International Journal of Psychoanalytic Psychotherapy*, 1, 1972: 61–75. For a family therapy understanding of the same concept, see Murray Bowen: *Family Therapy in Clinical Practice*, Aronson, 1978: 295–6.

Chapter Nine

[1] *'Success stories: Healing from Childhood Trauma'* 30 minute DVD (Cavalcade).

[2] Sarah Ferguson: *A Guard Within* (Chatto & Windus, 1973); Maria Cardinal: *The Words to Say It* (Van Vactor & Goodheart, 1983); Irvin Yalom and Ginny Elkin, *Every Day Gets a Little Closer* (Basic Books, 1974); Jewel Jones: *Now You See Me*.

[3] Joni Mitchell: 'Both Sides, Now' recorded on *Clouds* LP, 1969.

Must-Read Books

The books listed below are ones that we have found particularly valuable in our own professional lives. A few are self-help books that have proved their worth; most of them address professionals, but in a way which is engaging and personal. They bring theory to life. Most of these are books to buy and have on your shelf (or keep loaded on your iPad). As you gain experience and knowledge, you will find that they grow with you. The list doesn't try to cover every topic. If we couldn't think of a really good book on a particular topic, then we didn't include that topic.

Neurobiology and brain functioning

Bonnie Badenough: *The Brain-savvy Therapist's Workbook* (Norton, 2011).

Attachment and parenting

Patricia Crittenden: *Raising Parents*, Willan Publishing, 2008; Routledge, 2012.
Robert Karen: *Becoming Attached: First Relationships, and How They Shape Our Capacity to Love* (Oxford University Press, 1994; first published by Warner Books, 1994).
Dan Siegel and Mary Hartzell: *Parenting from the Inside Out: How a Deeper Understanding Can Help You Raise Children Who Thrive* (Doubleday, 2003).

Siblings and birth order

Dorothy Rowe: *My Dearest Enemy, My Dangerous Friend: Making and Breaking Sibling Bonds* (Routledge, 2007).

Growing up, and therapy with children and young people

Virginia Axline: *Dibs: In Search of Self* (Ballantine Books, 1964).
Peter Blake, *Child and Adolescent Psychotherapy*, 2nd Edn, Karnac Books, 2011).
Alice Miller: *The Drama of Being a Child: The Search for the True Self*, (Virago, 1987). (First published in German; first published in English 1979; variously titled in different editions).

Families and family therapy

Harriet Goldhor Lerner: *The Dance of Connection: How to Talk to Someone When You're Mad, Hurt, Scared, Frustrated, Insulted, Betrayed or Desperate* (HarperCollins, 2001).
Augustus Y. Napier with Carl A. Whitaker: *The Family Crucible* (Harper & Row, 1978).

Couples and couple therapy

David Shaddock: *From Impasse to Intimacy: How Understanding Unconscious Needs Can Transform Relationships* (Jason Aronson, 1998).
David Schnarch: *Passionate Marriage: Sex, Love and Intimacy in Emotionally Committed Relationships* (Norton, 1997).
Stan Tatkin: *Your Brain on Love: The Neurobiology of Healthy Relationships* (Sounds True, Audible, 2013).

Development in adulthood

Daniel J. Levinson, with Charlotte N. Darrow, Edward B. Klein, Maria H. Levinson and Braxton McKee: *The Seasons of a Man's Life* (Ballantine Books, 1978).

Daniel J. Levinson with Judy D. Levinson: *The Seasons of a Woman's Life* (Ballantine Books, 1996).

Addictions

John Bradshaw: *Homecoming: Reclaiming and Championing Your Inner Child* (Bantam, 1990).
Karen Walant, *Creating the Capacity for Attachment: Treating Addictions and the Alienated Self* (Aronson, 1977).

Trauma

Judith L. Herman: *Trauma and Recovery: From Domestic Abuse to Political Terror* (Pandora, 1992).
Bessel van der Kolk: *The Body Keeps the Score: Mind, Brain and Body in the Transformation of Trauma*, London, Allen Lane, 2014.

Depression

Dorothy Rowe: *Depression: The Way Out of Your Prison* (3rd edn, Routledge, 2003; first published 1983).
Andrew Solomon: *The Noonday Demon: An Anatomy of Depression* (Chatto & Windus, 2001).

Mental Illness

Richard P. Bentall: *Doctoring the Mind: Why Psychiatric Treatments Fail* (Allen Lane, 2009).
Hannah Green: *I Never Promised You a Rose Garden* (Gollancz, 1964). A novel based on the author's own experience of psychosis. There was also a movie version.)
Kay Redfield Jamison: *An Unquiet Mind: A Memoir of Moods and Madness* (Knopf, 1995).

Suicide

Kay Redfield Jamison: *Night Falls Fast: Understanding Suicide* (Knopf, 1999).

One-to-one therapy

Carl R. Rogers: *On Becoming a Person: A Therapist's View of Psychotherapy* (Constable, 1967; first published in the US, 1961).
Irvin Yalom: *The Gift of Therapy: Reflections on Being a Therapist* (HarperCollins, 2001).
Irvin Yalom and Ginny Elkin: *Every Day Gets a Little Closer: A Twice-Told Therapy* (Basic Books, 1974).
David Mearns and M. Cooper, *Working at Relational Depth in Counselling and Psychotherapy* (Sage, 2005).

Controversies and evidence

Colin Feltham: *Critical Thinking in Counselling and Psychotherapy* (Sage, 2010).
Nick Totton: *Not a Tame Lion: Writings on Therapy and its Social and Political Contexts* (PCCS Books, 2012).

Index

Note: on some occasions, you may find that a page reference does not actually contain the head word you were searching for. That page will still be relevant to the head word, even though it doesn't contain it. Read the page and you'll see why.

'intensity markers', see reflecting, skills of

In Treatment (HBO TV series) 20, 71, 166, 175, 189

Iser, Wolfgang 190

Ivey, Allen 190

Ivey, Mary 190

J

Jacobs, Michael 188

Janov, Arthur 54

James, Oliver 6

Jamison, Kay Redfield 168

Jeffers, Susan 133, 190

Jenkins, Alan 181

Jones, Jewel 176

K

Kandel, Eric 13

Karen, Robert 73

Kell, Bill 191

Kiesler, D. 190

Kirschenbaum, H. 190

Klein, Melanie 6

Klosko, Janet 57

Kohut, Heinz 95, 189

L

Lang, Moshe, 123

Le Doux, Joseph 57

left hemisphere, see brain, left hemisphere in

Lerner, Harriet Goldhor 6

Levinson, Daniel J. 13

Lewis, Ione 4

Licherman, Paul 190

life coaching 7, 131, see also coaching, skills of

limbic lobe, see brain

limit-setting 109

Linehan, Marsha 158

locus of control 140, 150

long-term therapy 132, 177–187, passim

     advice giving in 185

     consequences of 182–185

Q

R

www.ingramcontent.com/pod-product-compliance
Lightning Source LLC
Chambersburg PA
CBHW080644270326
41928CB00017B/3191